The Geneva Conventions Under Assault

THE GENEVA CONVENTIONS UNDER ASSAULT

Edited by
Sarah Perrigo and Jim Whitman

www.plutobooks.com

First published 2010 by Pluto Press
345 Archway Road, London N6 5AA and
175 Fifth Avenue, New York, NY 10010

www.plutobooks.com

Distributed in the United States of America exclusively by
Palgrave Macmillan, a division of St. Martin's Press LLC,
175 Fifth Avenue, New York, NY 10010

British Library Cataloguing in Publication Data
A catalogue record for this book is available from the British Library

ISBN   978 0 7453 2914 7   Hardback
ISBN   978 0 7453 2913 0   Paperback

Library of Congress Cataloging in Publication Data applied for

10   9   8   7   6   5   4   3   2   1

Designed and produced for Pluto Press by
Chase Publishing Services Ltd, 33 Livonia Road, Sidmouth, EX10 9JB England
Typeset from disk by Stanford DTP Services, Northampton, England
Printed and bound in the European Union by
CPI Antony Rowe, Chippenham and Eastbourne

To Georgia

Your courage, good humour and consideration for others
in the face of adversity continue to inspire me.

Contents

Preface   ix
Abbreviations and Acronyms   xv

1. The Geneva Conventions and the Normative Tenor
   of International Relations   1
   Sonia Cardenas

2. The History and Status of the Geneva Conventions   18
   Wade Mansell and Karen Openshaw

3. The Principle of Proportionality in the Law of Armed
   Conflict   42
   Françoise Hampson

4. Civilian Protection – What's Left of the Norm?   74
   Stuart Gordon

5. The Protection of Detainees in International
   Humanitarian Law   99
   Keiichiro Okimoto

6. Non-Lethal Weapons: A Rose by any Other Name   136
   Nick Lewer

7. From 'Total War' to 'Total Operations' –
   Contemporary Doctrine and Adherence to IHL   155
   Björn Müller-Wille

8. The Paradox of Value Discourses   179
   Helen Dexter

9. Freeing Force from Legal Constraint   201
   Jim Whitman

10. Undermining International Humanitarian Law and
    the Politics of Liberal Democracies   222
    Sarah Perrigo

About the Contributors   248
Index   250

Preface

Sarah Perrigo and Jim Whitman

Not all of the contributors to this volume subscribe to the idea that the Geneva Conventions are under assault, as we have chosen to describe the current state of affairs – even though all of us have particular concerns over their comprehensiveness, their resilience in the face of serious and repeated violations and/or their adaptability with respect to a range of practical and political developments. Our decision to adopt this phrase was based not so much on the number and seriousness of recent violations, but on the stand of outright defiance and contempt that have accompanied a few recent instances in particular. Our own view, as several of the chapters in this volume argue in detail, is that the relegation of the Geneva Conventions either to inadequacy (most notably with respect to the 'war on terror') or irrelevance in the face of declared, overriding exigencies, undermine the Geneva Conventions as an internationally shared, normative expectation much more seriously and quickly than the fact of any one or a number of recent violations of its strictures. Moreover, although we recognize that within the compass of international humanitarian law (IHL), the laws that concern the protection of the victims of armed conflict and those that concern the means and methods of warfare are distinct, our principal concern is with the integrity of a normative movement that is concerned with unnecessary and preventable human suffering during war. For this reason the 'Geneva Conventions' of the title encompasses both the four Geneva Conventions of 1949 and the two additional protocols of 1977.

Yet at the outset, some readers might consider that 'under assault' overstates either the intentions or the effects of violations of the Geneva Conventions. However, we regard the standing, meaning and force of the Geneva Conventions as an ongoing normative enterprise as much as a binding legal document – distinct from, but closely bound up with the other great normative movement that has shaped lived expectation throughout the world: the human rights regime. To dismiss the particulars of one or the other, or to resort to forms of instrumental reasoning or declarations of exceptionalism for their repeated violation is a challenge to the integrity of those legal orders, not merely violations of them. Because both IHL and human rights have as their substance the worth and integrity of human life and limits on the ends and means of the exercise of power, brutal and callous acts in one sphere can hardly be viewed as free-standing from the other, except on the narrowest of legal understandings – and nor are they. It is hardly a surprise that even as the Geneva Conventions have come under pressure, torture has re-entered our political vocabularies. 'Assault' in the sense in which we have employed it here does not mean 'acting with the intent to destroy' – indeed, even the most powerful states have evinced a desire to ensure that the protections of the Geneva Conventions continue to apply to their own soldiers and citizens. But we must distinguish between violations of the law and outright challenges to its compass and applicability; and when the two occur in combination as they have in recent years, it is not an exaggeration to characterize the effect as an assault.

We are also concerned about the wider, corrosive effects of our coarsened and normatively weakened political cultures. It is a grim irony that states that can rightly be regarded as beacons of the liberal democratic ideal have seen fit to undermine the principles so painstakingly conceived and fought for over centuries, as an acceptable price for the 'war on terror' – not least those articulated and codified in IHL and human rights. The realms of international, constitutional and domestic law that enshrine standards of humane decency as the *sine qua non* of the organization of political community are themselves dependent on normative expectation that cannot persist without renewal; and without rising to challenges as large as those now confronting us. In a world of intensifying human relatedness of every description, it is not plausible to suppose that actions that undermine fundamental norms pertaining to one legal realm can be insulated from those embodied in others, or from the perceptions of states and peoples everywhere. The same dynamics that are viewed by many as instruments for constructing a global civil society can also serve to drive a downward spiral toward the kinds of force-based politics that have marked so much of human history. This line of thinking also informed our choice of the word 'assault'.

At the same time, we recognize that neither nations nor individual combatants are required to place themselves in positions of reckless self-endangerment; that field-based military assessments are made in conditions that are tense and sometimes chaotic; and that life-and-death decisions cannot always await the unambiguous confirmation of intelligence-gathering. The Geneva Conventions regulate the conduct of war – they were not conceived to ensure that innocent civilians are not killed and injured. When they are, it is not always the result of an illegal act, but often part of the pity and horror of war. Popular misunderstandings of the scope and applicability of the Geneva Conventions, together with a misplaced faith in the ability of militaries to conduct reconnaissance and targeting with routine precision add to a feeling that the Geneva Conventions are a thin reed against both military technology and the political disposition of some states and/or belligerent parties. But not all such disquiet is without foundation: at the same time, national militaries and combatants of various stripes can and do violate the Geneva Conventions quite explicitly, which includes placing combatant personnel or operational sites in civilian areas or in protected buildings, or by using human shields.

In addition, much larger, strategically disposed and/or politically directed actions that appear to violate the Geneva Conventions certainly require investigation into whether the *prima facie* evidence of war crimes is conclusive – of which the Israeli blockade of Gaza is at the time of writing the most prominent as well as the most urgent.[1] According to Richard Falk, the UN Special Rapporteur on the situation of human rights in the Palestinian territories,

[I]t is a criminal violation of international law for elements of Hamas or anyone else to fire rockets at Israeli towns regardless of provocation, but such Palestinian behavior does not legalize Israel's imposition of a collective punishment of a life- and health-threatening character on the people of Gaza...

Indeed, writing in December 2008, Falk argued:

And still Israel maintains its Gaza siege in its full fury, allowing only barely enough food and fuel to enter to stave off mass famine and disease. Such a policy of collective punishment, initiated by Israel to punish Gazans for political developments within the Gaza strip, constitutes a continuing flagrant and massive violation of international humanitarian law as laid down in Article 33 of the Fourth Geneva Convention.[2]

A spiral of deeply disturbing action and reaction with little apparent regard for IHL has also become embedded in Sri Lanka. As government forces hasten to bring an end to their campaign against the Tamil Tigers (LTTE), the two sides appear to be committing war crimes as a matter of routine. According to Human Rights Watch,

> The Sri Lankan armed forces and the LTTE appear to be engaged in a perverse competition to demonstrate the greatest disregard for the civilian population. Retreating from Sri Lankan Army (SLA) advances, the LTTE has forcibly taken along all civilians under its control. As the territory held by the LTTE has shrunk – now a short, narrow strip on the northeast coast of the island – the civilian population has been dangerously forced into a smaller and smaller space. In violation of the laws of war, the LTTE has refused to allow civilians to flee the fighting, repeatedly fired on those trying to reach government-held territory, and deployed forces near densely populated areas. The civilians who remain under LTTE control, including children, are subject to forced recruitment into LTTE forces and hazardous forced labor on the battlefield. The LTTE's grim practices are being exploited by the government to justify its own atrocities. High-level statements have indicated that the ethnic Tamil population trapped in the war zone can be presumed to be siding with the LTTE and treated as combatants, effectively sanctioning unlawful attacks. Sri Lankan forces have repeatedly and indiscriminately shelled areas crowded with civilians. This includes numerous reported bombardments of government-declared 'safe zones' and the remaining hospitals in the region.[3]

It is not possible to determine the extent to which these and similar outrages arise from, or contribute to, a weakening of routine, normative adherence to the Geneva Conventions – or both; and whether such cases and a parallel weakening of human rights norms are causally related. But the adoption of torture as well as cruel and degrading treatment of prisoners is prohibited under both the Geneva Conventions and human rights law; and whatever the particulars of justifications for such behaviours, both legal orders are thereby debilitated. Of course, there was never a 'golden age' of state and non-state combatant adherence to the Geneva Conventions; and both the letter and the spirit of laws can survive egregious violations. But recent events hardly support the assumption of a blithe attitude. We note in particular the political disposition of the administration of President George W. Bush over eight years and the work of its lawyers to minimize the applicability of the provisions of the Geneva Conventions. One of the first acts of US

President Barack Obama was to order the closure of Guantánamo Bay. That the newly elected President clearly understands the legal, political and symbolic meanings that have attached to that place is clearly heartening. Yet the review ordered by Obama – to determine whether the conditions at Guantánamo are 'in conformity with all applicable laws governing conditions of confinement' – met the response in an 81-page Pentagon report that 'the conditions of confinement in Guantánamo are in conformity with Common Article 3 of the Geneva Conventions' – which does not addresses the remit fully, even in respect of the Geneva Conventions.[4]

Clearly, we are only at the start of addressing some of the very serious reversals, legal and normative, that have occurred in the last decade. The full extent of normative weakening is likely to manifest itself only gradually – and the ongoing 'war on terror', together with serious conflicts in which the Geneva Conventions appear to have little purchase, and new developments in strategic thinking and new weapons developments hardly provide propitious circumstances. Yet the level and extent of international revulsion over the kinds of excesses that the photographs from Abu Ghraib came to stand for; and the indications of a more general turn of the political tide (the election of Barack Obama not least), offer some hope that the values and principles enshrined in the Geneva Conventions are more deeply embedded in popular expectation than those tasked with circumventing and undermining them might ever have supposed. We are pleased to offer this volume in the hope of adding to that normative momentum.

We are very grateful to all of the contributors, whose early and enthusiastic support of this project was central to its initiation. We are conscious that every one has a range of commitments, many of which, on any sensible calculation, would preclude setting aside time for the research and writing of a book chapter. It is the measure of their own scholarly and personal engagement with the place of the Geneva Conventions in contemporary affairs that made the conception and completion of this book possible.

NOTES

1. Chris McGreal, 'Demands grow for Gaza war crimes investigation', *Guardian* (13 January 2009), available at: http://www.guardian.co.uk/world/2009/jan/13/gaza-israel-war-crimes.
2. United Nations Press Release, 'Gaza: Silence is not an option', 9 December 2008. Available at: http://www.unhchr.ch/huricane/huricane.nsf/0/183ED1610B2BCB80C125751A002B06B2?opendocument.

3. Human Rights Watch, 'War on the Displaced: Sri Lankan Army and LTTE Abuses against Civilians in the Vanni', 19 February 2009. Available at: http://www.hrw. org/en/embargo/node/80899?signature=ad26786effb2ac69849df06fb1997da1& suid=6.

4. Warren Richey, 'Pentagon report on Guantánamo detainees: incomplete? The Pentagon should have included more laws in its assessment of conditions, some experts argue', *Christian Science Monitor* (27 February 2009).

Abbreviations and Acronyms

ADS	Active Denial System
APM	Anti-Personnel Landmines
ATACMS	Army Tactical Missile Systems
ATCSA	Antiterrorism, Crime and Security Act
AU	African Union
BBC	British Broadcasting Corporation
CAT	Convention Against Torture
CCWC	Certain Conventional Weapons Convention
CIA	Central Intelligence Agency
CJCSI	Chairman of Joint Chiefs of Staffs Instruction
DE	Directed Energy Weapons
DNA	Deoxyribonucleic Acid
DoD	Department of Defense
DRC	Democratic Republic of Congo
EBA	Effects Based Approaches
EBO	Effects Based Operations
ECHR	European Convention on Human Rights
ECOWAS	Economic Community of West African States
EU	European Union
HIDA	High Intensity Directed Acoustic Device
HPM	High Power Microwave
HRA	Human Rights Act
IAC	International Armed Conflict
ICC	International Criminal Court
ICCPR	International Covenant on Civil and Political Rights
ICISS	International Commission on Intervention and State Sovereignty
ICJ	International Court of Justice
ICRC	International Committee of the Red Cross
IDF	Israeli Defense Force
IDP	Internally Displaced Person
IED	Improvised Explosive Device
IHL	International Humanitarian Law
IHRL	International Human Rights Law
IICK	Independent International Commission on Kosovo
ISAF	International Security Assistance Force

KE	Kinetic Energy
LOAC	Law of Armed Conflict
LRAD	Long-Range Acoustic Device
LTTE	Liberation Tigers of Tamil Eelam [Tamil Tigers]
MCA	Military Commissions Act
MEP	Member of the European Parliament
MLRS	Multiple Launch Rocket Systems
MoD	Ministry of Defence
MSF	Médecins Sans Frontières
NATO	North Atlantic Treaty Organization
NEC	Network Enabled Capabilities
NGO	Non-Governmental Organizations
NIAC	Non-International Armed Conflict
NLW	Non-Lethal Weapon
OC	Oleoresin Capsicum
OLC	Office of Legal Counsel
POW	Prisoner of War
R2P	Responsibility to Protect
RCA	Riot Control Agent
RIPA	Regulation of Investigative Powers Act
SACEUR	Supreme Allied Commander in Europe
UAV	Unmanned Aerial Vehicle
UDHR	Universal Declaration of Human Rights
UK	United Kingdom
UN	United Nations
UNCCPR	United Nations International Covenant on Civil and Political Rights
US	United States

1
The Geneva Conventions and the Normative Tenor of International Relations

Sonia Cardenas

The Geneva Conventions have come under assault in recent years. Critics depict them as outmoded treaties, incompatible with twenty-first-century wars. Indeed, in an age of 'global terror', the Conventions often conjure up archaic images of prisoners of war and an idealistic Red Cross. Some observers have gone so far as to suggest that while the Conventions may have been relevant during the days of 'knights and chivalry' they are woefully inadequate for modern warfare.[1]

More specifically, the perception is that the 1949 Conventions have three dominant characteristics that make them largely irrelevant in contemporary world politics: they are mostly prohibitive documents, restricting a range of state action; they are isolated treaties, prone to legalism and abstractness; and they derive largely from an ethical impulse to protect humanity. These popular notions, in turn, feed into the assumption that the Conventions are misguided and inappropriate doctrines for a post-Cold War world, dominated by a global 'war on terror' in which states may have to act exceptionally to protect their national security.

In fact, a close analysis of the broader politico-normative context underlying the creation and evolution of the Geneva Conventions suggests otherwise. This chapter advances three arguments, which together challenge critical views of the Conventions. First, the Geneva Conventions have been as important for generating new international norms as they have been for constraining state action. Second, the Conventions cannot be understood without examining the significance of two parallel and reinforcing developments – the United Nations Charter (1945) and the Universal Declaration of Human Rights (1948). Third, while clearly invoking ethical conceptions, the Geneva Conventions have always been rooted in a pragmatic interest in limiting war.

Reconceptualizing the Conventions as central normative instruments, linked closely to prominent international institutions and reflecting states' political interests, has profound implications. On the one hand, this view provides a more complete and accurate picture of the Geneva Conventions. On the other hand, it reveals that, far from being anachronistic documents ill suited to contemporary political imperatives, the Conventions' basic premises are as relevant today as they were last century.

A NEW NORMATIVE ORDER

As the first set of international treaties to address humanitarian issues, the Geneva Conventions have long been considered basic constraints on state behavior. Yet despite their obvious restrictions, it would be a mistake to view the Conventions as exclusively prohibitive in nature. Taken in their broader historical context, the Geneva Conventions of 1949 have been most remarkable in generating a set of expectations to govern global relations. They have created international standards regulating how states should treat civilians (i.e., human rights) during armed conflict. In particular, they have differentiated between combatants and non-combatants; defined the legitimate objectives of war; and stipulated how prisoners of war should be treated. These standards, in turn, have been a cornerstone of the post-Second World War international normative order, elevating the status of regular human beings and reconstituting the traditional contours of state sovereignty.

The prohibitive aspects of the Geneva Conventions are readily apparent. Indeed, on one level, the Conventions clearly forbid states from acting inhumanely during armed conflict. For example, states may not mistreat members of the armed forces who fall sick or are wounded in the battlefield (First Geneva Convention) or at sea (Second Geneva Convention), those who are taken prisoners of war (Third Geneva Convention), or civilians during war (Fourth Geneva Convention). Two protocols added in 1977 further limit what states can do during international armed conflicts (Protocol I) and non-international conflicts (Protocol II).

Additionally, Common Article 3, which appears in all four of the Geneva Conventions, expressly prohibits a catalogue of acts:

violence to life and person, in particular murder of all kinds, mutilation, cruel treatment and torture; (b) taking of hostages; (c) outrages upon personal dignity, in particular humiliating and degrading treatment; (d) the passing of sentences and the carrying out of executions without previous judgment pronounced by a regularly constituted court, affording all the judicial guarantees which are recognized as indispensable by civilized peoples.

In determining the extent to which the Geneva Conventions are prohibitive international instruments, it is crucial to compare the 1949 Conventions to previous developments. The Conventions certainly have deep roots in international affairs, especially in the nineteenth century, but the extent to which the Conventions are similar to and different from its precursors still needs to be clarified.

The Geneva Conventions can be traced in part to previous international developments restricting the scope of state action in armed conflict.[2] The most direct antecedent was the 1864 Geneva Convention for the Amelioration of the Condition of the Wounded and Sick in Armed Forces in the Field. More indirectly, however, a large body of customary rules had evolved over the centuries to regulate armed conflicts, whether in the form of codes of conduct or bilateral treaties between belligerents. And between the 1864 Convention and the adoption of the four Geneva Conventions in 1949, relevant international legal documents prohibited the use of weapons (such as the 1868 Declaration of St Petersburg and the 1925 Geneva Protocol), behaviors contrary to the laws and customs of war (The Hague Conventions of 1899 and 1907), and the inhumane treatment of prisoners of war (the 1929 Geneva Convention).

Despite building on important precedents, the 1949 Geneva Conventions also represented a crucial break from the past. Substantively, two important innovations are notable: the Fourth Geneva Convention and Common Article 3. While numerous aspects of the other 1949 Conventions could be found in earlier documents, the Fourth Convention's focus on the treatment of civilians was unique. Earlier instruments had referred only to members of the armed forces; states and their agents were still the only actors recognized and endowed with rights. The Fourth Geneva Convention, in contrast, shattered the state-centric consensus of international law, now according civilians unprecedented status.

Likewise, Common Article 3 delegitimized a set of behaviors not previously associated with international humanitarian law. This included the use of torture and degrading treatment, as well as violations of due process. The scope of protection thus extended substantially: from shielding from harm those who could no longer fight (i.e., those wounded, sick, or taken as prisoners of war) to protecting civilians who did not partake in the fighting (non-combatants). Moreover, the latter group of non-combatants was to be protected both in a 'negative' and a 'positive' sense. While state parties were not to harm them in any way, they also were to afford them basic rights of due process.

These normative innovations cannot be understood apart from the pivotal experience of the Second World War, as further sections elaborate. The horrific discovery of concentration camps, along with changes in technology that raised the specter of total war, led to a consensus on the part of post-war international architects. Those subjected to humane treatment during war now had to encompass a much broader segment of humanity. As Theodor Meron describes the Fourth Geneva Convention, it was partly '[a] result of the universal condemnation of the Nazis' treatment of civilians in occupied Europe during the Second World War'.[3]

The Geneva Conventions' emphasis on differentiating between combatants and non-combatants was also connected to the post-1945 rise of nuclear weapons. In particular, the Geneva Conventions closely complemented emerging norms of non-proliferation and an eventual taboo against the use of 'weapons of mass destruction'. The term 'weapons of mass destruction' itself was first articulated in 1948 by the UN Convention on Conventional Armaments, before the 1949 Geneva Conventions went into effect.[4]

Indeed, recognition that large-scale devastation could come to civilian populations was a central rationale behind both non-proliferation efforts and the Geneva Conventions. Just as the 1925 Geneva Convention banning the use of chemical weapons in war was partly a response to their wide-scale use on the battlefields of Europe during the First World War, the 1949 Geneva Conventions' focus on protecting civilians certainly was motivated by the use of nuclear weapons.[5] The use of nuclear weapons, after all, rendered meaningless the distinction between combatants and non-combatants.

The categories of combatants and non-combatants became increasingly significant during the Cold War, as a normative taboo gradually delegitimized the use of weapons of mass destruction.[6] It is true that US military doctrine supported the notion of deterrence through fear, i.e., convincing the other side that the use of nuclear weapons would result in punishment and retaliation. And while deterrence sometimes entailed threatening civilians through counter-value targeting, the ultimate goal was still one of avoiding nuclear conflict altogether.

Rising support for the Geneva Conventions therefore developed alongside an evolving normative taboo against the use of nuclear weapons. Not only did international institutional initiatives eventually seek to limit nuclear proliferation, a development discussed in the next section, but a transnational anti-nuclear movement arose in the 1950s that vehemently opposed nuclear weapons. Normatively, both the taboo against weapons of mass destruction and the rise of a non-proliferation regime reinforced the idea that war in a nuclear age had to be strictly limited. Far from undermining the Geneva Conventions, the rise of nuclear weapons only elevated the significance of the Conventions.

While many people associate the Geneva Conventions with an era of conventional warfare, the 1949 Conventions introduced standards – at the nexus of the laws of war and human rights – in direct response to changes in non-conventional technology. Consequently, just as the Conventions emphasized the differential treatment owed to combatants and non-combatants, norms limiting the use of nuclear weapons were influenced by a similar view: these weapons were so devastating precisely because they eroded all lines between civilians and non-civilians in conflict. The Geneva Conventions may have had their roots in the nineteenth-century battlefield, but the 1949 Conventions were inextricably embedded in the new normative order that arose after the Second World War.

International relations experts contend that new norms can arise in the aftermath of crises and systemic shocks, which call into question the ongoing viability of pre-existing standards.[7] The cataclysm of the Second World War and the advent of nuclear weapons made it clear that unbridled state power was no longer appropriate in the mid-twentieth century. The humane treatment of civilians, broadly defined, was to be a prerequisite for membership in the international community of 'civilized' states.

In this sense, the Conventions were 'constitutive' of the new international normative order erected after 1945. Far from merely restricting state behavior, the Geneva Conventions created a new set of expectations – or norms – about the *appropriateness* of state action post-1945. They differentiated between combatants and non-combatants, outlined the legitimate goals of war, and elaborated how prisoners of war were to be treated. They were an essential part of a new international normative order. Most fundamentally, the Geneva Conventions redefined prevailing conceptions of state sovereignty, elevating the status of individual human beings in international law and broadening the scope of state responsibility during armed conflict.

PARALLEL INSTITUTIONAL DEVELOPMENTS

If the Geneva Conventions of 1949 were essential in generating new international norms, they were not alone in this regard. It is common to view the Conventions, a complex set of documents comprising the centerpiece of international humanitarian law, as a realm unto themselves. In fact, however, they were part and parcel of the most fundamental post-1945 international institutional developments. The Geneva Conventions were linked, in particular, to two other seminal and mutually reinforcing documents: the UN Charter of 1945 and the 1948 Universal Declaration of Human Rights. Together, these three key documents and the institutions they spawned defined the conditions for international peace and security, including the importance of restricting war and treating individuals humanely in international relations.

The UN Charter of 1945, as its Preamble unequivocally states, combined a concern for avoiding war with protecting human rights and promoting compliance with international law. David Kennedy confirms this: 'The system of the United Nations Charter was more than a political regime of collective security – an institutional framework for diplomatic management of conflict. It was also a new legal order that inaugurated a new law of war.'[8] Like the UN Charter, the Geneva Conventions were essential in creating an innovative normative order, profoundly recasting expectations about state action during armed conflict.

In terms of the laws of war, the UN Charter and the Geneva Conventions complemented one another. While the UN Charter called on states to avoid using force or threatening to use force (Article 2(4)), it also identified the conditions under which the use of force could be used justifiably (*jus ad bellum*).[9] The Geneva Conventions in turn specify appropriate conduct during armed conflict (*jus in bello*). As such, these two essential instruments went hand in hand, serving as integral aspects of post-war international peace and security.

Given the UN Charter's concern with limiting war, UN-driven anti-proliferation efforts were also essential complements to the Geneva Conventions. Beginning in early 1946, the United Nations became the focal institutional actor for regulating the proliferation of nuclear weapons. These efforts only intensified over time. As newly independent states joined the United Nations and a transnational anti-proliferation network grew, a complex system of treaties was created to regulate the use and diffusion of weapons of mass destruction – from the 1968 Treaty on the Non-Proliferation of Nuclear Weapons to the 1993 Chemical Weapons Convention. These anti-proliferation institutional developments, under the UN umbrella, reinforce the Geneva Conventions' emphasis on mitigating war and shielding civilians from war's devastating effects.

If the UN Charter was one pillar of the post-war international normative order, the Universal Declaration of Human Rights (UDHR) was another. Approved by the UN General Assembly, the UDHR elaborates the full range of rights owed to all people. It so doing, it recognizes these rights as 'the foundation of freedom, justice and peace in the world'.[10] The linkage between international peace and security, human rights and international law is deemed fundamental.

While the UDHR lists a broad set of rights (civil, political, economic, social and cultural) and it is not legally binding, its direct influence on the Geneva Conventions is difficult to overlook. In particular, the rights enshrined in Common Article 3 of the Geneva Conventions can be traced to the UDHR, including prohibitions against cruel treatment and torture as well as guarantees of due process. Moreover, just as the UN Charter and the Geneva Conventions both emphasize the laws of war, the UDHR and the Geneva Conventions challenge the primacy of the state by elevating the status of civilians and human rights. Put simply, international humanitarian law, as enshrined in the Geneva Conventions, applies the human rights standards of the UDHR to situations of armed conflict.

Beyond the UDHR, a large corpus of human rights laws and institutions has emerged since the 1940s, consistent with the Conventions. For example, the 1977 Protocols themselves arose during a period when international human rights law was quickly evolving. The two international covenants, devoted to civil and political rights, on the one hand, and economic, social, and cultural rights, on the other, entered into force in 1976. Likewise, the Standard Minimum Rules for the Treatment of Prisoners were approved by the United Nations in 1957 and 1977. Other human rights norms, recognized in Common Article 3 of the Geneva Conventions, continued to evolve over time – for example, the pivotal Convention against Torture and Other Cruel, Inhuman or Degrading Treatment or Punishment, which entered into force in 1987.

Even after the end of the Cold War, the status of human rights law has progressed in ways that reinforce the Geneva Conventions. In particular, international standards have been formalized for the administration of justice and the treatment of prisoners, the rights of children and the implications of war crimes. The latter is of course evident in the recent creation of the International Criminal Court, a watershed in international law. As a Red Cross insider predicted on the eve of the new millennium, 'The growing convergence between international humanitarian law and human rights law will continue, providing greater protection for individuals in emergency situations of all types, from internal violence to international armed conflicts.'[11]

It is at the interstices of the constraints on war and the promotion of human rights, two central pillars of the post-war institutional order, that the Geneva Conventions are therefore situated. In a concrete sense, each of these institutional developments did not emerge in isolation. They arose during the same period, so that those drafting the various texts were acutely aware of parallel trends. The Geneva Conventions themselves represented four years of intense negotiations and research, beginning before the war even ended in mid-February 1945.[12] The degree of consensus surrounding these documents was also comparable. In 1949, both the UN Charter and the Geneva Conventions had 59 signatories; the UDHR had been enacted the previous year after 48 states signed it.[13]

These developments represented a trend toward post-war inter-state cooperation and institution-building, increasingly viewed as essential for assuring a stable international order. This differed from earlier epochs in which the distinction between states and non-state actors, or the public and private spheres, was drawn sharply; and international law only extended to protecting states and regulating their relations with each other. After the Second World War, however, political, legal and ethical considerations increasingly merged in global governance, evident in the concomitant rise of the UN Charter, the Universal Declaration of Human Rights and the Geneva Conventions.

It was indeed a new system where international law was to play a central role. For the first time, international law would systematically elaborate standards on a global scale and attempt to regulate state–society relations. States might still be the primary actors in world politics, but the era of absolute state power was in principle defunct.

Just as the erection of a post-war international economic order was an attempt to assure predictability and stability in the international system, so it was with the Geneva Conventions and related treaties. After the Second World War, the twin goals of limiting conflict and protecting human beings took on new urgency. As François Bugnion notes, 'Like the Universal Declaration of Human Rights ... the new Geneva Conventions were a response by the international community to the tremendous suffering and devastation brought about by the Second World War.'[14]

Put differently, existing institutions had failed to prevent countless atrocities. Even the International Committee of the Red Cross (ICRC) was accused of tacit complicity in failing to expose the horrors of the concentration camps. It was clear that drastic improvements would require broader institutionalization. Thus, for the first time, the Geneva Conventions explicitly included a monitoring mechanism to assure implementation. 'Protecting powers', or neutral states, would defend civilians, alongside the vigilance of the ICRC. Like other post-war institutions, the goal was partly to enhance certainty and predictability in an increasingly volatile world.

While the ICRC played a leading role in drafting the Geneva Conventions, treaty signatories were ultimately state parties – determined to manage a system that had become far too dangerous and complex to handle on an ad hoc or limited basis.[15] A web of related institutions, taking the form of treaties, was the preferred response. It is in this broader institutional legal context, rather than as an isolated set of treaties, that the Geneva Conventions must be understood.

POLITICAL INTERESTS AND ETHICAL PURPOSES

The temptation today is to portray humanitarian law as belonging to the realm of ethics, divorced from the realities of state power and security. The view is that war is an exceptional event; where national security and even survival may be at stake, humanitarian concerns must necessarily take a back seat to state prerogatives. Yet the origins of the Conventions suggest an alternative interpretation of humanitarian law, in which states define their *long-term* interests in terms of minimizing the impact of war.

The Geneva Conventions must be understood in terms of two motive forces: a social consensus about the importance of mitigating the effects of war and an interest on the part of even powerful states in avoiding large-scale war. These concerns are themselves inextricable from the unprecedented experience of the Second World War. The war introduced new fears for the international community, arising out of unprecedented technological developments fused with extreme nationalism.

The atrocities associated with the Holocaust, the targeting of civilian populations during the war and the advent of nuclear weapons all raised the specter of total war. The discovery of concentration camps shocked the conscience of humankind, leading to promises that such atrocities would never again be tolerated by the international community. Unlike previous acts of barbarity, however, the genocide committed by Nazi Germany may have been especially disturbing to powerful states. Not only was it massive in scale, but ethnic cleansing occurred in the very heart of Europe.

Driven by fear as much as moral outrage, states may have had an interest in using international law and institutions to tame the unbridled power of extreme nationalism, which could spill over into their territory and that of their allies. Jean Pictet, former director of the International Committee of the Red Cross, concurs that this interest lay behind the creation of the Fourth Geneva Convention:

> The establishment of a new Convention for the Protection of Civilians in Wartime was an imperative necessity. After the bitter experiences of the last conflict and the horrors of the concentration camps, there was no need to stress the urgency and capital importance of international rules in this particular field.[16]

Changes in the technologies of warfare also had a profound effect on state interests. On the one hand, the lines between combatants and non-combatants all but disappeared in the Second World War, as civilians were deliberately targeted and aerial bombings caused widespread devastation. On the other hand, the use of the atomic bomb introduced an unfathomable threat and shifted permanently the calculus of state interests. In a bipolar world, the costs of all-out war mounted, just as the benefits of avoiding war (and at a minimum, protecting civilians) rose substantially.

Even before the Second World War, however, states' interests vis-à-vis the Geneva Conventions arguably were shaped by changes in the material context of warfare, not simply humanitarian concerns. For example, the 1864 Geneva Convention recognized the importance of medical neutrality in warfare. Rather than being driven strictly by benevolence, some scholars have suggested a different dynamic:

In an age of conscript armies and more rapid communications, state representatives realized that they had to do more for wounded soldiers. The battle of Solferino, which gave rise to the idea of the Red Cross, was part of an era in which European armies had more veterinarians to care for horses than doctors to care for the wounded. If states did not improve their military medical services, the very institution of war might be undermined by social unrest.[17]

According to historian John Hutchinson's account of the Red Cross, in the mid-nineteenth century, 'Realpolitik was every bit as important as humanitarianism…'[18]

Against the backdrop of the Second World War, political events only elevated the importance of the Geneva Conventions. As one commentator notes, Cold War threats to international stability were soon evident, raising the value of the Geneva Conventions:

> In 1948 this confrontation intensified dramatically at the time of the coup in Prague and the blockade of Berlin, the civil wars in Greece and China, the war in Indochina and the nuclear arms race. It paralyzed nearly all aspects of international relations and brought the threat of a third world war long before the wounds left by the second had been able to heal. And yet, despite this menacing background – or maybe because of it – the nations of the world managed to rally around the red cross and red crescent emblems and adopt new treaties protecting the victims of war.[19]

The context of ongoing threat suggests that state interests in supporting the Geneva Conventions were partly political. In an increasingly dangerous world, where virulent ideologies mixed with potent technologies, states ultimately wanted to protect their civilian populations during armed conflict.[20]

The actual exercise of drafting the Geneva Conventions also reflected a combination of ethical and pragmatic considerations. It was a joint exercise by state and non-state actors, who collected vast amounts of data on their cumulative experience during the Second World War. Governments, Red Cross societies and commissions of experts all cooperated to incorporate the lessons of the war into humanitarian law. All told, the spirit that dominated the 1949 Conference was 'a spirit of reprobation of war'.[21] Ethical concerns clearly underlay this condemnation of war, but political consider-ations cannot be discounted in a new climate where warfare posed unrivaled threats. Even the International Committee of the Red Cross, accused by some of failing to expose the horrors of the Holocaust, must have had an interest in institutionalizing its role in the post-war world and further legalizing the humanitarian norms of warfare.

The degree of overall consensus surrounding the Geneva Conventions reflects these political underpinnings. The Conventions have consistently enjoyed a high degree of support, despite existing international divisions. When the Conventions were first opened for signature in 1949, all five permanent members of the Security Council signed them. By 1960, 114 countries had ratified the Conventions; two decades later, the number of state parties stood at 154. Since the 1990s, over 30 countries have joined the Conventions, giving the Conventions universal support.[22]

Since in a closely interconnected world almost all states can be affected by war, it is in most states' interests to protect civilian populations during armed conflict. Otherwise, according to the logic of retaliation, free rein in attacking a country's civilian population could translate into attacks against one's own civilians. The horrors of the Second World War made the avoidance of war an ethical concern, but this does not negate the real political incentives that states faced to humanize war. If this were not the case, human rights treaties would all enjoy the same degree of universal support, but this is not so. International humanitarian law, as encapsulated in the Geneva Conventions, has enjoyed unprecedented levels of global backing.

Precisely because warfare has traditionally been the prerogative of states, one would not expect states readily to accept treaties that limit their monopoly in this area. Ethical considerations surely motivated some individuals in their drive to humanize war and protect civilians during armed conflict – witness the historic role of Henry Dunant in founding the Red Cross. But for the states that signed the Geneva Conventions in 1949 and subsequently, political calculations about the costliness of unrestrained warfare also must have weighed heavily.[23]

In short, just because the Geneva Conventions protected the interests of individual non-combatants against the interests of states does not mean that the Conventions were driven exclusively by ethical considerations. The ethical purposes underlying the Conventions should not obscure their political origins. The Geneva Conventions were adopted and continue to enjoy widespread support because they resonated with the post-1945 international community *and* they have helped self-interested states maintain international peace and security.

DEMYSTIFYING THE CONVENTIONS: PRAGMATISM AND RELEVANCE

Rather than being isolated and utopian instruments, anathema to state interests, the Geneva Conventions should be seen through a much broader prism. The evidence suggests that these Conventions were central to the post-war normative order. They created new expectations about the appropriateness of state behavior, defining how states should treat non-state actors. They also were a key component of the international system after the Second World War, serving as an institutional bridge between the laws of war and emerging human rights norms. And they were supported by powerful states that deemed it in their interest to mitigate the costliness of war in a new era. This demystified view of the Conventions – norm-generating more than prohibitive, institutionally central versus exceptional, and driven by politics as much as ethics – has important implications.

The primary criticism launched against the Conventions today is that they constrain states unnecessarily, limiting their capacity to defend the national interest in an era of non-state terrorism.[24] The US government, for example, has charged that the nature of war today is no longer limited to battles between uniformed soldiers from regular state armies. Instead, as Renée de Nevers describes the need to modernize the Geneva Conventions,

> [W]ars today range from wildly unbalanced conflicts pitting highly trained and technologically sophisticated armies like that of the United States against irregular combatants on horseback, to conflicts in which paramilitaries and criminals intermingle and terrorize local populations to achieve their own goals. Moreover, today, war in much of the world takes place against the backdrop of failed states, and is fought by warlords, mercenaries, and children.[25]

While legal experts continue to debate the limits and relevance of the Conventions, and whether the Conventions should be revised to reflect changes in warfare, it remains unclear whether the introduction of new participants in armed conflict actually poses a significant challenge.

Critics make two essential assumptions to bolster their claims about the irrelevance of the Conventions. First, they assert that non-conventional actors will engage in non-conventional acts against states, requiring the latter to defend themselves by any means necessary. Second and closely related, they presume that non-conventional actors are far less likely to follow international rules like the Geneva Conventions, risking greater uncertainty and insecurity in the international system.

Perhaps compelling at first glance, these assumptions remain problematic. Both of these assumptions emphasize the presumed motives and actions of non-state actors, whereas states are treated as highly reactive actors. Yet there has never been any guarantee that state parties to the Conventions themselves would abide by the rules of war, as violations of the Conventions in the past 60 years indicate. Likewise, states still have access to much more lethal uses of force, with the potential to threaten large segments of a population, than non-state actors. The new emphasis on terrorists and other non-conventional fighters may not be as crucial as critics of the Convention have presumed.

Would states today be better off if they were free to treat suspected terrorists detained in armed conflicts inhumanely? Critics of the Conventions focus on the apparent short-term benefits of rejecting the Geneva Conventions, disregarding a global normative consensus about the value of the Conventions and the long-term benefits that states historically have associated with the Conventions. In creating standards about the way states should act in armed conflict, the Conventions have defined an essential set of expectations that now have global reach. One has to look no further than support for the Conventions, which enjoy universal consensus: 194 states today have acceded to them. These expectations reflect a complex mix of realist calculations and ethical considerations, and they remain as relevant today as they did in the late 1940s. Indeed, the humane treatment of civilians, even suspected terrorists who might not comply with the Geneva Conventions, is still pertinent today, despite the asymmetry of many contemporary conflicts.

While rejecting the Conventions might provide powerful states with short-term gains, it also would prove potentially costly to states' reputations and to broader international stability and order. Given the strong normative consensus that the Conventions enjoy, deeply embedded in both the laws of war and human rights, any state that rejects the Conventions would likely suffer costs to its reputation. More generally, if states are permitted to act inhumanely in armed conflict, the possibility of retribution and increased militarization increases. In either case, rejection of the Conventions leads to greater insecurity.

Recent actions by the United States – illustrated vividly by the treatment of prisoners in Guantánamo – are therefore destabilizing. When basic rights of due process and personal integrity, guaranteed in the Geneva Conventions and a host of major international human rights instruments, are routinely violated, the stability of the past six decades is undermined. New technologies of warfare also challenge longstanding humanitarian laws. For example, attempts to regularize the use of nuclear weapons by introducing tactical versions for the battlefield could threaten the existing normative order. Like other so-called 'smart' bombs and weapons, 'mini-nukes' purportedly can be used only against military targets, maintaining the illusion that civilian casualties are purely accidental (i.e., 'collateral damage'). While there is nothing inherent in the apparent rise of a global terrorist threat that makes the Geneva Conventions obsolete, contemporary responses to terrorism (from the treatment of detainees to the use of new battlefield technologies) do threaten the prevailing international normative order.

Rather than being wholly humanitarian documents with little relevance for realist-driven states, the Geneva Conventions' political and normative origins suggest their potential to play a pragmatic and enduring role in world politics. The Geneva Conventions define central international standards, support a network of major international institutions and reflect states' interests in avoiding conflict – they are not primarily prohibitive, isolated treaties, inspired solely by a humanitarian impulse. Rejecting them necessitates a fundamental shift in the normative tenor in international relations: permitting states to unleash inhumane treatment and force against ordinary human beings.

At the intersection of the laws of war and human rights, the Conventions have set essential standards for 60 years that have helped to mitigate armed conflict and maintain international peace and security. Dramatic changes in warfare, including the rise of new terrorist threats, only bolster their relevance in world affairs. Far from becoming obsolete, the Geneva Conventions must remain a cornerstone of the contemporary international order.

NOTES

1. John Dwight Ingram, 'The Geneva Convention is Woefully Outdated', *Pennsylvania State International Law Review* 23, no. 1 (Summer 2004), pp. 79–84.
2. For relevant background material, see Angela Bennett, *The Geneva Convention: The Hidden Origins of the Red Cross* (Stroud: Sutton Publishing, 2006).

3. Theodor Meron, 'The Geneva Conventions as Customary Law', *American Journal of International Law* 81 (1987), p. 364.
4. Nina Tannenwald, *The Nuclear Taboo: The United States and the Non-Use of Nuclear Weapons Since 1945* (Cambridge: Cambridge University Press, 2007).
5. For the evolution of a normative taboo against the use of chemical weapons, including the role of the Geneva Conventions, see Richard M. Price, *The Chemical Weapons Taboo* (Ithaca, NY: Cornell University Press, 1997).
6. On the nuclear taboo, see also Thomas C. Schelling, 'The Nuclear Taboo', *MIT International Review* (Spring 2007), pp. 8–11.
7. See, for example, Jeffrey Legro, *Rethinking the World: Great Power Strategies and International Order* (Ithaca, NY: Cornell University Press, 2005).
8. David Kennedy, *Of War and Law* (Princeton: Princeton University Press, 2006), p. 77.
9. For a comprehensive guide to the laws of war, see *Documents on the Laws of War*, ed. Adam Roberts and Richard Guelff, 3rd edn (Oxford: Oxford University Press, 2000). See also Christine Gray, *International Law and the Use of Force*, 2nd edn (Oxford: Oxford University Press, 2004).
10. Preamble, Universal Declaration of Human Rights (1948).
11. Michael A. Meyer, 'The Relevance of the 50th Anniversary of the Geneva Conventions to National Red Cross and Red Crescent Societies: Reviewing the Past to Address the Future', *International Review of the Red Cross*, no. 835 (30 September 1999), pp. 649–68. Available at http://www.icrc.org/Web/eng/siteeng0.nsf/html/57JQ3J.
12. Jean S. Pictet, 'The New Geneva Conventions for the Protection of War Victims', *American Journal of International Law* 45 (1951), pp. 462–75.
13. State parties to the Geneva Conventions, and their dates of accession, can be found at the website of the International Committee of the Red Cross: http://www.icrc.org/eng/party_ccw.
14. François Bugnion, 'The Geneva Conventions of 12 August 1949: From the 1949 Diplomatic Conference to the Dawn of the New Millennium', *International Affairs* 76, no. 1 (2000), p. 42.
15. For a definitive study of the International Committee of the Red Cross, see David P. Forsythe, *The Humanitarians: The International Committee of the Red Cross* (Cambridge: Cambridge University Press, 2005).
16. Pictet, 'The New Geneva Conventions', p. 473.
17. David P. Forsythe, 'Human Rights and the Red Cross in Historical Perspective', *Human Rights Quarterly* 19, no. 3 (1997), p. 686.
18. John F. Hutchinson, *Champions of Charity: War and the Rise of the Red Cross* (Boulder, CO: Westview Press, 1996), p. 29.
19. Bugnion, 'The Geneva Conventions', p. 42.
20. A related argument suggests that, in the aftermath of major wars, multilateral institutions such as the Geneva Conventions reflect the presence of a global hegemon with foreign democratic allies. See G. John Ikenberry, *After Victory: Institutions, Strategic Restraint, and the Rebuilding of Order after Major Wars* (Princeton: Princeton University Press, 2001).
21. Pictet, 'The New Geneva Conventions', p. 475.
22. *Ibid.*, note 13.
23. Martha Finnemore describes how non-state actors like Dunant and the International Committee of the Red Cross reconstituted state interests to accommodate humanitarian concerns. Finnemore, 'Norms and War: The

International Red Cross and the Geneva Conventions', in Martha Finnemore, *National Interest in International Society* (Ithaca, NY: Cornell University Press, 1996).

24. For a contemporary analysis of the Geneva Conventions, see especially Derek Jinks, *The Rules of War: The Geneva Conventions in the Age of Terror* (Oxford: Oxford University Press, 2008).

25. Renée de Nevers, 'The Geneva Conventions and New Wars', *Political Science Quarterly* 121, no. 3 (Fall 2006), p. 369. See also Renée de Nevers, 'Modernizing the Geneva Conventions', *Washington Quarterly* 29, no. 2 (Spring 2006), pp. 99–113.

2
The History and Status of the Geneva Conventions

Wade Mansell and Karen Openshaw

The use ... of the words 'and to ensure respect for'[1] was, however, deliberate; they were intended to emphasize the responsibility of the Contracting Parties. ... It follows, therefore, that in the event of a Power failing to fulfil its obligations, the other Contracting Parties (neutral, allied or enemy) may, and should, endeavour to bring it back to an attitude of respect for the Convention. The proper working of the system of protection provided by the Convention demands in fact that the Contracting Parties should not be content merely to apply its provisions themselves, but should do everything in their power to ensure that the humanitarian principles underlying the Conventions are applied universally. It is clear that Article 1 is no mere empty form of words but has been deliberately invested with imperative force. It must be taken in its literal meaning.[2]

The Geneva Conventions of 1949 were the then international community's response to what were seen to have been the exposed shortcomings of international humanitarian law in the course of the Second World War.[3] Earlier Geneva Conventions of 1864[4] (revised in 1906) and a replacing Convention of 1929 following the experience of the First World War, considered not only the treatment of sick and wounded but also (in 1929) the question of the treatment of prisoners of war.[5] The 1949 Conventions were not therefore without a history. Indeed, they are best seen as a further development of a preoccupation with the laws of war that had long concerned European states. The 'international community' of 1949, although changing as decolonisation began, was obviously very different from the current United Nations with 192 states. Indeed, the Conventions were drawn up by delegations from only some 60 nations, but this did not mean that there was total, or even general consensus as to what was desirable, what was possible or even what was practical. Early and significant divisions between the strategy and views of the 'first' and 'second' world states quickly appeared.

Motivation for the new Conventions continued a preoccupation with the laws of war that had its origins in the nineteenth century. Unless this history is appreciated it is scarcely possible to understand the role and place of the 1949 Conventions. In turn this history has to be placed alongside the startling new developments concerning human rights and international law.

Curiously, the preoccupation with *how* war was to be waged has a history that pre-dates questions of *when* it might be permissible to wage it. It is curious because it seems strange that international law should be concerned with limiting the inhumanity of war rather than with the prosecution of war itself. In a book published by the Council on Foreign Relations from the United States titled *Right v. Might*[6] the Foreword began:

> Man's readiness to settle differences by force of arms has been a feature of society since prehistory. Man's attempt to place rational bounds on the use of force, emerging from his revulsion against the scourge of war, is almost as old. This struggle to impose 'rationality on reality' was a central feature of the Enlightenment and the 'Age of Reason' in the eighteenth century.[7]

But it failed to go beyond this undoubted truth to observe the fact that a right to wage war remained unconstrained until after the First World War.

One might have thought that the Treaty of Westphalia,[8] bringing as it did the concept of sovereign equality, might have at least implicitly affected this position. How, after all, could sovereignty be equal if the powerful states were entitled to wage war on the powerless? Such inconsistency was at the very heart of the Westphalian system, however, and the idea that international law could constrain the prerogative of sovereign states to wage war would have been unimaginable.

Endemic European wars were an enduring feature of the seventeenth, eighteenth and nineteenth centuries, both waged within Europe and without. Conquest was the means by which territory was acquired and colonies won. But the ferocity of battle came to be greatly enhanced by the development of ever more fearful weaponry and the beginnings of the 'weapons of mass destruction'. The ability to kill and maim enemies and civilians alike 'progressed' in a remarkable way. The revulsion at the result of this 'progress' led to the founding of the International Red Cross in 1863. Coinciding with the formation of the International Red Cross was another important development. In the United States an American lawyer by the name of Francis Lieber drafted what he wanted to be a statement of the laws and customs of war (not insignificantly, he apparently had friends and relatives on both sides of the American Civil War). The resulting Lieber Code was issued as 'Instructions for the Government of Armies of the United States in the Field'. In the words of Brian Simpson,

> The Lieber Code stated a fundamental principle: 'Men who take up arms against one another in public war do not cease on that account to be moral beings, responsible to one another and to God.' It laid down principles designed to reduce suffering by non-combatants, to limit reprisals, to provide for the humane treatment of prisoners and wounded, to regulate the use of flags of truce, and to limit the severity of measures taken under martial law. Versions of the Code were adopted by other armies, for example by Germany, and so it acquired an international character. In any case it purported to state international law, not American law. Lieber's innovative attempt to express the demands of humanity in legal form encouraged the powers to produce formal agreements (variously called Declarations, Conventions and Protocols) on aspects of the laws of war...[9]

Nevertheless, as long as many armies remained essentially mercenary (and where not, the overwhelming percentage of casualties remained impoverished recruits), there was little impetus to develop rules as to when war might be waged.

One further development was important in the rise of humanitarian law. As Oppenheim observes, whereas in warfare in the Middle Ages

> war was a contention between the whole populations of the belligerent States ... [and] in time of war every subject of one belligerent, whether an armed and fighting individual or not, whether man or woman, adult or infant, could be killed or enslaved by the other belligerent at will,

by the twentieth century war had become, almost invariably 'a contention of States *through their armed forces*'.[10] This led to an increase in awareness that private subjects of belligerent states, not involved in the 'contention' could reasonably expect some protection.

International law responded by developing customary international laws not as to when war might or might not be waged but concerning *how* it might be waged, and, to a lesser extent, against whom it might be waged.[11] These laws were ultimately codified in treaties beginning only in the second half of the nineteenth century. The first of these was the 1856 Paris Declaration on the subject of maritime war, and it was followed by the 1864 Geneva Convention concerned with the wounded and sick and the St Petersburg Declaration of 1868 concerned with explosive projectiles. In 1874, at the instigation of Russia, an international conference was held in Brussels that adopted an International Declaration Concerning the Laws and Customs of War. While a lack of ratifications meant that it never entered into force it was important as a precursor to the crucial Hague 'First International Peace Conference' of 1899, and the 'Second International Peace Conference' of 1907. These Conferences, again held at the invitation of the Russian Government, adopted numerous international instruments codifying (and sometimes adding to) international law. The 1907 Conference alone adopted 13 conventions and a declaration.[12]

Because these Conventions primarily codified the law relating to warfare they were, when this was the case, binding on all states.[13] Prominence was also given here to the so-called 'Martens Clause', which appeared in the Preamble in 1899. While the origin of this clause is disputed, what it did was to assert that where law was not yet sufficiently complete, the parties nevertheless wished to declare that in cases outside those covered by the declarations and regulations, populations and belligerents remained under the protection of international laws 'as they result from usages established among civilized peoples, from the laws of humanity, and the dictates of the public conscience'.[14] This clause was later to be reformulated in the 1949 Geneva Conventions, where it is stated that

in cases not covered by [the Geneva Conventions and Protocols] or by other international agreements, civilians and combatants remain under the protection and authority of the principles of international law derived from established custom, from the principles of humanity and from dictates of public conscience.

Humane sentiments notwithstanding, there are obvious tensions between a state determined to win a war and the demands of humanity. To be required to prosecute a war humanely smacks of oxymoronism. It is the reality of this that has 'necessitated' a limitation upon humanitarian objectives and is encompassed within the concept, apparently antithetical to international humanitarian law, of 'military necessity' – a concept recognised as early as 1868 in the St Petersburg Declaration, where it is stated that there are 'technical limits at which military necessities ought to yield to the requirements of humanity'. As Ingrid Detter observes, 'By implication, there are thus cases when such limits will not yield.'[15] It is not difficult to imagine dilemmas when even a cost/benefit analysis will fail to determine whether military necessity could or should be a justification for what would otherwise be a breach of humanitarian obligation.[16]

Such tensions were inevitably present in the drafting of the 1949 Geneva Conventions. At the drafting conference many different interests had to be accommodated. Those attending represented states that were directly engaged in the Second World War, some of which had been battlefields, some of which had 'merely' been bombed, some of which had 'merely' provided armed forces, and a number of which had been occupied. There were also states that had remained uninvolved in the war. Not surprisingly, these different experiences led to different priorities, which in turn necessarily led to compromise. States that had been occupied were acutely aware of the inadequacy of international humanitarian law for such situations. In particular, the question of the 'right' to resist belligerent occupation in the face of the argued need of an occupier to promote order within unpopularly occupied territory, led to much dispute – particularly as some of the participants were now in the situation of being occupiers themselves, not least in Germany and Japan. Again the thorny problem of 'military necessity' tempered the enthusiasm for the unrestrained protection of inhabitants of occupied territories.

While the preparation of the Geneva Conventions continued, it was against the background of the war crimes trials at Nuremburg and elsewhere. These affected the negotiations in two ways. Firstly, they acted as a constant reminder of the need to be able to call to account those who violated international humanitarian law – and the gruesome evidence presented could hardly have been more graphic. Secondly, they highlighted the need for international humanitarian law to be supplemented with human rights protection.[17] As has been observed, international humanitarian law confined itself to the effect of the rules of warfare – rules that at that stage were almost entirely assumed to be concerned with international conflict between warring states. The rise of international concern with human rights arose from the very clear evidence that citizens not involved in warfare might yet require clear protection from the decisions and conduct of their own governments[18] – though quite how this was to be secured remained unresolved, with the strain between sovereignty and mandatory international obligation (which was the obligation human rights protection implied) apparently almost insuperable.

Unsurprisingly, then, no delegation was entirely happy with the outcome at Geneva but the result, if less than perfect, was still impressive. The crucial, traditional distinction between combatant and non-combatant was retained and remained central. The four separate Conventions aimed at protecting the wounded and sick on land (Geneva Convention I), the wounded, sick and shipwrecked at sea (Geneva Convention II), defining and refining the correct treatment of prisoners of war (Geneva Convention III), and providing for the protection of civilian persons (non-combatants) in a time of war (Geneva IV). It is with Geneva III and Geneva IV that this book is most concerned, together with the two 1977 Geneva Protocols.

The necessity for these protocols is itself instructive concerning developments unforeseen in 1949. Between 1949 and 1977 many armed conflicts occurred that did not fit easily within the warfare envisaged. Some at least were non-international in character, and there was also a rise in guerrilla activities, consequently challenging definitions for combatant status. The effect of Protocol I, by no means unanimously supported, was to expressly extend international conflict status to 'armed conflicts in which peoples are fighting against colonial domination and alien occupation and against racist regimes in the exercise of their right of self-determination'.[19] Protocol II recognised the rise of civil conflicts and provided rules intended to constrain the range of violence that states might use while suppressing civil unrest. In so doing it clearly entered into areas that might have been thought to be within the preserve of human rights law. Also, in the words of Stephen Neff,

> it supplemented Common Article Three by expanding the range of protections available to persons in detention. More importantly, it placed various restrictions on the waging of the conflict, largely in the interest of protecting civilians.[20]

Before proceeding to consider the status of the Geneva Conventions after the terrorist attacks upon the US of 11 September 2001, it is important to briefly consider examples of their operation elsewhere, not least because some idea of their significance, limitations and enforceability may be illustrated. The first concerns the application of Geneva IV in the Palestinian Occupied Territories – territory that has been occupied by Israel since 1967. In 1991 Falk and Weston, two eminent international lawyers, argued persuasively in an article in the *Harvard International Law Journal*, not only that Geneva IV applied to Israel's occupation but that there was irrefutable evidence of clear breaches of that Convention.[21] The authors argued that these transgressions could not be justified by 'military necessity'. Convincing though the arguments were, they proved to be inconsequential. Israel was shielded from any effective action (which could only come from the Security Council) by at least one 'veto power' upon whom Israel could always rely (the USA).

A subsequent article by Ardi Imseis in the same journal in 2003 made many of the same arguments notwithstanding the changed circumstances (which in fact remained depressingly similar).[22] Beyond observing the many transgressions both continuing and new,[23] Imseis attempted to discover remedies that might be available, or at least solutions that might be identified, and how, if at all, Geneva IV might be enforced. Fairly observing that the primary purpose of Geneva IV is 'the effective and impartial protection of victims of armed conflict rather than the punishment of war crimes and other violations after they have been committed',[24] Imseis nevertheless concludes that where compliance is demonstrably and unapologetically absent, questions of enforcement become crucial, and this is inferable from Article 1 of the Convention, which provides an obligation upon High Contracting Parties 'to respect and to ensure respect for the present Convention in all circumstances'.

But how might this be achieved? The first possibility lies in the domestic jurisdiction of the allegedly non-compliant state. This is discussed with reference to the US below but was of little avail in Israel. The second possibility, at least for Geneva IV, is the enforcement mechanism found in Article 9. This provides for the appointment of 'Protecting Powers' that are to have the duty 'to safeguard the [humanitarian] interests of the parties to the conflict'. Unfortunately, no Protecting Power has ever been appointed in any conflict. A third relevant but unlikely possibility might be the use of the International Criminal Court, which includes in the list of the most serious international crimes for which perpetrators could be brought to justice in the ICC, stated in Article 8 of the Rome Statute, acts defined as 'grave breaches' in Article 146 of Geneva IV. As neither Israel nor the US is a party to the ICC (Israel voted against its creation, and the US initially signed but then famously unsigned), it would require Security Council action if it was to have effect.[25] Finally, the matter could be considered by the International Court of Justice. In fact, this did happen and the advisory opinion of the ICJ was given in 2004.[26] As will be seen, this did not directly deal with all the issues raised in the Imseis article but it did assert that the building of the 'security wall' was contrary to the obligations found in Geneva IV.[27] Such a decision might have been expected to lead to attempts to give effect to the advisory opinion, as indeed it did, but again without significant effect. Israel's manifest and unpunished breaches of Geneva IV might be seen to have encouraged the US to pay less attention to the Conventions' requirements than could have been hoped after the events of September 11.

A brief legal point needs to be briefly explained at this juncture concerning the relationship between domestic and international law. The principle of *pacta sunt servanda*[28] underlies international law. But this of course refers to a state's international obligations and does not necessarily affect domestic law. An example may be helpful. The United Kingdom was an early ratifier of the European Convention on Human Rights. As such it entered into an international obligation to enforce the Convention. But this did not give UK citizens the right to rely upon the Convention in UK courts because it was not (without legislation) a part of domestic (internal) UK law. The Convention was not entirely without meaning in a domestic context, as the courts had held that in the light of international obligation, legislation or common law should be interpreted *insofar as it was possible* in a manner consistent with such international provision, while recognising that the accurate application of domestic law was the first responsibility. To be incorporated into domestic law required legislation.[29] Thus until the Human Rights Act,[30] which enacted many of the provisions of the Convention, UK citizens had first to exhaust any domestic remedies and then pursue their remedies under the Convention at Strasbourg, with the UK state then having a treaty obligation to give effect to whatever ruling came from the European Court of Human Rights.

The position in the US is similar but marginally more complicated. At first sight it seems straightforward, with Article VI, Clause 2 of the US Constitution stating:

This Constitution, and the Laws of the United States which shall be made in Pursuance thereof; and all Treaties made, or which shall be made, under the Authority of the United States, shall be the supreme Law of the Land; and the Judges in every State shall be bound thereby, any Thing in the Constitution or Laws of any State to the Contrary notwithstanding.

It might be inferred that such treaties as the Geneva Conventions automatically become part of domestic law. In general, however, this is not true. A treaty duly signed and ratified does bind the state in its dealings with other states that have ratified mutual obligations, but ordinarily if it is to become a part of domestic law it will require enactment through legislation. The Geneva Conventions may, however, be different. In the case of *USA v Noriega*[31] a court had to determine whether Geneva III could provide General Noriega with any protection in domestic, federal law. Here the court held that, exceptionally, the Geneva Conventions were 'self-executing'[32] and so could provide Noriega with a right of action in a US court. It held that this was so because, unlike most other multilateral treaties, not to hold that the Geneva Conventions were self-executing would be 'inconsistent with both the language and spirit of the treaty' and could not be reconciled with the professed support of its purposes by the administration.[33]

This, then, was the legal setting of the operation of the Geneva Conventions before 2001. Shortly after the attacks on US territory carried out by members of the terrorist group al-Qaeda on 11 September 2001, President George W. Bush announced the instigation of a 'war on terror'. That the language employed was not merely figurative (as in a 'war on drugs' or 'war on crime') was seemingly confirmed by the US Congress a few days later in its joint resolution[34] empowering the President 'to use all necessary and appropriate force against those nations, organizations, or persons he determines planned, authorized, committed, or aided the terrorist attacks that occurred on September 11, 2001…'. Thus, from the very beginning, the Bush administration signalled its determination to treat the terrorist atrocities perpetrated by al-Qaeda not, as might have been expected, as crimes best tackled under domestic and international criminal law, but as the opening salvos in an armed conflict, governed by the laws of war.

This confusion between criminal law and the laws of war has been a persistent theme of the war on terror, illustrative of the fact that combating terrorism sits uneasily within a humanitarian law framework premised on the belief that conflicts take place between states or between governments and insurgents within the boundaries of one country,[35] have identifiable end-dates, and enable a clear distinction to be maintained between those who are actively involved in hostilities and those who are not. Moreover, the Bush administration's attempts to capitalise on this confusion, arrogating to itself the powers of a nation at war while denying those captured in the course of the conflict the basic protections provided for under the Geneva Conventions, has greatly undermined the post-war humanitarian law consensus, which, ironically, the US played a principal role in constructing. In the process, the rights of detainees have been considerably eroded, establishing damaging precedents for the treatment of captured individuals in future conflicts.

Indeed, while past conflicts have prompted attempts to correct inadequacies and close loopholes in the existing legal regime governing the conduct of war and the treatment of those who, for one reason or another, are not active participants in the hostilities (the suffering of civilian populations at enemy hands during the Second World War being the main impetus for the implementation of the Geneva Conventions themselves),[36] the Bush administration instead chose to attempt to manipulate humanitarian law to its own advantage in the war against terror, cynically exploiting any apparent ambiguities or omissions in order to minimise the safeguards the Conventions intended to provide. This has been especially evident in its insistence that the various protections contained in the Conventions are not applicable to those termed enemy combatants, detained at the US naval base at Guantánamo Bay, Cuba, and its attempts to reclassify certain interrogation methods as acts not amounting to torture.

Ironically, given the role of the US in drafting the Conventions, the Bush administration exhibited a determination to focus on the letter rather than the spirit of Geneva, maintaining that those held at Guantánamo Bay do not fall within the ambit of the Conventions, and so are undeserving of even the most minimal of the protections that the Geneva framework was intended to provide. Thus, the Bush government argued[37] that, because the conflict with members of al-Qaeda does not amount to a war between one or more states as required by Article 2 common to each of the four Conventions,[38] the main provisions of the Conventions do not apply. In addition, it has also denied that the minimum safeguards contained in Article 3 (also common to the four Conventions) have been activated, since the conflict is not of the intra-state type apparently contemplated by

Article 3,[39] being not confined to US territory or indeed within the borders of any one nation alone.[40] Consequently, detained members of al-Qaeda (or those alleged to be so) have found themselves in a sort of humanitarian limbo, seemingly involved in neither an international nor non-international conflict for the purposes of the Conventions, and so not entitled to the benefit of any of their safeguards.

In fact, the Bush administration was reluctant to extend the protection of the Geneva Conventions to any individual captured during the course of the conflict in Afghanistan between the US and its allies and members of the Taliban forces and their Afghan and non-Afghan sympathisers,[41] whether members of al-Qaeda or not. Even after it had conceded that the Conventions were applicable to the conflict between the US and Taliban forces,[42] the administration refused to regard those who had fought on behalf of the Taliban as prisoners of war, since, it contended, they had failed to fulfil the criteria entitling them to such status as set out in Geneva Convention III,[43] most notably by violating the customs of war through their association with a terrorist group (al-Qaeda), and by failing to wear an identifiable uniform.[44] Similarly, the US administration routinely refused to grant prisoner of war status to those fighting against US forces and its allies in Iraq, even former members of Saddam Hussein's regime who were 'continuing to fight for their "legitimate" government, and who would almost certainly be entitled to treatment in accordance with the law of war and the Geneva Convention on the treatment of prisoners ...'[45] Nor had the administration been prepared to entertain the notion that there might be any doubt in such matters, thereby enabling it to ignore Geneva Convention III's requirement that, where it is uncertain whether a detainee is a prisoner of war or not, he or she must be treated as such pending determination of the matter 'by a competent tribunal'.[46]

Moreover, attempts by individual detainees to test the legality of their detention by way of a petition of habeas corpus prompted the administration to deny that the jurisdiction of the US courts extended to Guantánamo, so creating a legal lacuna in which detainees could be held for an unlimited length of time (potentially for the rest of their lives, there being, unlike in the case of conventional warfare, no obvious end to a war directed against terrorist acts) without being informed of the evidence against them or provided with the opportunity and means to challenge such evidence.[47] In so doing, the Bush administration also violated the provisions of Article 75(3) of

Additional Protocol I to the Geneva Conventions,[48] which stipulates that anyone detained for reasons relating to a conflict must be informed promptly of the reasons why they have been detained and released as quickly as possible, unless a criminal offence has been committed.[49]

As a result, it has generally been left to members of the US judiciary to resist the excesses of the executive in the war against terror, albeit that the applicability of the Geneva Conventions to those held at Guantánamo Bay remains unresolved by the US courts, which are seemingly reluctant to confront the matter directly. In *Rasul v Bush*[50] the US Supreme Court asserted that the US courts did possess the necessary jurisdiction to entertain habeas corpus petitions from those held at Guantánamo, holding that the naval base fell within the exclusive jurisdiction and control of the US (Cuba's sovereignty over the territory reviving only when the treaty leasing the base to the US is finally terminated). The Supreme Court also confirmed (in *Hamdi v Rumsfeld*)[51] that a detainee classified as an enemy combatant was entitled, notwithstanding the fact that the hostilities in which he was involved were still ongoing, to challenge the executive's right to hold him without trial or access to legal representation. This in turn led to the Bush administration setting up 'combatant status review tribunals' to establish whether individuals held at Guantánamo could in fact be categorised as enemy combatants and therefore detained until the relevant hostilities had ceased.

Similarly, it was left to the US Supreme Court in *Hamdan v Rumsfeld*[52] to bring the al-Qaeda detainees within the ambit of the Geneva Conventions by opting for a much more expansive interpretation of Common Article 3's remit, in which the court asserted that the Article's provisions applied to all armed conflicts not of an international character (whether confined within the boundaries of one state or not) and hence operated as a mop-up provision, ensuring minimum standards were adhered to in any conflict not caught by Article 2.[53] As a consequence, the court was able to conclude that the military commissions set up by the Bush administration to try detainees such as Hamdan[54] did not comply with Common Article 3 (incorporated into US domestic law, together with other provisions of the law of war, by Article 21 of the Uniform Code of Military Justice),[55] since they violated Article 3's stipulation that such tribunals be 'regularly constituted'[56] – a requirement that could be met under US law only by adhering to the standards of a court martial, with any deviation from this allowable only when justified by 'some practical need', any such need not being demonstrated in Hamdan's case.[57] Among other matters, the court noted that the military commissions failed to comply with regular court-martial practice and the minimum standards of Common Article 3 by permitting the accused and his counsel to be excluded from parts of the proceedings at the discretion of the presiding officer, and by preventing the accused from being informed of what evidence was presented against him during such 'closed' sessions.

Nevertheless *Hamdi* and *Hamdan* both failed to clarify the question of whether the Geneva Conventions can be relied on directly by individuals before US courts (i.e., whether the Conventions are 'self-executing' as had been held in *Noriega*), as opposed to being enforceable only if incorporated into US law by means of implementing legislation. In *Hamdi*, as Aya Gruber notes, the Supreme Court adopted a distinctly selective approach to the laws of war, consulting them in order to determine the nature of the President's authority to detain individuals involved in hostilities, but then failing to consider the other side of the coin – the extent to which such laws, including the Geneva Conventions, applied to protect those individuals during the period of detention.[58] Meanwhile, in *Hamdan*, the Court was able to sidestep the issue of whether the Conventions could be relied on directly by holding that certain provisions of the Conventions (set out in Common Article 3) applied by virtue of their being incorporated into US domestic law via the Uniform Code of Military Justice.[59]

This failure to determine whether the Geneva Conventions can be enforced directly before US courts has inevitably undermined the status of the Conventions, ultimately weakening rather than strengthening the humanitarian protection afforded to the detainees at Guantánamo. In the case of *Hamdi*, the outcome has been the invocation of 'the law of war to avoid prosecuting terrorist suspects in civilian courts, while ignoring the limits that the law of war imposes on the detention, treatment and trial of prisoners',[60] while *Hamdan*, by refusing to hold that the applicability of the Conventions rests on anything firmer than the approval of the US legislature, set the scene for Congress to determine when and in what form the Geneva framework would take effect at the domestic level.

Consequently, the Military Commissions Act of 2006 (MCA),[61] enacted to try those designated as alien unlawful enemy combatants,[62] effectively overruled the decision in *Hamdan*, allowing Congress to baldly assert that any military commission established under the MCA would be deemed fully compliant with the provisions of Common Article 3,[63] notwithstanding the fact that the Act sanctions several departures from regular court-martial practice, and arguably fails to provide 'the judicial guarantees ... recognized as indispensable by civilized peoples'. In particular, the MCA permits the exclusion of defendants and their counsel from the commission's proceedings in certain circumstances, allows classified information to be presented while restricting defendants' ability to challenge such evidence, renders hearsay evidence admissible in certain cases, and refuses to regard as inadmissible statements obtained by ill treatment falling short of torture. Unsurprisingly, the MCA also precludes defendants from relying on any of the provisions of the Geneva Conventions directly before a military commission,[64] thus ousting the Conventions completely, and making its own interpretation of humanitarian law definitive.[65] Moreover, other provisions of the MCA deviate from the standards of the Geneva Conventions in important ways, making further damaging inroads into humanitarian law. Most notably, the Act takes an overly restrictive view of those entitled to prisoner-of-war status,[66] while widening the definition of an unlawful enemy combatant to include an individual 'who has purposefully and materially supported hostilities against the United States or its co-belligerents who is not a lawful enemy combatant (including a person who is part of the Taliban, al-Qaeda, or associated forces)'.[67] It also includes a much wider definition, in defiance of internationally accepted norms, of what constitutes a war crime, thereby unilaterally extending this most serious category of criminal act, and demonstrating in the process the way in which conventional crimes and violations of the law of war became dangerously blurred under the Bush administration – an administration that was more than willing to prosecute terrorist suspects under the laws of war rather than domestic criminal law, but was much less eager to afford those individuals the complementary humanitarian protections embodied in the Geneva Conventions.

Significantly, the military commission convened to try Hamdan in December 2007 (i.e., after the passage of the MCA) decided that it was obliged to entertain the defendant's claim that he was entitled to prisoner-of-war status in accordance with Article 5 of the third Geneva Convention,[68] in spite of the fact that the MCA had apparently barred defendants from relying on any provisions of the Conventions directly. This in turn may indicate the extent to which the US government's attempt to exclude the provisions of the Conventions and other concepts of humanitarian law from situations in which they would ordinarily be thought to apply is alien to those charged with adjudicating such matters (even those presiding over tribunals specifically set up in order to circumvent the niceties of the Conventions). This would seem to leave the way open for further assaults on the MCA and its attempt to redefine humanitarian law as it applies to a certain category of detainee.

The double standards evident in the Bush administration's efforts to combat terrorism – an insistence that it is prosecuting a war, matched with a refusal, whenever possible, to grant those captured, prisoner-of-war status, or any of the protections set out in the Geneva Conventions – has also enabled it to justify the use of harsh interrogation methods, undermining basic prohibitions against torture and ill treatment. Indeed, characterizing terrorist acts as illustrative of a new type of war (rather than as the commission of criminal acts) enabled the administration to argue that the Geneva rulebook was simply irrelevant. Thus, explained Alberto Gonzales, General Counsel to President Bush, the war on terrorism, in contrast to conventional warfare:

> ... places a high premium on other factors, such as the ability to quickly obtain information from captured terrorists and their sponsors ... this new paradigm renders obsolete Geneva's strict limitations on questioning of enemy prisoners and renders quaint some of its provision ...[69]

In effect, the Bush government, with the help of certain legal advisers, sought to deny the applicability or reinterpret its international and domestic legal obligations prohibiting the use of torture and ill treatment in order to expand the range of interrogation techniques available to use against suspected terrorists. Such a strategy was implemented in defiance not only of the prohibitions on torture and ill treatment contained in Geneva Convention III and Geneva Convention IV,[70] as well as in various human rights treaties,[71] but also contrary to the more specific requirements contained in the Convention Against Torture (CAT),[72] to which the US is a party.

Most notoriously, Assistant Attorney General Jay Bybee, in advising as to whether the treatment meted out to certain detainees thought to be high-level al-Qaeda operatives was sufficiently severe as to amount to torture, offered an extremely narrow definition of the concept. Taking CAT's definition of torture as codified into US federal law as his starting point – 'severe physical or mental pain or suffering'[73] – he argued that only acts that produced physical pain equivalent to that accompanying 'serious physical injury such as death or organ failure' or gave rise to mental suffering resulting in 'lasting psychological harm, such as seen in mental disorders like post-traumatic stress disorder' would be sufficient to constitute torture.[74] Setting the bar for committing torture so high thereby enabled a greater range of maltreatment to slip through the net.[75] In any event, Bybee asserted, legal constraints on the way in which information could be gleaned from detainees represented an unconstitutional interference with the President's commander-in-chief powers, obstructing him 'from gaining the intelligence he believes necessary to prevent attacks upon the United States',[76] and could therefore be ignored. Moreover, even if this were not the case, interrogators who committed acts of torture would not necessarily be criminally liable for their actions, provided they were able to raise a defence of necessity (that the act of torture was necessary to avert a great harm, such as occurred on 9/11)[77] or show that they were acting in self-defence on behalf of the country, so as to prevent further terrorist attacks.[78] That the Bybee memo was aimed not so much at providing impartial legal advice as at sanctioning the use of interrogation methods bordering on torture and beyond was highlighted by one senior government lawyer, who commented that the document read 'like a bad defense counsel's brief, not an OLC [Office of Legal Counsel] opinion'.[79]

The Bush administration also sought to deny, extraordinarily, that any of its international legal obligations regarding the outlawing of torture applied to those detainees held at Guantánamo. This was partly because the administration had determined that the Geneva Conventions did not apply to such individuals, but also, in the case of various human rights treaties, because their provisions were held not to be effective in US domestic law. This was either because such treaties were deemed to be non-self-executing, with the US having failed to pass implementing legislation, or because the US had made it a condition of entering such treaties that its own interpretation of what amounts to inhumane treatment would apply.[80]

Arguably, therefore, instances of torture and ill treatment that occurred in various US-run detention camps were not merely the inadvertent consequences of a casual disregard for the basic principles of humanitarian and human rights law, but the logical outcome of a culture eager to extend the boundaries of permissible interrogation techniques in order to extract as much information as possible from suspected terrorists. Thus it was argued that subjecting a detainee to an interrogation method intended to reproduce the effects of drowning (the use of so-called waterboarding or simulated drowning techniques) does not amount to torture. This surely emphasises the extent to which departure from the fundamental protections contained in the Geneva Conventions leads to an appalling degradation in the treatment meted out to those caught up in the course of a conflict. The fact that such treatment may return to haunt the US if its own military or other personnel are captured did not move the Bush administration. Nor, with such attitudes prevalent in the highest echelons of that US administration, is it surprising that soldiers on the ground came to believe that inflicting both physical and psychological pain on their charges (resulting in death in some cases), as occurred in particular at the Abu Ghraib detention centre in Iraq, was acceptable behaviour, ultimately justified by the goal of obtaining useful intelligence.

This chapter concludes by emphasising once more the initial quotation. The Geneva Conventions are dependent for their effect upon the good faith of the international community. That such good faith has been lacking in the case of the US is a matter of profound regret for all who believe that the principles of international humanitarian law are in the interests of all mankind. On an optimistic note, it is difficult to believe that the incoming administration, with its new President a sometime Professor of Constitutional Law at Chicago, will wish to uphold the policies of the old. At the same time the lesson of the ease with which cherished rights can be lost should never be forgotten.

NOTES

1. Article 1 of the Fourth Geneva Convention states 'The High Contracting Parties undertake to respect and to ensure respect for the present Convention in all circumstances.'
2. Taken from the International Committee of the Red Cross commentary regarding the object and purpose of the Fourth Geneva Convention. Quoted in A. Imseis, 'On the Fourth Geneva Convention and the Occupied Palestinian Territory', *Harvard International Law Journal* 44, no. 65 (2003), p. 137.
3. International humanitarian law may be briefly defined as a set of rules intended for humanitarian reasons to limit the effects of armed conflict.
4. Convention for the Amelioration of the Condition of Soldiers wounded in Armies in the Field.
5. These Conventions entered into force and were binding between most belligerents during the Second World War, though not as between Germany and Soviet Russia. See *Oppenheim's International Law*, edited by Sir Hersch Lauterpacht, 7th edn (London: Longman, 1969), p. 369.
6. Louis Henkin, *Right v. Might* (New York: Council on Foreign Relations Press, 1989), Foreword by John Temple Swing.

7. *Ibid.*, p. vii.

8. There are many qualifications, beyond the scope of this chapter, that need to be made concerning the meaning and significance of this 1648 'Peace of Westphalia'. For an excellent introduction into the complexities, see L. Miller, *Global Order: Values and Power in International Politics*, 2nd edn (Boulder, CO: Westview, 1990).

9. A.W.B. Simpson, *Human Rights and the End of Empire* (Oxford: Oxford University Press, 2001), p. 97. For a discussion of the Lieber Code, see R.S. Hartigan, *Lieber's Code and the Laws of War* (Piscataway, NJ: Transaction Publishers, 2006).

10. *Oppenheim's International Law*, ed. Lauterpacht, p. 204.

11. This emphasis upon controlling conduct in the course of war rather than controlling resort to war has been argued by David Kennedy to be explicable in the distinction between public and private acts. He suggests that

> These humanitarian limitations on war were thus part of a broader reorganization of legal thought, sharpening the distinction between the public and private sphere, hardening private rights and limiting public powers to their respective sphere. ... The result was a legal conception of war as a public project *limited to its sphere*. It seemed reasonable to expect that warriors *stay* over there, and that protected persons, even women soldiers stay *outside* the domain of combat.

See David Kennedy, *Of War and Law* (Princeton: Princeton University Press, 2006).

12. At its broadest the distinction between so-called 'Hague law' and 'Geneva law' (although they do overlap) has been described as 'Hague law' being concerned with the laws of war in the strict sense, i.e., law 'that regulated the conduct of hostilities as between the contenders (by, for instance, prohibiting certain types of weapons or certain types of tactics)', while 'Geneva law' was humanitarian law that began its life as a body of rules distinct from the laws of war and concerned with relief for the victims of war. See S. Neff, *War and the Law of Nations: A General History* (Cambridge: Cambridge University Press, 2005).

13. Generally speaking, as customary international law is binding upon all states (with only rare exceptions) it remains so even if codified in a document to which all states are not parties. See *Nicaragua v USA* [1986] ICJ Rep.

14. Preamble to Hague Convention II on the Rules of Land Warfare, 1899.

15. I. Detter, *The Law of War*, 2nd edn (Cambridge: Cambridge University Press, 2000), p. 393.

16. An obvious case is the dropping of atomic bombs in Japan in 1945 with the objective of shortening the war and actually saving lives – albeit allied lives.

17. For an incisive discussion on the relationship between international human rights law and humanitarian law, see H.J. Steiner, P. Alston and R. Goodman, *International Human Rights in Context*, 3rd edn (Oxford: Oxford University Press, 2008), pp. 395–401.

18. Nowhere more clearly illustrated than in the Nazi genocide. The 1948 United Nations Genocide Convention on the Prevention and Punishment of Genocide is to be considered as a part of human rights law as well as the laws of war, in particular the law on crimes against humanity. See A. Roberts and R. Guelph, *Documents on the Laws of War*, 3rd edn (Oxford: Oxford University Press, 2000), p. 179.

19. Protocol I Art. 1(4).

20. Neff, *War and the Law of Nations*.

21. R. Falk and B.H. Weston, 'The Relevance of International Law to Palestinian Rights in the West Bank and Gaza: In Legal Defense of the Intifada', *Harvard International Law Journal* 32 (1991), pp. 129–58.

22. A. Imseis, 'On the Fourth Geneva Convention and the Occupied Palestinian Territory', *Harvard International Law Journal* 44 (2003), pp. 65–138.

23. *Ibid.,* pp. 100–21.

24. Quoting from Hilaire McCoubrey, addressing a United Nations International Meeting on the Convening of the Conference on Measures to Enforce the Fourth Geneva Convention in the Occupied Palestinian Territory, including Jerusalem, held in Cairo, June 1999.

25. See Imseis, 'On the Fourth Geneva Convention', p. 130.

26. Advisory Opinion of the ICJ concerning the Legal Consequences of the Construction of a Wall in the Occupied Palestinian Territory, 9 July 2004.

27. The ICJ has two types of jurisdiction. It can give decisions in contentious cases between state parties under particular circumstances (usually effectively requiring the consent of the parties to the dispute to the ICJ's jurisdiction), or it can provide advisory opinions on points of international law, if requested to do so by a relevant body of the UN.

28. Roughly translated as 'every treaty in force is binding upon the parties and must be performed by them in good faith', or even more roughly as 'in international law, promises must be honoured'.

29. A point also made in *Pinochet* where the House of Lords held that the 1984 Convention Against Torture could only be relevant in extradition proceedings when it had been incorporated into domestic law (as it had been in the Criminal Justice Act of 1988). See *ex parte Pinochet (No 3)* [2000] 1 AC 147.

30. The Human Rights Act, 1998.

31. 808 F. Supp. 791 (S.D. Fla. 1992). One aspect of this case concerned whether General Noriega, who had been captured by US forces in Panama and removed to the US where he was charged with a number of offences, was entitled to claim to be treated as a prisoner of war under Geneva III.

32. This means that the treaty was incorporated into domestic law without further legislation being required.

33. For an accurate summary of *United States of America v Manuel Antonio Noriega,* see M. Reisman and C.T. Antoniou, *The Laws of War* (London: Vintage, 1994), pp. 220–30.

34. Authorization of Use of Military Force (AUMF) of 18 September 2001 (Public Law 107-40, 115 Stat. 224).

35. As Sean Murphy notes:

    ... the two dominant paradigms that operate within the Geneva Conventions – one concerning 'international' armed conflict (i.e. conflict between two or more states) and the other concerning 'noninternational' armed conflict between a state and nonstate actors (typically understood as conflict internal to a single state) – do not fit the phenomenon of global terrorism, where the dominant paradigm concerns transnational armed conflict between state and nonstate actors.

    Sean D. Murphy, 'Evolving Geneva Convention Paradigms in the "War on Terrorism": Applying the Core Rules to the Release of Persons Deemed

"Unprivileged Combatants"', *George Washington Law Review* 75 (2006–07), pp. 1105–64. Cf. Eran Shamir-Borer, 'Revisiting *Hamdan v Rumsfeld*'s Analysis of the Laws of Armed Conflict', *Emory International Law Review* 21 (2007), pp. 601–2.

36. See Geoffrey Best, *War and Law Since 1945* (Oxford: Oxford University Press, 1994), p. 115.

37. *Hamdan v Rumsfeld*, 126 S. Ct. 2749, 29 June 2006.

38. According to which, '… the present Convention shall apply to all cases of declared war or of any other armed conflict which may arise *between two or more of the High Contracting Parties …*'. Emphasis added.

39. Article 3 commencing: 'In the case of armed conflict *not of an international character occurring in the territory of one of the High Contracting Parties, …*'. Emphasis added.

40. It did, however, pledge to treat those detained at Guantánamo 'in a manner consistent with the principles of the Third Geneva Convention of 1949'. See White House Fact Sheet of 7 February 2002, available at: http://www.whitehouse.gov/news/releases/2002/02/20020207-13.html.

41. The initial attack on Afghanistan in October 2001 by the US and certain of its allies was prompted by the refusal of the ruling Taliban administration to cooperate in locating and handing over Osama bin Laden, the Saudi Arabian architect of the 9/11 attacks, who had been operating from Afghanistan. The attack did not receive the prior approval of the UN Security Council (as required under Chapter VII of the UN Charter) but was effectively sanctioned by the Security Council after the event, being described as an instance of 'self defence' (permissible under Article 51 of the UN Charter) in UN SC Resolution 1368 of 12 September 2001 and Resolution 1373 of 14 November 2001. In arriving at this conclusion, the Security Council seems, rather surprisingly, both to have accepted that the anticipatory use of force by the Bush administration could constitute a legitimate act of self-defence for the purposes of Article 51, and also that the reference to an 'armed attack' under the Article covered terrorist attacks of the type perpetrated by al-Qaeda, as opposed to an attack by another nation.

42. The Bush government initially denied that the Conventions applied, on the ground that the US had never recognized the Taliban administration in Afghanistan, and that the latter was a 'failed state' not capable of being a party to the Conventions. See memorandum from John Yoo, Deputy Assistant Attorney General, and Robert J. Delabunty, Special Counsel, to William J. Haynes II, General Counsel, Department of Defense, *Application of Treaties and Laws to al Qaeda and Taliban Detainees*, 9 January 2002, reproduced in Karen J. Greenberg and Joshua L. Dratel (eds), *The Torture Papers: The Road to Abu Ghraib* (New York: Cambridge University Press, 2005), p. 39. However, the government was later prepared to confirm that 'Afghanistan is a party to the Convention [i.e., Geneva Convention III], and the President has determined that the Taliban are covered by the Convention'. See White House Fact Sheet, 7 February 2002, note 7.

43. Geneva Convention (III) relative to the Treatment of Prisoners of War, 12 August 1949.

44. Under Article 4(A)(2) of Geneva Convention III, '[m]embers of other militias and members of other volunteer corps, including those of organized resistance

movements, belonging to a Party to the conflict …' are deserving of prisoner-of-war status only if they comply with the following four conditions:

(a)   that of being commanded by a person responsible for his subordinates;
(b)   that of having a fixed distinctive sign recognizable at a distance;
(c)   that of carrying arms openly;
(d)   that of conducting their operations in accordance with the laws and customs of war.

Many commentators, however, have argued that the Taliban do operate independently of al-Qaeda, making it wrong simply to conflate the two. Leslie Green, for example, suggests that members of the Taliban are in the position of 'insurgents or rebels and not … terrorists, thus distinguishing them from members of Al Qaeda'. Leslie C. Green, 'Relevance of Humanitarian Law to Terrorism and Terrorists', in *International Humanitarian Law: Prospects*, ed. John Carey, William V. Dunlap and R. John Pritchard (New York: Transnational Publishers, 2006), p. 25. In addition, the distinctive style of dress adopted by most of the Taliban arguably makes them recognizable as belligerents. Moreover, if Taliban fighters are actually classified as '[m]embers of the armed forces of a Party to the conflict' under Article 4(A)(1), then it is a moot point whether they need meet the conditions listed in Article 4(A)(2) (which deals only with militias and other non-regular forces), unless compliance with such conditions is viewed as implicit in Article 4(A)(1). See Aya Gruber, 'Who's Afraid of Geneva Law?', *Arizona State Law Journal* 39 (Spring 2007), pp. 1023–6.

45.   Green, 'Relevance of Humanitarian Law', p. 35.
46.   Geneva Convention III, Article 5. This also contradicts the US's own rules on the law of land warfare (set out in *Field Manual 27–10*), stating that such a doubt for the purposes of Article 5 must be deemed to arise whenever a captured individual claims the right to be treated as a prisoner of war. See Philippe Sands, *Lawless World: America and the Making and Breaking of Global Rules* (London: Penguin, 2005), p. 149. For a defence of the view that the interpretation of treaties to which the US is a party remains a presidential prerogative, see J. Yoo, *The Powers of Peace and War* (Chicago: University of Chicago Press, 2005), pp. 211–14.
47.   Denying that the US courts enjoy jurisdiction over territory outside the US also prevented Guantánamo detainees from pursuing any claims judicially, including those based on human rights law. See Sands, *Lawless World*, p. 145.
48.   Protocol Additional to the Geneva Conventions of 12 August 1949, and relating to the Protection of Victims of International Armed Conflicts (Protocol I), 8 June 1977. Although the US has not ratified the Protocol, it does accept that the provisions set out in Article 75 form part of customary international law, and are therefore binding on all nations.
49.   Sands, *Lawless World*, p. 150.
50.   124 S. Ct. 2686 (2004).
51.   542 U.S. 507 (2004).
52.   *Hamdan v Rumsfeld*, 126 S. Ct. 2749, 29 June 2006.
53.   For doubts as to whether the court interpreted Article 3 correctly, see Shamir-Borer, 'Revisiting *Hamdan v Rumsfeld*', pp. 608–12, emphasising in particular the drafting history of the Article, which suggests that it was intended to deal with internal, civil war-type conflicts only.

54. Such commissions, set up to try non-US citizens suspected of belonging to al-Qaeda or to have engaged in terrorist activities against the US, were established under a military order issued by the President on 13 November 2001, bearing the somewhat Kafkaesque title 'Detention, Treatment, and Trial of Certain Non-citizens in the War Against Terrorism'. As a result, suspected terrorists were denied the opportunity of being tried either before a court martial or before the US federal courts.

55. 10 U.S.C. §§801–946.

56. The actual wording of the relevant provision, set out in Article 3(1)(d), prohibits 'the passing of sentences and the carrying out of executions without previous judgement pronounced by a regularly constituted court, affording all the judicial guarantees which are recognized as indispensable by civilized peoples'.

57. See Peter J. Spiro's commentary on the case in *American Journal of International Law* 100 (2006), p. 891. The court also concluded that the President lacked congressional authority to set up such military commissions, thereby rejecting the government's arguments that such authority was implicit in the AUMF resolution passed by Congress (see note 1, above). Furthermore, the court denied that the conspiracy charges brought against Hamdan were sufficient to amount to a violation of the law of war, which in turn meant that the commission lacked the authority to try him.

58. Gruber, 'Who's Afraid of Geneva Law?', pp. 1030–2.

59. *Ibid.*, pp. 1037–8. Gruber contends that the court in fact misinterpreted Article 21 of the UCMJ, which was meant only to confirm the President's common-law power to set up military tribunals, and was never intended to expressly authorise their establishment or to prescribe the standards by which they were to operate.

60. *Ibid.*, at p. 1056, quoting Jonathan Hafetz.

61. 10 U.S.C. §§948(a)–950w.

62. U.S.C. §948(a).

63. U.S.C. §948b(f).

64. U.S.C. §948b(g).

65. As Matthew Happold points out, the MCA, notwithstanding its apparent binding effect in terms of US municipal law, cannot serve to weaken the US's legal commitments at the international level, since 'it is a basic rule of international law that a State cannot determine for itself the extent of its international obligations …'. Consequently, for Happold, 'the Supreme Court's decision in *Hamdan* remains a better analysis of US international obligations, whatever the situation might be under its domestic law'. Matthew Happold, '*Hamdan v Rumsfeld* and the Law of War', *Human Rights Law Review* 7, no. 2 (2007), p. 431.

66. 'The MCA defines lawful combatants narrowly to include only roughly the first three categories of those qualifying for protected prisoner of war status under GPW [i.e. Geneva Convention III] …'. See John C. Dehn, 'Why Article 5 Status Determinations are not "Required" at Guantánamo', *Journal of International Criminal Justice* 6, no. 2 (1 May 2008), p. 375.

67. Military Commissions Act of 2006.

68. This Article stipulates that any doubt as to whether an individual qualifies as a prisoner of war or not is to be 'determined by a competent tribunal', with such individual enjoying prisoner-of-war status until such time as the determination is made. That Article 5 was deemed to be applicable to Hamdan's case at all, since it is relevant only to international armed conflicts, with the

Supreme Court in *Hamdan v Rumsfeld* only willing to hold that Common Article 3 applied (relevant to non-international conflicts) was not addressed directly by the court and may be explained by the fact that the charges against Hamdan were widened to include unlawful hostilities in support of the Taliban in Afghanistan, thus bringing him within the ambit of an international armed conflict and hence the provisions of Geneva Convention III. See Dehn, 'Article 5 Status Determinations', pp. 372–3.

69. Memorandum from Albert R. Gonzales to President George W. Bush, *Decision re Application of the Geneva Convention on Prisoners of War to the Conflict with Al Qaeda and the Taliban*, 25 January 2002, reproduced in Greenberg and Dratel, *The Torture Papers*, note 9, p. 119.

70. Article 17 of Geneva Convention III forbids, inter alia, the infliction of physical or mental torture on prisoners of war, with any such acts classified as grave breaches of the Convention (under Article 130). Meanwhile, Geneva Convention IV relative to the Protection of Civilian Persons in Time of War of 12 August 1949 outlaws, under Article 3(1)(a), any acts that cause 'violence to life and person', including 'cruel treatment and torture' while Article 32 prohibits any action that would cause 'physical suffering or extermination', including, inter alia, murder, torture and corporal punishments.

71. In particular, the International Covenant on Civil and Political Rights of 19 December 1966, Article 7.

72. Convention against Torture and Other Cruel, Inhuman or Degrading Treatment or Punishment of 10 December 1984. The Convention entered into force on 26 June 1987. In particular, the Convention defines torture as 'any act by which severe pain or suffering, whether physical or mental, is intentionally inflicted on a person' (Article 1), and obliges states to prevent acts of torture or acts of cruel, inhuman or degrading treatment or punishment occurring in any territory under their jurisdiction (Articles 2 and 16). The US ratified the Convention on 21 October 1994.

73. 18 U.S.C. §2340.

74. Memorandum from Jay S. Bybee, Assistant Attorney General, to Alberto R. Gonzales, Counsel to the President, *Standards of Conduct for Interrogation under 18 U.S.C. §§2340–2340A*, 1 August 2002, reproduced in Greenberg and Dratel, *The Torture Papers*, note 9, pp. 213–14. According to Jack Goldsmith, a former Assistant Attorney General within the Bush administration, the memo was in fact drafted for Bybee by his subordinate, John Yoo. See Jack Goldsmith, *The Terror Presidency* (New York: W.W. Norton, 2007), p. 142.

75. As the Bybee memo acknowledged: 'Because the acts inflicting torture are extreme, there is a significant range of acts that though they might constitute cruel, inhuman, or degrading treatment or punishment fail to rise to the level of torture.' *Standards of Conduct for Interrogation under 18 U.S.C. §§2340–2340A*, note 41, p. 214.

76. *Ibid.*, p. 207.

77. *Ibid.*, pp. 207–9.

78. *Ibid.*, pp. 209–13. The various justifications for committing acts of torture set out in the Bybee memo are neatly summarized by Goldsmith: '... violent acts aren't necessarily torture; if you do torture, you probably have a defense; and even if you don't have a defense, the torture law doesn't apply if you act under color of presidential authority'. Goldsmith, *The Terror Presidency*, p. 144.

79. Cited in *ibid*., p. 149. Goldsmith also notes that the memo's interpretation of the torture legislation was over-broad, and not, as would be usual, confined to determining whether particular practices violated its provisions or not. Consequently, it 'in effect gave interrogators a blank check'. *Ibid*., p. 151.
80. See memorandum of Diane E. Beaver, Staff Judge Advocate, to Commander, Joint Task Force 170, Legal Brief on Proposed Counter-Resistance Strategies, 11 October 2002, reproduced in Greenberg and Dratel, *The Torture Papers*, note 9, pp. 229–30.

3
The Principle of Proportionality in the Law of Armed Conflict

*Françoise Hampson**

The concept of proportionality appears to be hard-wired into the moral and/or legal thinking of human beings, or at least of lawyers and diplomats. It is used in a wide range of legal contexts, from public law to international law. Wherever the law uses the idea of the reasonable man or the man on the Clapham omnibus, it is in effect using the same or a closely related idea. That said, proportionality does not have precisely the same meaning or work in the same way in every context in which it is used.

Some years ago, Professor Michael Reisman of Yale University tried an interesting exercise with some of his students.[1] He asked them to identify an international incident in which law was relevant. He then asked them to examine not the law but the reactions of the affected states and third parties. What emerged in every case was that the reaction depended on proportionality. In some cases, the relevant legal rule left no room for proportionality. Nevertheless, the international reaction depended on that concept. In some cases, a state might be criticised for a lawful act that was viewed as disproportionate. In other cases, third states would not complain about a violation provided that the act was not seen as disproportionate.

Clearly, the situation with regard to the law itself is different. While it may, in certain circumstances, leave room for the application of proportionality, that is not always the case. In some cases, there is a violation of the relevant legal rule, however apparently insignificant the result of the act in question.

This chapter discusses the meaning of and the role played by the principle of proportionality in the law of armed conflict. It is important at the outset to indicate what is not included. The law makes a sharp distinction between the rules applicable to the lawfulness of the resort to armed force (the *jus ad bellum*) and the rules applicable to the conduct of the resultant conflict (the *jus in bello*). Only the latter is being examined here. That said, two recent conflicts suggest that there may be a link, in popular perception, between the two. It is possible that part of the severe criticism of the conduct of the Israeli campaigns in Lebanon and Gaza resulted from the perceived lack of overall proportion in the response to the particular provocations (i.e., the *jus ad bellum*).

It is first necessary to locate the principle of proportionality in its context. That requires that brief consideration be given to the nature and function of the law of armed conflict (LOAC).[2] Again, some of the criticisms made of recent military operations may flow from misunderstandings of what LOAC seeks to do. The relationship between the principles of distinction and proportionality will also need to be discussed briefly. There will follow a more detailed analysis of the form taken by the legal rules that encapsulate the principle of proportionality. There will, finally, be an examination of some of the difficulties to which the rule gives rise in practice. The discussion will focus on the concept of proportionality as defined under treaty law applicable in international armed conflicts (IACs).[3] At the end, there will be a brief discussion of the concept in customary international law and also in non-international armed conflicts (NIACs).[4]

THE NATURE AND FUNCTION OF LOAC

LOAC is not human rights law in situations of conflict. It does not start from a rule on the protection of civilians, from which there are exceptions, which should be narrowly construed, permitting certain forms of military activity. Nor does LOAC have as a hidden agenda making wars impossible to fight lawfully. LOAC takes the fact of conflict as a given. LOAC represents a balance between acts that are militarily necessary and humanitarian considerations. Generally speaking, there is no presumption in favour of one side or the other.[5] Equally, the rules as they stand encapsulate that balance. There can be no appeal to military necessity outside the rules.[6] LOAC is not aspirational. It represents rules by which armed forces have agreed to be bound. Those rules, including the interpretation of those rules, must be capable of being applied in the situations that confront armed forces. If the rules give rise to insuperable difficulties, armed forces are not going to adhere to them. That will result in either revised interpretation of the rules or general abandonment of the law. There can be no doubt that civilians have more to lose from the latter.

The focus of LOAC is on the member of the armed forces. It is designed principally for the operator, rather than the policy-maker. It seeks to guide his decision-making at the time at which action is or is not taken. This cannot be sufficiently emphasised. In some cases, there is a tendency to assume that a high civilian death toll necessarily involves a violation of LOAC.[7] Responsibility will in fact depend upon what individuals knew or ought to have known at the time at which they acted.

The current body of LOAC rules represents the bringing together of two different types of rules, designed for significantly different contexts within armed conflict. Historically, international humanitarian law (IHL) was applied to the rules on the protection of the victims of war. These rules were the province of the International Committee of the Red Cross (ICRC) and were sometimes called 'the law of Geneva'. The concept of victim related to vulnerability. People were victims if they had been adversely affected by the conflict and were in the hands of the opposing party. They were not victims if in the power of their own side. On that basis, and oversimplifying somewhat, victims were the military wounded, sick and shipwrecked, prisoners of war and civilians either in occupied territory or in the power of an opposing party to the conflict. IHL afforded no protection to civilians generally and, in particular, did not protect them from the effects of the fighting.[8] These rules did not interfere significantly in the conduct of military operations. Clearly, there were implications for conduct on the battlefield in the rules on providing care for the wounded and sick and the running of prisoner-of-war camps might involve the diversion of resources that could otherwise have been used in the fighting. Subject to those caveats, IHL rules could be seen principally as operating away from the battlefield. Given the context in which the rules are applicable, it is usually possible to frame the necessary rules in terms of strict rules of behaviour – 'thou shalt' and 'thou shalt not'. There is limited need for any concept of proportionality.

That is not the case with the other strand of the rules. They were designed to regulate the conduct of military operations. Originally, they concerned primarily the relationship between the fighting parties, although there were rules for when civilians found themselves in a conflict zone, such as in a town under siege.[9] The rules addressed what could be targeted and how. While there is clearly scope for some absolute prohibitions, such as the prohibition of intentional attacks against civilians, there is a need for criteria to guide decision-making, rather than absolute rules of behaviour.

These rules are sometimes known as 'the law of The Hague', owing to the location of the negotiations preceding some of the treaties.[10]

In 1977, these two strands were brought together in the Additional Protocols to the Geneva Conventions of 1949. Civilians were seen as potential victims of the fighting. In order to protect them, it was necessary to make more precise the rules on the conduct of hostilities. As was seen above, however, the culture of the two types of rules was significantly different. The Geneva rules were more absolute and did not interfere with the conduct of operations, while the Hague rules provided criteria for decision-making and did restrict military choices. It is possible that some of the current disagreements over the scope and implementation of the principle of proportionality derive from the application, by some commentators, of a Geneva mindset to what is a Hague type of rule.

THE RELATIONSHIP BETWEEN THE PRINCIPLE OF DISTINCTION AND THE PRINCIPLE OF PROPORTIONALITY

The principle of proportionality is not a free-standing legal rule, in the sense that it becomes relevant as a particular step in the decision-making process. Before considering its application, the military operator first has to consider whether the persons or objects that he wishes to target are legitimate objects of attack. If not, the attack will be unlawful, however proportionate the impact on civilians. In other words, there is a logical order in which the questions need to be asked.

Where concern is expressed at the number of civilian casualties, the issue might, superficially, appear to concern proportionality but, in many cases, that may disguise a more complicated reality. If an attacking party regards all members of an organisation that contains a military wing as members of that wing, the result will be that many of those killed will be claimed by the other side to have been civilians.[11]

If an attacking party attaches an overriding priority to guarding against casualties in its own ranks, this may dictate a choice of tactics that makes it more difficult to determine accurately whether a building does contain a military observer or not and will narrow the range of options regarding the means of attack.[12] The result is likely to be a higher civilian toll and greater destruction of civilian property, but this is not the result of problems with applying the concept proportionality. It is attributable, rather, to prior decisions regarding who is a legitimate target of attack and what constitutes a military objective and, ultimately, to the priority attached to avoiding casualties on one's own side, which may have contributed to those decisions.

The definition of a military objective in Additional Protocol I (API) is generally accepted as reflecting customary international law.[13] There do, however, appear to be differences in the interpretation of part of the definition.[14] This is of particular relevance in coalition operations. The degree to which the differences give rise to difficulties in practice depends in part on the type of military operation and the political context.[15] It should be noted that the definition requires a threshold to be crossed.

> [M]ilitary objectives are limited to those objects which by their nature, location, purpose or use make an effective contribution to military action and whose total or partial destruction, capture or neutralization, in the circumstances ruling at the time, offers a definite military advantage.[16]

If the threshold is crossed, the thing is a military objective. If it is not, the object cannot be attacked at all. Anything that is not a military objective is, by definition, a civilian object.[17] Nothing can fall between the two.

Legally speaking, there is no such thing as a dual-use object. If, for example, a bridge is used by both civilians and the armed forces, the first question is whether the military use that is made of the bridge is such as to cross the threshold in the definition of a military objective. The question of civilian use is not relevant to that determination. If the military significance of the bridge takes it across the threshold, it is a military objective and can be attacked. The second question, which must be answered before any attack can be carried out, concerns the way in which the target is to be attacked. At that point the issue of proportionality comes into play and the use made of the bridge by civilians will be taken into account.

It appears that proportionality has no relevance in establishing which *things* can be attacked but it may be relevant in determining *how* they can be attacked. The law with regard to the *people* who can be attacked is both more complicated and more contested.

The first difficulty concerns the number of different categories into which people may come. The British view is that there are only two categories: combatants and civilians.[18] A combatant may, exceptionally, lose the entitlements of that status but he remains a combatant. Civilians may, on account of their activities, lose the protection normally attaching to civilian status but they remain civilians. In recent years, the United States has chosen to characterise civilians who lose protection as some form of combatant.[19] It is not clear whether that is to be reviewed by the Obama administration. This text will adopt the British approach.

The armed forces of a state can target the armed forces of an opposing state, irrespective of what the latter are doing at the time and whether or not they constitute a threat. Simplifying somewhat, the armed forces of each state have a right to take part in the fighting.[20] In certain circumstances, militia that satisfy several cumulative and rigorous requirements have the same status.[21] Such forces have the status of combatants, which is a technical term in LOAC and does not simply mean anyone who fights. Combatant can only be used to describe those who have the *right* to fight.

Another group of people may also be lawfully targeted, although it may be more accurate to describe them as not being protected from attack. Those with civilian status may, on account of their behaviour, forfeit the protection from attack normally attaching to that status. The behaviour that gives rise to this result is taking a direct part in hostilities, and the loss of protection only applies for such time as they take such a part.[22] It should be noted that there is a presumption that someone who appears to be a civilian is in fact a civilian.[23] In other words, evidence is needed that a person has forfeited protection; that cannot simply be assumed.

The definition of the loss of protection gives rise to a range of legal and practical difficulties. The first problem is what, legally speaking, constitutes taking a direct part in hostilities. The second difficulty is the factual one of determining whether an individual is engaged in whatever are agreed to be the relevant activities. These problems are compounded by the temporal restriction in the formula for loss of protection. It only applies 'for such time as' they engage in the behaviour in question. In other words, if an individual detonates an improvised explosive device (IED) and then walks away, he has stopped taking a direct part in hostilities. This does give rise to very real problems for armed forces, which may be exposed to several attacks by the same individual simply because they should not target him as he leaves the scene of his attack and they cannot do so until he takes a direct part in hostilities again.

There is no need for a new rule but there may be a need for informal agreement as to the scope of the existing rule. In an attempt to clarify the concepts, the Asser Institute and the ICRC convened a series of meetings over a few years to explore the problems and to see whether there was a consensus as to their solution.[24] There has been a measure of agreement about the activities covered. The temporal problem has proved more intractable. One of the suggestions made revolved around the notion of membership of a group. Where an individual is known to be a member of an armed group that engages in attacks, the individual could be targeted until he takes steps to dissociate himself permanently from the group. This approach seeks to make protection depend on status, as in the case of combatants, rather than behaviour. It also fails to recognise that even organised armed groups may require tea-boys and cooks. It is also far from clear how a person is supposed to enable the opposing forces to learn of his dissociation from the activities of the group. It has not proved possible to reach agreement but at least the issues have been explored.

A practical example will show the impact that the rules on who can be attacked may have on 'civilian' casualties. During the recent conflict in Gaza, there was an apparently intentional attack against new members of the police in Gaza, at their passing-out ceremony.[25] The police are generally regarded as civilians. There is an exception in the case of police forces that become part of the defence forces in time of conflict, such as a large proportion of gendarmerie forces.[26] There appears to be no evidence that the police in Gaza are that type of force. The Israeli argument appears to be rather that by virtue of their alleged close link with Hamas, they were in effect operatives of the organisation. This illustrates the danger of adopting a status approach, rather than one based on behaviour, except in the case of armed forces. In the eyes of the IDF, simply by virtue of being policemen in Gaza, they were a legitimate target. As such, they could be attacked without regard to what they were doing at the time or the threat they posed. At the same time, it is most unlikely that Israel would have regarded them as combatants, that is to say as having the right to fight. In the eyes of the majority of outsiders, civilian casualty figures include the police who were killed. That is not attributable to a breach of the principle of proportionality. It is the result of regarding them as a legitimate target of attack.

There is no doubt that there are genuine difficulties in applying the rule regarding the circumstances in which civilians forfeit protection. In part, that arises from uncertainty as to the scope of the rule, particularly its temporal scope. Insofar as the problems arise owing to uncertainties of fact, that is not a legal problem. The function of the law is not to take the commander's decisions for him. It cannot resolve problems of fact. In deciding whether or not to target an individual who may be taking a direct part in hostilities, the commander has to take account of a range of factors. They include the evidence available to him as to such participation and also the implications for his mission of getting it wrong, and the possibility of avoiding the problem by, for example, removing his forces out of harm's way. In some cases, however, the explanation for civilian casualties is not the difficulty in applying the rule. It is because parties choose to put people into a category that is said to have forfeited protection, not on the basis of what individuals have done but on the basis of their status or alleged links to another party.

THE LEGAL FORMULATION OF THE PRINCIPLE OF PROPORTIONALITY [27]

When a commander has determined that the target of his intended attack is a military objective, he has to take a second step. He has to consider how he intends to attack it. He is required to take into account the likely effect on civilians and civilian property. In other words, no attack can be undertaken until both questions have been addressed. Unlike certain formulations of the doctrine of double effect, it is not enough for the military operator not to intend or desire the harm to civilians.[28] He is positively required to consider the undesired but foreseeable effect of his action.

While the concept at issue is the principle of proportionality, the legal rule is not formulated in those terms. It does not require proportionality but rather prohibits attacks whose effects are likely to be *in*discriminate. This suggests a possibly significantly lower threshold. That said, there is no presumption that civilian casualties are acceptable provided that they are not indiscriminate. There is a positive requirement to avoid indiscriminate attacks.

There are, broadly speaking, two types of indiscriminate acts. If a person enters a room and fires randomly, the objection is the failure to fire aimed shots. A similar problem can arise where a party to a conflict treats a town containing five, geographically separated, military objectives as one large objective.[29] Again, what is objectionable is the failure to fire at a specific objective. That is different from a person firing a shell into a room, with the intention of killing a person taking a direct part in hostilities, killing ten other persons also in the room in the process. In the first type of case, the large number of casualties is the result of the failure to target precise military objectives. In the second case, a precise person is targeted but the means chosen foreseeably results in the killing or injuring of a large number of civilians. Both are examples of indiscriminate attacks but only the second is an example of a lack of proportionality. The law prohibits both types of indiscriminate attack.[30] This chapter only looks at the second type of attack.

The rule, expressed in the same way, occurs in two contexts. Attention is to be paid to the likely effects of an attack at the planning stage of the operation.[31] It is also a requirement when the operation is to be executed.[32] In other words, the person with responsibility for carrying out the operation cannot simply rely on what has been decided by the planners.

[A]n attack which may be expected to cause incidental loss of civilian life, injury to civilians, damage to civilian objects, or a combination thereof, which would be excessive in relation to the concrete and direct military advantage anticipated

is regarded as indiscriminate and indiscriminate attacks are prohibited.[33] In the carrying out of an attack, precautions have to be taken to spare the civilian population. To that end,

With respect to attacks, the following precautions shall be taken:
(a) those who plan or decide upon an attack shall: ...
(ii) take all feasible precautions in the choice of means and methods of attack with a view to avoiding, and in any event to minimizing, incidental loss or civilian life, injury to civilians and damage to civilian objects;
(iii) refrain from deciding to launch any attack which may be expected to cause incidental loss of civilian life, injury to civilians, damage to civilian objects, or a combination thereof, which would be excessive in relation to the concrete and direct military advantage anticipated;
(b) an attack shall be cancelled or suspended if it becomes apparent ... that the attack may be expected to cause incidental loss of civilian life, injury to civilians, damage to civilian objects, or a combination thereof, which would be excessive in relation to the concrete and direct military advantage anticipated.[34]

Unlike the threshold involved in the definition of a military objective, what is at issue here is a balance. On one side of the scales is the likely impact on civilians, including both death and injury and also including harm to civilian property. As already mentioned, in order to evaluate the likely impact on civilians, it is necessary to have a particular method of attack and a particular weapon in mind. On the other side of the scale is the specific military gain expected from the operation.[35]

There is an interesting difference between the formulation used in this context (concrete and direct military advantage) and that used to define a military objective (definite military advantage). The commentaries on the Protocols suggest that the use of concrete and direct to qualify the military advantage anticipated implies something tangible, not abstract and brought about as a direct effect of the operation itself. In contrast, a definite military advantage only implies something both real and significant.[36] In other words, more is required of the claimed advantage for it to constitute a military advantage for the purposes of the proportionality requirement. It should be emphasised that the military advantage, in this context, has to have these qualities to constitute a military advantage *at all*. Then the qualifying advantage has to be weighed against the likely impact on civilians.

This still leaves the question of the use of the word 'military'. It implies that the advantage must relate to the outcome of the military operation, rather than to the wider context. For example, if the RTS television station in Belgrade was only broadcasting propaganda and the building and broadcasts were not fulfilling any military purpose, then the attack against it would appear to have been unlawful.[37] Again, this is a case where the objection is not to the proportionality of the attack but to the characterisation of the building as a military objective.

There are, however, situations in which even a narrow definition of 'military' could result in attacks that do significant harm to civilians and also harm the operation as a whole. Imagine a hypothetical attack against an Afghan village in which seven members of al-Qaeda are believed to have gathered. The military advantage in killing those seven might be thought to be proportionate to the death of, hypothetically, twenty civilian villagers. There is a risk, of course, that the intelligence regarding the presence of the seven fighters is unreliable. If, however, the context is taken into account, most notably the concern among Afghans at the rate of civilian casualties, then that casualty rate might appear to be disproportionate, particularly given the accepted need to win the hearts and minds of the population.

This raises the question of whether proportionality can mean different things in LOAC in different types of operations or whether it should do. It might be that this is asking too much of law. It should be recalled that the law simply indicates what is lawful and unlawful. It is not a substitute for the exercise of discretion by a commander. He needs to know that conduct is lawful; that does not mean that it would be right or wise, morally or militarily.[38]

The United States is alleged to have a computer program to assist in the determination of proportionality.[39] It is submitted that there is a possible danger in reliance on such a technical solution. Even assuming that it is possible to include in the program variations for the degree of certainty attaching to the intelligence and for the nature of the operation, can a machine make a sufficiently nuanced determination? It is easy to show how often human judgment gets things wrong.[40] Since a computer is programmed by humans, it is difficult to see how a computer could deliver a better judgment than humans.

Perhaps the same solution should be adopted as proposed above in a different context. On the one hand, the operator should not be able to carry out an attack which the computer says will result in disproportionate casualties but, on the other, the commander should be free not to order or execute an attack that the computer program claims to be lawful. A computer can assist in the decision-making process but it is not a substitute for the exercise of individual judgment, and it would certainly not be a defence if charged with a criminal offence.

It is immediately apparent that two unconnected and fundamentally different types of things have to be balanced. This is not always the case with proportionality. Under human rights law, for example, in determining the proportionality of a killing, the human rights body has to evaluate the proportionality of the harm caused to the individual in the light of the risk that he himself poses to others.[41] The person who will be harmed is responsible for bringing that upon himself. To that extent, he is not 'innocent'. Under LOAC, however, the victims may be wholly 'innocent'.

It should be noted that there is no 'bottom line'. There is no level of harm to civilians that must be ruled out, however great the military advantage. Does this mean that the end of a war and the avoidance of thousands of casualties, both military and civilian, would justify use of nuclear weapons?

The pivot on which the two sides balance is excessiveness. A lower standard could have been chosen, such as reasonable or proportionate. The rule has to be capable of being applied in real time in conflict situations. The lower the threshold, the more difficult it would be for an operator to determine the precise balance. It is possible that the treaty law, which imposes obligations on states and is civil in character, may be interpreted more rigorously than the equivalent criminal offences.[42] In other words, it may be that an attack could be found to be excessive in civil proceedings but that the perpetrator would be acquitted in criminal proceedings.

It is obvious that, in making the evaluation, an operator can only judge and be judged on the basis of what he knew or ought to have known at the time. He can be expected to know the likely kinetic impact of the weapon he is proposing to use in the context in which he will use it. When it comes to evaluating how many civilians may be in or around a military objective, he will be dependent on intelligence. The first difficulty is that in many conflict situations armed forces operate in an environment of considerable uncertainty. They are lucky if they know what they don't know. To add to that problem, the person making the decision will usually have to rely on intelligence gathered and evaluated by others. He will not be in a position to make the initial evaluation himself. That suggests that, at the implementation stage, a member of the armed forces can only be expected to call the plan into question if he has evidence that the basis on which the plan was conceived does not correspond with reality. In other words, it may be the case that he does not have to be satisfied as to the lawfulness of the operation but only as to its not being unlawful. That raises the question of how much he should be expected to do to put himself in a situation where he can make such an evaluation.

If a pilot has been told that his target is a column of military vehicles and he is flying at twenty thousand feet, he may not be in a position to confirm the composition of the column.[43] If he flew much lower, he might be able to see that the convoy was in fact composed principally of civilian vehicles and that any attack, even against the few military vehicles, would be likely to cause significant civilian casualties. Does the prohibition of indiscriminate attacks *require* the pilot to fly at a lower altitude? Is it relevant to know the risk of anti-aircraft fire?

This raises the question of the priority to be attached to the protection of the attacking state's own forces. The law makes no reference to the issue. There may well be a certain degree of hypocrisy surrounding the issue. Those who complain about the number of civilian casualties may also be the same people who complain about commanders 'throwing away' the lives of their men in the First World War. Clearly, some concern for the safety of their men is necessary and desirable, both morally and militarily. That is reinforced by human rights law, which requires that states

54 THE GENEVA CONVENTION UNDER ASSAULT

protect the right to life of those in their jurisdiction.[44] Soldiers run the risk of being killed, but that does not mean that no regard should be paid to their safety, even in conflict. It is clearly a matter of degree. How is the balance to be achieved between the desire to protect one's own forces, which is likely to result in increased civilian casualties, and the obligation to protect civilians from unnecessary harm? It is likely that measures to protect one's own forces will not take the form of a direct violation of the rules but will rather lead to a choice of method of attack that will result in a higher level of civilian casualties than would have occurred had a different method been chosen.[45]

The rule seeks to minimise civilian casualties. It recognises that it is not possible to eliminate such casualties. If the defending state is fighting from an urban environment, it is certain that the state will be attacked, with probably inevitable civilian casualties. On occasion, when issues of proportionality are raised with an attacker, the spokesman appears to suggest that the other party has, in some sense, 'cheated' by not fighting in the way that was expected. This is a bizarre accusation. Surely, the object in war is to surprise the other side. One example is the tactics resorted to in an asymmetric conflict. They are not necessarily unlawful but may on occasion involve the location of military assets in civilian areas or the movement of civilians to military objectives. This will be considered further below.[46]

While it is easy to point to the difficulties with the formulation of the rule, this does not mean that it is necessarily unworkable in practice. Proportionality could be like an elephant – difficult to define but easy to recognise. It is not clear that there would be any value in trying to clarify further the scope of the rule itself.[47] It should also be remembered that many of the incidents that appear to suggest a failure to respect the principle of proportionality are in fact the result of decisions as to whether a thing or person is a military objective and of the concept of operations.

DIFFICULTIES IN APPLYING THE RULE IN PARTICULAR SITUATIONS

This section concerns not difficulties with the rule itself but rather situations in which the application of the rule raises particular problems. It is not the rule but the situations that constitute the problem. Seven situations will be examined.

1. Innocent Co-location

This is the situation for which the rule appears to have been designed and, as such, poses no particular problem. So far as possible, states are required to try to locate military objectives away from civilian centres of population.[48] The dependence of the military on means of communication, together with the inevitable accretion of human settlement around military bases, makes it inevitable that some military objectives will be located close to civilians. There is no suggestion that the situation is being exploited by the armed forces, far less that the civilian presence constitutes a 'human shield'.[49] The rules provide criteria for every type of attack. The same criteria apply to war in a desert as to war in an urban environment. If fighting occurs in an urban environment, it is likely to result in a significant level of civilian casualties. This does not make attacks against military objectives in densely populated areas necessarily unlawful. LOAC is not 'motherhood and apple pie' law. It is accepted as binding precisely because it is realistic. There would be no point in seeking to ban fighting in urban environments. Such a rule would not be accepted by most and would be disregarded by those accepting it in theory.

2. Civilians in a Military Facility

As indicated above, there is a difference of view between the military lawyers of the United Kingdom and United States with regard to this category. The former regard them as civilians, whereas the latter are, at best, less sure and may even regard them as 'quasi-combatants'. What is less clear is how much of a difference this makes in practice. That depends on whether the British military lawyers apply the proportionality principle in the same way to 'ordinary' civilians and to those located in such a facility.

As a hypothetical example, imagine an attack against a munitions factory. The foreseeable effect on civilians outside the factory area, given the choice of weapon, is no more than 50 killed and injured. The attack is, however, likely to kill or injure all 200 of the civilian employees. They are working a shift system and the factory is working 24 hours a day, seven days a week. The obvious solution of attacking at night would not, therefore, make a difference to the casualties among the employees. When determining the proportionality of the planned attack, is the toll among civilians evaluated at 50 (disregarding the employees), 250 (treating the employees in the same way as the civilians in the vicinity) or somewhere in between?

The denial of protection associated with 'quasi-combatant' status presumably means that the answer of American military lawyers would be 50. What is less clear is whether the British military lawyers treat all civilians as having the same 'value' for the purposes of the proportionality principle or whether the employees, while recognised as having civilian status, have a lower 'value'. If, for example, they were given a 'value' half that of 'normal' civilians, the casualty toll would be reduced to a notional 150 civilians instead of 250.

Depending on the importance of the military advantage anticipated, this difference could be decisive. The law offers no guidance at all. It simply refers to civilians and combatants. If the American military lawyers knew that a different 'value' was to be ascribed to the life of a civilian in a military objective solely for the purpose of the rule of proportionality, they might be willing to revisit the question of the status of such workers.

3. Exploited Co-location

In the previous two types of situation, there is no suggestion that the defending state has done anything wrong. In this situation, that state has not deliberately manipulated events so as to obtain protection for military objectives and combatants but rather seeks to exploit a situation that has arisen naturally. Rather than moving civilians to the objective, in the natural course of events the combatants have been driven towards the civilian population. An example of such a situation would be where forces were originally stationed outside a town but were forced to retreat into the town and continued to fire at the enemy. The fact that the opposing combatants are suddenly in a civilian area does not affect *whether* the attacking forces can target them but does affect *how* they can do so. The defending forces did not choose to expose the civilian population to danger in the process of attempting to protect themselves. There would appear to be no reason to depart from the normal application of the proportionality principle. Nothing better illustrates the fact that, in war, there are inevitably 'innocent' civilian casualties. Civilians cannot guarantee their protection by locating themselves away from military objectives. The conflict may come to them. Should they be killed, that will not necessarily be in violation of LOAC.

4. Deliberate Co-location

This situation is different in that one party to the conflict has deliberately moved military personnel and/or equipment to a civilian area in order to seek to protect the former. The defending party is acting in breach of LOAC in acting in this way. Article 58 of Additional Protocol I requires a party, to the maximum extent feasible, to move civilians away from military objectives and to avoid locating military objectives in the vicinity of civilians. Even more specifically, Article 51.7 of the Additional Protocol requires that the presence of civilians not be used to render military objectives immune from attack. *Deliberately* to move military personnel and equipment to a civilian area *with a view to* obtaining some protection from the presence of civilians is clearly incompatible with these requirements.[50]

The difficulty for the attacking party is that the defending state may obtain a military advantage from its own breach of the rules. The attacking state may be prevented from taking action on account of the risk of disproportionate civilian casualties. In the meantime, the defending state can use the military assets against the other party. While it is possible that the military advantage will be sufficient to make an attack proportionate, that will often not be the case. The civilians in this case are wholly 'innocent'. There is no basis on which they can be regarded as 'quasi-combatants'. They have not chosen to be in the middle of the fighting.

If a party is able to obtain an advantage by breaching the rules, there is a real risk that the other side will simply ignore the rules. That is not likely to be to the benefit of the civilian population. It is not clear how this situation should best be addressed, but it is important that consideration be given to it as a matter of some urgency. An agreed compromise may reduce the benefit gained by breaching the rules, without abandoning altogether the protection of civilians in the process.

It may be difficult in practice to distinguish this situation from the previous one. It is important to do so because important consequences may flow for the protection of civilians. That being the case, there should perhaps be a presumption that a situation is one of exploited co-location rather than deliberate co-location. That would result in a presumption of the applicability of the usual proportionality rule, rather than any compromise that may emerge with regard to deliberate co-location.

5. Involuntary Human Shields[51]

The term 'human shields' was originally used to describe a very specific phenomenon. In the Gulf War 1990–91, Saddam Hussein had certain foreign detainees put in and around military objectives in order to secure their protection. In other words, the civilians were moved to the objective; this occurred deliberately and the civilians were obliged to play this role. The phenomenon bears a certain resemblance to hostage-taking. More recently, notably in the conflict in Gaza, the term has been bandied around indiscriminately, at least by some commentators, and appears to be used to cover any case of co-location.

The failure to use the term sufficiently precisely is likely to give rise to confusion. It is not a technical term, but it would be helpful if there could be agreement to use it in the way outlined above. Involuntary human shields are not only used by a weaker party to protect military objectives. They have also been used by ground forces to protect themselves, particularly when engaged in search operations.[52] In some cases, the argument may be made that the use of human shields reduces the civilian casualties that will be incurred if an operation is carried out from a greater distance.[53] In the case of operations in which winning the hearts and minds of the civilian population is important, using local civilians to conduct operations in the midst of the civilian population is likely to be counter-productive. Using involuntary human shields is not a solution.

The use of involuntary human shields raises similar legal issues to deliberate co-location. In the case of the former, the civilians are moved to the objective and, in the case of the latter, the military personnel and equipment are moved to the civilian area. In both cases, the act is deliberate and is done with a view to protecting military assets by increasing the risk that any attack will result in disproportionate civilian casualties. This again would appear to be a breach of Articles 51.7[54] and 58 of Protocol I.

This raises the same problem for the attacking state. The other party may obtain a military advantage by its own breach of the rules. Again, there is a need for agreement to be reached on the application of the proportionality rule in such a situation, if the attacking state is to be deterred from abandoning the rule altogether.

6. Voluntary Human Shields

This is the same phenomenon as the one discussed above but, in this case, the civilians are willing participants. They may have been encouraged to behave in this way by the state or this may be an entirely civilian initiative. The state that encourages but does not compel is still putting civilians in jeopardy. It is not clear whether the law requires states to take positive measures to prevent civilians from acting as human shields. If not, it might be worth considering whether there could be agreement to interpret the existing rules as containing this requirement.

One example of the use of voluntary human shields was the occasion when a group of civilians in Gaza surrounded a mosque to prevent fighters inside from being detained by the Israeli Defence Forces.[55] Another example was when civilians in Belgrade chose to position themselves on bridges so as to protect them from attack during the conflict with NATO over Kosovo.[56]

The state probably has no responsibility for purely civilian initiatives, on the assumption that a state does not, at present, have an obligation to prevent civilians from jeopardising their own safety but only an obligation not to do so itself.

The question in this context is whether the civilians have forfeited their right to protection. The problem is that their participation in hostilities is entirely passive. It is by their mere presence that they intend to achieve an effect. That effect, however, is on the military operations of an opposing state. Are there any circumstances in which that constitutes taking a direct part in hostilities?[57] If so, the civilians have forfeited their right to protection, and likely casualties among them do not need to be taken into account in assessing the proportionality of an attack against a military objective. Indeed, they expose themselves to the risk of being made a target themselves.

If they are not regarded as taking a direct part in hostilities, they retain their protection from attack. That still leaves the question of whether the normal rule should be applied in the usual way, as in the case of innocent co-location. While no state is implicated in the manipulation of events, there has still been a deliberate act. The civilians are likely to choose significant military objectives to protect. Even if the defending state is not obtaining a benefit from its own breach of the rules, the attacking state is at the same disadvantage. While in some military contexts, refraining from causing significant civilian casualties in this type of situation may be the wisest solution, states are unlikely to accept that across the board. There is a risk that they will treat the civilians as having reduced 'value' as compared to 'normal' civilians. In other words, the situation resembles that discussed at subsection 2, civilians in a military objective. As in that case, it is possible that an agreed compromise would provide a solution that avoids the complete abandonment of their protection as civilians.

In many cases, the opposing forces may not know whether the human shields are voluntary or involuntary. In view of the implications, it is important that there should be a presumption that human shields are involuntary.

7. Other Issues

This subsection concerns assorted issues in which the principle of proportionality is relevant.

a) Reprisals and Proportionality[58]

Reprisal is a technical term in LOAC. It does not simply mean a response to a prior act. At customary law, where a party to a conflict has repeatedly breached a rule of LOAC, the victim is expected to call upon the other party to desist but, if all else fails, may itself breach a LOAC rule in order to try to persuade the perpetrator to return to lawful ways of fighting, on condition that its own response is proportionate. The rule is forward-looking. It is based on the future return to lawfulness and not on revenge for past violations. Parties that have ratified Additional Protocol I without reservations or declarations regarding proportionality have accepted never to engage in reprisals in the face of attacks against the persons and objects protected from attack by the Protocol. That only leaves combatants and military objectives as lawful targets of belligerent reprisals, and they can be attacked anyway. Some states have attached reservations or declarations to their ratification, leaving open the possibility of reprisal action where it exists at customary law.[59] Customary law precludes the taking of reprisals against targets protected by the Geneva Conventions, in other words the wounded and sick, the shipwrecked, prisoners of war and civilians in the power of the opposing side.[60] That would still leave the possibility of reprisal action against civilians and civilian property.[61] Those states that have not ratified Additional Protocol I are bound by the customary law on belligerent reprisals.

Two separate issues arise in relation to proportionality. The first is whether a state is entitled to take reprisal action when the rule violated by the perpetrator state is the principle of proportionality. As noted above, the restrictions on reprisal action are imposed by adding to the list of prohibited targets of reprisal action. The limitations do not attach to the nature of the original wrongdoing. A party to the Additional Protocols, without declarations or reservations, would not be able to take reprisal action save against members of the armed forces and military objectives. Those parties that have ratified subject to relevant reservations or declarations or who have not ratified at all would only be prohibited from taking reprisal action against targets protected by the Geneva Conventions. They could, in other words, take reprisal action against civilians or civilian property for the repeated violation of a LOAC rule, including the principle of proportionality. By virtue of the restrictions imposed on reprisals, their own response would itself have to be proportionate. Those who have not ratified Additional Protocol I would be in the same position.

That raises the second issue: proportionality as a requirement of a lawful belligerent reprisal. Treaty law only identifies the prohibited targets of reprisal action. The requirement that the reprisal response be proportionate is part of customary law. Proportionality is not defined.[62] Reprisals do not need to be taken against the same type of target as was the victim of the original unlawful act. That compounds the difficulties inherent in the concept of proportionality. It might be useful to consider the possibility of requiring that, if possible, reprisal action should be taken against the same type of target as that which was the victim of the original wrong.[63] Given that the purpose of reprisals is forward-looking, the obvious test would be action that is necessary to persuade the other party to fight lawfully, rather than harm equivalent to the original wrong. That could, however, result in a higher level of civilian casualties being regarded as necessary and therefore proportionate. Requiring that reprisals be proportionate to the original wrong, however, would inevitably make them appear backward-looking and punitive.

b) Proportionality and Weapons

It has already been explained that, in order to determine the likely effect on civilians of an attack, it is necessary to have a particular weapon in mind. The general principle of proportionality starts from the assumption that weapons themselves are neutral. What matters, in terms of impact, is the use of a weapon in a particular context.

Certain weapons may, however, either be inherently indiscriminate or may involve particularly high risks of causing disproportionate casualties, either generally or when used in particular circumstances. In addition to general rules about attacks, there are specific rules about weapons and weapon use. While the general rules are set out in Additional Protocol I,[64] there is no known example of a weapon being prohibited on that basis alone. A treaty appears to be required to ban the use of a weapon. Where a weapon may be used in an indiscriminate way, it is subject to the general principles but, in addition, there may be more specific regulation of the weapon in a treaty.

There are few examples of inherently indiscriminate weapons. That requires that the weapon be incapable of being used in a discriminate way. An obvious example is gas, the use of which is prohibited in armed conflict, at least on a first-use basis.[65] Weapons of mass destruction are usually regarded as inherently indiscriminate. It is submitted that anti-personnel landmines (APMs) are not *inherently* indiscriminate. It may well be the case that they are routinely used in an indiscriminate way, and on that basis it is understandable that there should be a treaty banning their use.[66] Given that some states appear to have no intention of ratifying the treaty, it is important that efforts should continue to regulate more effectively the use of APMs.

A large part of the problem with the use of APMs is the failure to clear them after the conflict is over, thereby exposing returning civilians to the risk of injury and death long after the need for the mines has ceased. This raises an important question in relation to proportionality generally. In assessing the likely effect on civilians, should account be taken only of the effect on civilians at risk during the period of the attack, or also of the likely effect of the result of the attack, including the effect over time? The formula used, 'an attack which may be expected to cause' is ambiguous. It could be read as referring only to harm that is directly caused by the attack, which implies caused at the time. It could equally be read as referring to any result of the attack, provided that it was foreseeable at the time of the attack. It is submitted that the latter is to be preferred.[67]

The greater problem in practice is the use of potentially discriminate weapons in an indiscriminate way. Any weapon is capable of being used in such a way, but there is clearly much more of a risk with some weapons than with others. The regulation of conventional weapons is achieved principally through the protocols to the Certain Conventional Weapons Convention (CCWC), most notably those on landmines, incendiary weapons and a possible future text on cluster munitions.[68] The original second protocol dealt with booby-traps, anti-tank mines and APMs. It was subsequently replaced by a different protocol, which only deals with booby-traps and APMs. The status of the earlier provisions on anti-tank mines for a state that has ratified both protocols is not clear. The protocol starts by defining APMs.[69] It then reiterates the general rules on precautions in attack in the specific context of the use of APMs.[70] The protocol then distinguishes between remotely delivered and non-remotely delivered APMs. Minefields have to be marked or recorded in particular ways, depending on the type of delivery. There are also requirements as to detectability and self-destruction or self-neutralisation. There are provisions regarding responsibility for the removal of minefields. It is clear that the underlying goal behind these provisions is the effective protection of civilians, but it is not achieved solely by reference to that criterion. It is sought to be achieved by the detailed regulation of the manner in which APMs are to be used. The weakest provisions, unfortunately, are those on the removal of minefields.

Incendiary weapons are regulated by a protocol concluded at the time of the original Convention.[71] Again, the Protocol starts by defining its terms. In all these treaties regulating specific weapons, the focus of the definition is not on the effect of the weapon but rather on how it is designed to work or what it is designed to do. Nowhere is this better illustrated than in the third protocol to the CCWC. For example, incendiary weapons do not include '[m]unitions which may have incidental incendiary effects, such as illuminants, tracers, smoke or signalling systems'. To take the example of white phosphorous, if it is primarily designed to light up the battle space or to create smoke, it will not be an incendiary weapon, irrespective of how it is in fact used.[72] It is prohibited to use air-delivered incendiary weapons, as defined, when a military objective is located within a concentration of civilians and non-air-delivered incendiary weapons unless the military objective is located away from a concentration of civilians. Again, the law seeks to achieve the minimisation of civilian casualties by providing detailed rules as to how the weapon can be used, rather than by merely reiterating the general principle.

Cluster weapons pose a similar type of problem to APMs. Certain states agreed in 2008 on a text that bans the use and transfer of cluster weapons, as defined.[73] Other states are in the process of negotiating an additional protocol to the CCWC, which has the aim of reducing the risk to civilians by imposing restrictions on use.

The treaties that ban and regulate the use of specific weapons provide a very useful addition to the more general rules regulating the conduct of military operations. They are, of course, subject to ratification. In the case of non-parties, reliance can only be placed on the general rules and on such provisions of the weapons treaties as represent customary law.

*c) Proportionality and Customary Law in International Armed
   Conflicts (IACs)*

The discussion so far has focused principally on treaty law. Internationally, 168 states are party to Additional Protocol I, but this
still leaves certain significant players who are not, including the
USA and Israel. The question then arises as to the extent to which
the rules prohibiting indiscriminate attacks are part of customary
law in international conflicts. It seems clear that there is a general
prohibition of indiscriminate attacks in customary law and that it
covers both senses of indiscriminate discussed above.[74] Specifically,
the rule of proportionality appears to have customary law status.[75]
The question of the customary law status of the rule in NIACs will
be considered below.

*d) The Principle of Proportionality and Non-international Armed
   Conflicts (NIACs)*

The rules considered so far are treaty rules applicable in IACs.[76] The
treaty framework in NIACs is very limited. Most of the provisions
of Additional Protocol II of 1977, which supplements common
Article 3 of the Geneva Conventions of 1949, concern victims in
the traditional sense, that is to say persons in the power of the other
side, and/or conduct away from the battlefield. The only provision
that restricts the conduct of hostilities prohibits the targeting of
civilians and provides that civilians forfeit protection for such time
as they take a direct part in hostilities. There is no treaty provision
requiring that attacks not be indiscriminate.

There are two possible sources for a requirement of proportionality in NIAC; customary LOAC and human rights law. This is not the
place to enter into a discussion of the relationship between human
rights law and LOAC.[77] Suffice it to say that in a traditional NIAC,
i.e., a conflict involving opposing armed groups in the territory of a
state that may itself be involved in the fighting, there is a likelihood
that the state will have human rights obligations. Human rights
law only binds the state and not the non-state armed groups, in
contrast to LOAC. The application of the prohibition of arbitrary
killings in a conflict situation is likely to require the state to adhere
to a strict concept of proportionality. Human rights law will not
be further considered here.

The other potential source of such a requirement is the customary
law of NIACs. In its study, the ICRC refers to a significant body
of evidence suggesting that such a rule exists, including national

and international case law, and states that no official contrary practice has been found.[78] It is worth noting that the Statute of the International Criminal Court makes it a criminal offence intentionally to launch an indiscriminate attack in international but not in non-international conflicts.[79] This is not conclusive. It is possible for an international crime to exist but not to be within the jurisdiction of the court. It should also be remembered that a party may have an obligation under LOAC, as part of international civil law, which may not be translated into a rule of individual criminal liability. It seems unlikely that a party would dispute the existence of a prohibition of indiscriminate attacks in NIACs. While no firm conclusion can be reached, it would appear that the better view is that proportionality is a requirement of customary law in NIACs.

CONCLUSION

This chapter has sought to analyse the concept of proportionality in the context of military operations. It is easy to point to all sorts of difficulties in the formulation of the rule, never mind its application in practice. There are some issues that, it is suggested, could usefully be the subject of the same type of discussion as has occurred in relation to the loss of civilian protection. They do not include the formulation of the principle itself but rather how it is to be applied in difficult situations. The object would be clarification and not the creation of new legal rules. When called upon to evaluate a legal provision, it is all too easy to give a very negative impression. Just because things could be improved does not mean that they are bad. The improvement that would make most difference to civilian death tolls would be respect in practice for the existing rules, rather than making new ones. I have no doubt that, if I found myself in a conflict zone in which the parties to the conflict generally respected LOAC, my safety as a civilian would owe more to the principle of proportionality than it would to the principle of distinction.[80]

NOTES

*   Professor of Law at the University of Essex. I am very grateful to Theresa di Perna for her assistance with the notes.
1. M. Reisman and A. Willard, *International Incidents: The Law That Counts in World Politics* (Princeton: Princeton University Press, 1988).
2. LOAC is that part of international law that regulates the conduct (means/ methods) of armed conflict. The nature and function of LOAC serves the following purposes: to limit the effects of the conflict (reduce damage and

casualties); to protect combatants and non-combatants from unnecessary suffering; to safeguard fundamental rights of combatants and non-combatants and to prevent the conflict from becoming worse, thereby making it easier to restore peace when the conflict is over. See further below.

3. An international armed conflict (IAC) is defined in common Art. 2 of the Geneva Conventions, note 4, as involving an armed conflict between two or more states on opposing sides. It therefore does not include one or more states fighting against a non-state group, whether in the national territory of the state or outside it.

4. Originally, common Art. 3 of the Geneva Conventions was intended to apply to what in common parlance would be called civil wars. Commentary to Geneva Convention I of 1949, http://www.icrc.org/ihl.nsf/COM/365-570006?OpenDocument; Geneva Convention for the Amelioration of the Condition of the Wounded and Sick in Armed Forces in the Field, 12 August 1949, 75 U.N.T.S. 31 [hereinafter GCI]; Geneva Convention for the Amelioration of the Wounded, Sick, and Shipwrecked Members of the Armed Forces at Sea, 12 August 1949, 75 U.N.T.S. 85 [hereinafter GCII]; Geneva Convention Relative to the Treatment of Prisoners of War, 12 August 1949, 75 U.N.T.S. 135 [hereinafter GCIII]; Geneva Convention Relative to the Protection of Civilian Person in Time of War, 12 August 1949, 75 U.N.T.S. 287 [hereinafter GCIV]. The phrase used was 'armed conflict not of an international character'. It is now interpreted as applying to all armed conflicts that are not international as defined in the previous endnote.

   So, for example, following the transfer of authority from the CPA to the Iraqi government, the foreign forces in Iraq were regarded as fighting a non-international armed conflict (NIAC). Similarly, ISAF, in Afghanistan, is regarded as assisting the Afghan government and therefore as involved in an NIAC. The US regards itself as involved in two separate armed conflicts: the continuation of the previous armed conflict against the Taliban and al-Qaeda (Operation Enduring Freedom) in the east of the country, which is regarded as an IAC, and ISAF, which is assisting the Afghan government deal with an insurgency.

5. But see Protocol Additional to the Geneva Conventions of 12 August 1949, and Relating to the Protection of Victims of International Armed Conflicts, 7 December 1978, 1125 U.N.T.S. 3 [hereinafter API]; Articles 45(1), 50(1) and 52(3).

6. A.P.V. Rogers, *Law on the Battlefield*, 2nd edn (Manchester: Manchester University Press, 2004), pp. 3–7.

7. See, for example, Camillo Bica, *Collateral Damage: A Military Euphemism for Murder*, ZNet, 16 April 2007, available at: http://www.zmag.org/znet/viewArticle/1571 (asserting that the collateral damage resulting from the US bombing of a bunker deep beneath the al-Sa'ah restaurant and the overall 654,000 civilians killed in Iraq was unjustifiable murder of non-combatants). But see F. Hampson, 'Means and Methods of Warfare in the Conflict in the Gulf', in *The Gulf War 1990–91 in International and English Law*, ed. P. Rowe (Abingdon: Routledge, 1993), pp. 96–7; 'Needless Deaths in the Gulf War: Civilian Casualties During the Air Campaign and Violations of the Laws of War' (New York, Human Rights Watch, 1991).

8. But see GCIV4, above note 4, at Part II, General Protection of Populations Against Certain Consequences of War, at Articles 13–25.

9. Hague Convention IV, *The Laws and Customs of War on Land*, of 1907, Annex, at Articles 25–9.

10. It should be noted that the phrases 'the law of Geneva' and 'the law of The Hague' are used to describe the nature of the content of the treaty and do not always match the location of the negotiations. It is possible for a text with Geneva in the title to be an example of 'the law of The Hague', such as the Geneva Protocol for the Prohibition of the Use in War of Asphyxiating, Poisonous or Other Gasses, and of Bacteriological Methods of Warfare, 17 June 1925, 26 U.S.T. 571, 94 L.N.T.S. 65.

11. See, for example, 'Who are Hezbulla?', BBC News, 21 May 2008, available at: http://news.bbc.co.uk/1/hi/world/middle_east/4314423.stm; Adam Shatz, 'In Search of Hezbullah', *New York Review of Books*, 29 April 2004, available at: http://www.nybooks.com/articles/17060.

Hezbullah was created in response to Israel's invasion and subsequent occupation of Southern Lebanon in 1982. Hezbullah started as a small militia (military wing) but now holds a number of seats in the Lebanese Parliament (political wing), has an extensive social service network and a popular satellite television station called al-Manar. While the organisation garners support as a legitimate resistance movement throughout the Arab and Muslim world, the USA, Israel, Canada and the Netherlands do not make distinctions between Hezbullah's political/social and military factions, and it is deemed as a 'terrorist organization' as a whole. The UK distinguishes between these two wings and has only placed Hezbullah's 'military wing' on its list of terrorist organisations while Australia considers Hezbullah's external military structure (External Security Organization) as a terrorist organization.

See also, 'Backgrounder: *Hamas*', Council on Foreign Relations, 7 January 2009, available at: at http://www.cfr.org/publication/8968/#2 (comparing Hamas with Hezbullah; Hamas also has a military wing (Izz al-Din al-Qassam Brigade) and an extensive social services network making up 90 per cent of its activities). Raghida Bahnam, 'Washington Unhappy About UK Ties with Hezbollah', asharq alawsat, 15 March 2009, available at: http://www.asharq-e.com/news.asp?section=1&id=16071 (quoting US State Department Official, 'we do not see the distinctions the [British] see in the unified leadership of Hezbollah. … The US does not distinguish between military, cultural and political wings of Hezbollah, and our decision to avoid making such a distinction is premised on accurate available information indicating that all Hezbollah wings and branches share finances, personnel and unified leadership and they all support violence').

For some states, the situation is not the same with regard to Hamas. James Petras, 'The Politics of an Israeli Extermination Campaign: Backers, Apologists and Arms Suppliers', 2 January 2009, available at: http://petras.lahaine.org/articulo.php?p=1770 (quoting Israeli military officials in a report in the *Boston Globe* (30 December 2008) '... we are trying to hit the whole spectrum [Hamas's 'vast support network'], because everything is connected and everything supports terrorism against Israel'. Also quoting an IDF spokesman: 'Hamas has used ostensibly civilian operations as a cover for military activities. Anything affiliated with Hamas is a legitimate target'). See also note 25 and accompanying text.

12. Asa Kasher and Amos Yadlin, 'Military Ethics of Fighting Terror: An Israeli Perspective', *Journal of Military Ethics* 4, no. 1 (April 2005), pp. 3–32; this

may be part of the explanation for the incident referred to in Dion Nissenbaum, 'Israeli Fire Killed Interviewee's 3 Daughters just before Airtime', McClatchy Newspapers, 18 January 2009, available at: http://www.mcclatchydc.com/251/story/59962.html.

13. API, above note 5; see J. Henckaerts and L. Doswarld-Beck, *Customary International Humanitarian Law*, Volume I: *Rules* (Cambridge: Cambridge University Press, 2005), at Rule 8 at pp. 29–32. See further below.

14. To constitute a military objective, the object has to make an 'effective contribution' to military action. Economic activities may generate the resources that can be converted into military action, but is this a close enough connection for the purposes of the definition? See Horace B. Robertson, Jr, 'The Principle of the Military Objective in the Law of Armed Conflict', *United States Air Force Academy Journal of Legal Studies* 8 (1997), pp. 35–70, available at: http://www.au.af.mil/au/awc/awcgate/usafa/miloblac.doc.

15. For example, the attack on the RTS television station in Belgrade during the conflict between NATO and Yugoslavia over Kosovo and some of the other targets during that conflict. It is said that the US worked through EUCOM and not through the NATO authorisation chain when attacking sensitive targets. See M. Ignatieff, *Virtual War: Kosovo and Beyond* (London: Picador, 2001).

16. API, above note 5, at Article 52.2; ICRC Commentary (the ICRC Commentary is attached to the text of API), available at: http://www.icrc.org/ihl.nsf/FULL/470?OpenDocument; see also M. Bothe, K. Partsch, W. Solf, et al. (eds), *New Rules for Victims of Armed Conflicts* (The Hague: Kluwer Law International, 1982).

17. API, above note 5, at Article 52.1.

18. Rogers, *Law on the Battlefield*, pp. 7–8; UK *Manual of Military Law*, s. 5.31, chapter 4, para. 88 (referring to 'the division of the population of a belligerent State into two classes, namely, the armed forces and the peaceful population').

19. A. McDonald, *Yearbook of International Humanitarian Law – 2005* (Cambridge: Cambridge University Press, 2007), pp. 11–12 (stating that some civilians could be considered 'quasi-combatants' such as civilians working in a munitions factory. However, this view as been rejected and these types of factory workers cannot be targeted). See Memorandum of Jay S. Bybee, United States Attorney General Office of Legal Counsel, United States Department of Justice, Determination of Enemy Belligerency and Military Detention, 8 June 2002, available at: http://www.usdoj.gov/opa/documents/memomilitarydetention06082002.pdf (citing *Ex parte* Quirin, 317 U.S. 1, 31 (1942), referring to '[l]awful combatants' and '[u]nlawful combatants'); G. Aldrich, 'The Taliban, Al Qaeda, and the Determination of Illegal Combatants', *American Journal of International Law* 96 (2002), p. 892. Even before 9/11, the US appeared to recognise a category of 'quasi-combatants'. An example would be civilians working in a munitions factory. The British would regard them as civilians working in a military objective. The factory could be attacked. but they could not be. Whether the deaths of such civilians would be evaluated in the same way as civilians not in a military objective for the purposes of the proportionality rule will be discussed below.

20. API, above note 5, at Article 43(2); however, military medical personnel and military chaplains are not to take part in hostilities nor be subject to attack: Article 4 of GCIII, above note 4 and API, above note 5, at Articles 43 and 44.

21. GCIII, above note 4, at Article 4(A)(2); International Conferences (The Hague), *Hague Convention (IV) Respecting the Laws and Customs of War on Land and Its Annex: Regulations Concerning the Laws and Customs of War on Land*, 18 October 1907 at Article I.

22. API, above note 5, at Article 51(3).

23. API, above note 5, at Article 50(1).

24. International Committee of the Red Cross and the TMC Asser Institute, Summary Report, Third Expert Meeting on the Notion of Direct Participation in Hostilities, Geneva, 23–25 October 2005, available at: http://www.icrc. org/Web/eng/siteeng0.nsf/htmlall/participation-hostilities-ihl-311205/$File/ Direct_participation_in_hostilities_2005_eng.pdf; International Committee of the Red Cross and the TMC Asser Institute, Summary Report, Second Expert Meeting, Direct Participation in Hostilities under International Humanitarian Law, The Hague, 25–26 October 2004, available at: http://www.icrc.org/ Web/eng/siteeng0.nsf/htmlall/participation-hostilities-ihl-311205/$File/ Direct_participation_in_hostilities_2004_eng.pdf; International Committee of the Red Cross and the TMC Asser Institute, Summary Report, Direct Participation in Hostilities under International Humanitarian Law, Geneva, September 2003, available at: http://www.icrc.org/Web/eng/siteeng0.nsf/htmlall/ participation-hostilities-ihl-311205/$File/Direct%20participation%20in%20 hostilities-Sept%202003.pdf. See generally N. Melzer, *Targeted Killing in International Law* (Oxford: Oxford University Press, 2008).

25. Donald Macintyre, 'Sudden Attacks Lead to Territory's Highest Death Toll in a Single Day since Six Day War in 1967', *Independent (*28 December 2008), available at: http://www.stopdebezetting.com/wereldpers/different-articles-about-gaza-massacre-israeli-air-strikes-kill-200-and-leave-700-injured.html (describing television pictures that showed wounded police officers writhing in pain after Israeli air strikes hit at least one police compound in Gaza where a passing-out-ceremony was being held for recent recruits); see also above, note 7.

26. API, above note 5, at Article 43(1), (3).

27. See generally, J.G. Gardam, *Necessity, Proportionality and the Use of Force by States* (Cambridge: Cambridge University Press, 2004); W.J. Fenrick, 'The Rule of Proportionality and Protocol I in Conventional Warfare', 98 *Military Law Review* 91 (1982).

28. See generally, M. Walzer, *Just and Unjust Wars: A Moral Argument with Historical Illustrations* (New York: Viking, 1977). This book was written before the adoption of the Additional Protocols.

29. API, above note 5 at Article 51(5)(a).

30. *Ibid.*, at Article 51(4), (5).

31. *Ibid.*, at Article 51(5).

32. *Ibid.*, at Article 57(2), (3).

33. *Ibid.*, at Article 51(4).

34. *Ibid.*, at Article 57(2).

35. UK Letter dated 28 January 1991; UN Doc. S/22156, 28 January 1991, p. 1; UK Manual, pp. 54–7, at paras. 5.4 to 5.4.5; Steven Haines, 'The United Kingdom and Legitimate Military Objectives: Current Practice … and Future Trends?', in *International Humanitarian Law Facing New Challenges*, ed. Heintschel von Heinegg and Volker Epping (New York: Springer, 2007), pp. 132–3 (stressing that the British statement on its ratification of Additional Protocol I

defined 'military advantage' anticipated from an attack 'refers to the advantage anticipated from the attack as a whole and not only from isolated or particular parts of the attack. The advantage need not be immediate.').

36. C. Pilloud, Y. Sandoz, C. Swtnarski and B. Zimmerman (eds), *Commentary on Additional Protocol of June 8, 1977 to the Geneva Conventions of 12 August 1949* (1987); Bothe et al. (eds), *New Rules for Victims of Armed Conflicts.*

37. *Final Report to the Prosecutor by the Committee Established to Review the NATO Bombing Campaign Against the Federal Republic of Yugoslavia*, para. 76, available at: http://www.un.org/icty/pressreal/nato061300.htm. The British are said to have believed the target not to be a military objective; Ignatieff, *Virtual War*, pp. 194, 199 and 207.

38. See, for example, M. Walker, *The Iraq War as Witnessed by the Correspondents and Photographers of United Press International* (London: Brassey's, 2004), Introduction, at p. ix. For example, it was lawful to attack fleeing members of the Iraqi armed forces at Multa Ridge in 1991. The television footage of a 'turkey shoot' led to the attacks being stopped; see also Hampson, 'Means and Methods of Warfare'.

39. US/UK, Conduct of the 2003 War in Iraq, Case No. 153 at pp. 1592–601, available at: https://portfolio.du.edu/portfolio/getportfoliofile?uid=82266.

40. Lieutenant-Colonel Jay Stout, US Marine Corps (Retired), *Proceedings, Close Air Support Using Armed UAVs?* Military.com, July 2005, available at: http://www.military.com/NewContent/0,13190,NI_0705_Air-P2,00.html (an argument found in relation to the use of armed unmanned aerial vehicles, which poses analogous problems).

41. Noam Lubell, 'Challenges in Applying Human Rights Law to Armed Conflict', *International Review of the Red Cross* 860 (2005), available at: http://www.icrc.org/Web/eng/siteeng0.nsf/iwpList602/A6EE02D 5129949BCC125713F00420D1B.

42. See further below.

43. Human Rights Watch, 'Civilian Deaths in the NATO Air Campaign', 12, no. 1 (February 2000) (incident involving refugees on the Djakovica–Decane Road). See generally, William J. Fenrick, 'Attacking the Enemy Civilian as a Punishable Offense', *Duke Journal of Comparative and International Law* (1997), p. 546.

44. An English test case in April 2008 determined that the state owes an obligation to protect the right to life of its armed forces even in a conflict zone but its scope will be affected by the context; *Smith R. (on the application of) v Assistant Deputy Coroner for Oxfordshire and Secretary of State for Defence* [2008] EWHC 694 (Admin), 11 April 2008 [per Collins J. at para. 20: 'But the soldier does not lose all protection simply because he is in hostile territory carrying out dangerous operations. Thus, for example, to send a soldier out on patrol or, indeed, into battle with defective equipment could constitute a breach of Article 2. If I may take a historical illustration, the failures of the commissariat and the failures to provide any adequate medical attention in the Crimean War would whereas the Charge of the Light Brigade would not be regarded as a possible breach of Article 2.']. The case is currently under appeal. Other similar cases involving defects in equipment have also been lodged. *Observer*, 'Families Sue MoD over Air Victims' Rights', 31 August 2008, available at: http://www.guardian.co.uk/politics/2008/aug/31/defence.military.

45. See sources in note 12 above. An example of the tension between, on the one hand, the desire to protect one's own forces and achieve the object of the mission

and, on the other, to protect civilians is to be found in the two briefings given to a US Marine Reconnaissance Unit before the invasion of Iraq. Evan Wright, *Generation Kill* (London: Corgi, 2005), pp. 53, 54.

46. See pp. 55–7; on issues arising out of asymmetry, see the contributions by Michael Schmitt and W. Hays Parks in Heintschel von Heinegg and Epping, *International Humanitarian Law*.

47. That does not mean that clarification might not be useful in relation to the particular problems considered in the next section.

48. API, above note 5, at Article 58(b).

49. See further below on 'human shields'.

50. A farcical example is the positioning of an Iraqi military aircraft in the middle of a cultural monument during the Gulf War of 1990–91. It is not clear who had the last laugh. The coalition could not attack the aircraft but Saddam Hussein could not extricate it and use it either. See United States Department of Defence, *Report to Congress on the Conduct of the Persian Gulf War, Appendix O: The Role of the Law of War*, 31 ILM 612 (1992), at 626.

51. F. Hampson and M. Schmitt, *The Prohibition of Human Shields and the Precautions Against the Effects of Attacks*, Conference Report on The Conduct of Hostilities, 30th San Remo Round Table on Current Issues of International Humanitarian Law, 6–8 September 2007, at pp. 91–6; Michael Skerker, 'Just War Criteria and the New Face of War: Human Shields, Manufactured Martyrs and Little Boys with Stones', *Journal of Military Ethics* 3, no. 1 (2004), p. 27; Emanuel Gross, 'Use of Civilians as Human Shields: What Legal and Moral Restrictions Pertain to a War Waged by a Democratic State against Terrorism', *Emory International Law Review* 16 (2002), p. 445.

52. Human Rights Watch, *Israel: Gaza Ground Offensive Raises Laws of War Concerns*, 4 January 2009, available at: http://www.hrw.org/en/news/2009/01/04/israel-gaza-ground-offensive-raises-laws-war-concerns.

53. See sources cited in note 12 above.

54. API, above note 5, at Article 51(7) (specifying that 'The Parties to the conflict shall not direct the movement of the civilian population or individual civilians in order to attempt to shield military objectives from attacks or to shield military operations').

55. Andre Zantonavitch, 'Palestinian Human Shields', *American Thinker*, 22 November 2006, available at: http://www.americanthinker.com/2006/11/palestinian_human_shields.html.

56. Ignatieff, *Virtual War*, note 15, p. 139; Rewi Lyall, 'Voluntary Human Shields, Direct Participation in Hostilities and the International Humanitarian Law Obligations of States', *Melbourne Journal of International Law* 11 (2008), available at: http://www.austlii.edu.au/au/journals/MelbJIL/2008/11.html. In exceptional circumstances, civilians behaving in this way may form part of a *levée en masse*; Annex to Hague IV of 1907, Art. 2. As such, they might be entitled to combatant status, on condition that they respected the laws and customs of war.

57. See references in note 24.

58. See generally, Frits Kalshoven, *Belligerent reprisals*, 2nd edn (The Hague: Nijhoff, 2005); Françoise Hampson, 'Belligerent Reprisals and the 1977 Protocols to the Geneva Conventions of 1949', *International & Comparative Law Quarterly* 37 (1988), pp. 818–43; C.J. Greenwood, 'The Twilight of the

Law of Belligerent Reprisals', *New York International Law Journal* 20 (1989), pp. 35–69.

59. For example, many NATO states have made very similar, obscurely worded statements. See A. Roberts and R. Guelff, *Documents on The Laws of War*, 3rd edn (Oxford: Oxford University Press, 2000) at p. 507. The UK made a much clearer reservation; *ibid.*, p. 511.

60. *Legality of the Threat or Use of Nuclear Weapons*, Advisory Opinion of 8 July 1996 [1996] *IC Rep.* 257, para. 79. It should be noted that the Geneva Conventions have attained universal ratification.

61. See also API, above note 5, at Articles 53–6.

62. It is at least a requirement of proportionality rather than a prohibition of indiscriminateness. It is not clear how large is the difference between the two.

63. If the original wrong was committed against a group protected by the four Geneva Conventions, it would not be possible to make such a requirement since reprisals against such groups are expressly prohibited by the Conventions.

64. API, above note 5, at Articles 35–6; 1907 Hague Convention IV, Article 23.

65. Protocol for the Prohibition of the Use in War of Asphyxiating, Poisonous or Other Gasses, and of Bacteriological Methods of Warfare, above note 10; many state signatories made reservations that the treaty is only binding towards other state signatories (reciprocal obligation) and will cease to be binding if the signing state's allies or enemies fail to respect the prohibitions therein. The USA dissented against including tear gas as coming within the Protocol on the grounds that it would be inconsistent to prohibit the use of tear gas in warfare while it could still be used domestically during peacetime for law enforcement purposes such as is riot control situations; Roberts and Guelff, *Documents on the Laws of War*, note 58 at pp. 155–6.

66. Convention on the Prohibition of the Use, Stockpiling, Production and Transfer of Anti-Personnel Mines and on their Destruction (March 1999) (Ottawa treaty).

67. See generally Christopher Greenwood, 'Customary International Law and the First Geneva Protocol of 1977 in the Gulf Conflict,' in Rowe, *The Gulf War, 1990–91*, at pp. 76–9.

68. Convention on the Prohibition on the Use of Certain Conventional Weapons which may be Deemed to be Considered Excessively Injurious or to Have Indiscriminate Effects, Oct 10, 1980, UN Doc. A/Conf.95/15.

69. Protocol on Prohibitions or Restrictions on the Use of Mines, Booby-Traps and Other Devices (1980 Protocol II) at Art. 2 of amended Protocol 2.

70. *Ibid.*, at Article 3.

71. 1980 Protocol III on Prohibitions or Restrictions on the Use of Incendiary Weapons.

72. Human Rights Watch, however, has concluded that the white phosphorous used in Gaza was an incendiary; Human Rights Watch, *Rain of Fire: Israel's Use of White Phosphorous in Gaza* (2009), at p. 63.

73. Diplomatic Conference For The Adoption Of A Convention On Cluster Munitions ('Cluster Munitions Convention') CCM/77, 30 May 2008, available at: http://www.mineaction.org/downloads/1/CCM77_ENGLISHfinaltext_001%5B1%5D.pdf.

74. Henckaerts and Doswald-Beck, *Customary International Humanitarian Law*, Volume I: *Rules* note 13, at Rules 11–14, pp. 37–50.

75. *Ibid.*, at Rule 14.

76. By virtue of Protocol on Prohibitions or Restrictions on the Use of Mines, Booby-Traps and Other Devices (Protocol II as amended on 3 May 1996) adopted on 3 May 1996, that Protocol applies to both IACs and NIACs. As a result of Convention on Prohibitions or Restrictions on the Use of Certain Conventional Weapons Which May be Deemed to be Excessively Injurious or to Have Indiscriminate Effects, Geneva, 10 October 1989, Amendment article 1, 21 December 2001, the CCWC and its Protocols apply to both IACs and NIACs.

77. Robert Kolb, 'The Relationship between International Humanitarian Law and Human Rights Law: A Brief History of the 1948 Universal Declaration of Human Rights and the 1949 Geneva Conventions', *International Review of the Red Cross* 324 (30 September 1998), at pp. 409–19; René Provost, *International Human Rights and Humanitarian Law* (Cambridge: Cambridge University Press, 2002), at pp. 13–16; John Cerone, 'Jurisdiction and Power: The Intersection of Human Rights Law and the Law of Non-International Armed Conflict in an Extraterritorial Context', *Israel Law Review* 40, no. 2 (2007), pp. 72–128, and other contributions in that publication.

78. Henckaerts and Doswald-Beck, *Customary International Humanitarian Law*, Volume I: *Rules*, note 13, Rule 14, pp. 48–9.

79. Rome Statute of the International Criminal Court, Article 8(2)b.iv, UN Doc. PCNICC/1999/INF/3 (17 July 1998), available at: http://untreaty.un.org/cod/icc/statute/romefra.htm.

80. It is a waste of ammunition and military effort intentionally to target civilians. The requirement of proportionality is much more inconvenient for an attacking force. It has an impact on how a force may carry out an attack against a military, and therefore legitimate, objective. More civilians are likely to be harmed by attacks against military objectives than by intentional attacks against civilians, at least in the case of generally law-abiding forces.

4
Civilian Protection – What's Left of the Norm?

Stuart Gordon

IS THERE A CRISIS?

The theme of this book is that there is a crisis in the application of the Geneva Conventions. At first glance this is clearly a difficult conclusion to draw. Hersch Lauterpacht warned over three decades ago that 'if international law is ... the vanishing point of law, the law of war is even more conspicuously the vanishing point of international law'.[1] He continues,

> It is in particular with regard to the law of war that the charge of a mischievous propensity of unreality has been levelled against the science of international law. The very idea of the legal regulation of a condition of mere force has appeared to many incongruous to the point of absurdity.

If correct, such an analysis makes it intensely difficult to identify what a period of 'non-crisis' would even look like. Arguably IHL has never met the editors' fairly challenging criteria of being able to deal with breaches of the law while retaining the characteristic of routine adherence and a sense that the violations remain uncharacteristic. Nevertheless, perhaps we have still crossed a critical threshold – one in which the underlying assumptions of IHL itself have begun to erode. The editors may well be right in suggesting that the sum of the 'new' breaches may have undermined the integrity of significant elements in the overall framework of international law, particularly with regard to civilian protection.

But before unpacking the nature of this crisis it is worth identifying and contextualising a counter-trend. The past decade has witnessed the gradual coalescence of norms and institutions that do in fact contribute to the consolidation of civilian protection. The international community is actively considering its political and legal instruments – in particular a political consensus is developing around an obligation to protect civilians from the most serious of threats (genocide, crimes against humanity, etc.) and this itself represents a significant evolution of the limited concepts of protection enshrined in Geneva and Hague law.

The trend is significant: in September 2000, the UN Member States pledged in their Millennium Declaration to expand and strengthen the protection of civilians in complex emergencies. More recently the International Commission on Intervention and State Sovereignty (ICISS)[2] made the case in its 'responsibility to protect' (R2P) concept that 'protection from mass killings, ethnic cleaning and genocide should constitute grounds for military intervention, when peaceful means had failed'.[3] The Joint Declaration by Heads of Governments at the UN High Level Summit in September 2005 also recognised the collective obligation to protect populations from 'genocide, war crimes, ethnic cleaning and crimes against humanity'.[4] In a more practical sense, since 1999 there have been an increasing number of UN missions with explicit or implicit civilian protection elements in their mandates (Burundi, Haiti, Côte d'Ivoire, Democratic Republic of Congo, Sierra Leone, Liberia and Sudan and ISAF in Afghanistan) – although each of these has been characterised by a lack of clarity over precisely how force should be employed in the service of civilian protection.

While these changes are significant, there also appear to be growing threats, in particular the increasing proportion of civilians in conflict-related deaths.[5] Louise Fréchette argued that:

> Civilians account for an estimated 75 per cent of war victims. The ongoing human suffering inflicted by conflicts from Afghanistan to Angola, and from the Middle East to the Great Lakes and elsewhere, are daily reminders of the need for a new and concerted response at the highest political levels: from governments, which bear the primary responsibility for protecting civilians; from the Security Council; and from all others who can help cover the considerable distance still to be travelled if the international community is to find truly effective solutions in this area of acute human need.[6]

Civilians are not only victims of 'collateral damage' but they, and those who help them, have increasingly become the direct targets of military action by belligerents. In Sudan, Liberia, the DRC[7] and Sierra Leone civilian populations have been deliberately attacked or forcibly displaced by armed actors for control of resources or weakening the support base of an enemy or simply to enable exploitation (particularly sexual exploitation of women and children, forced labour and the conscription of children). These populations have also faced the traditional consequences of warfare: inadequate food, water, healthcare and sanitation – but increasingly these services have themselves been manipulated by belligerents seeking increased political or military leverage or economic benefits. Even in situations of conflict the primary responsibility for the protection of civilians lies with the sovereign state or the 'belligerent occupying' force. Nevertheless, some governments, such as the Sudanese, are complicit in attacks, while others simply lack the capacity to prevent them.

The norms regulating the transference of responsibility for civilian protection to the international community remain in their infancy, and there remain significant challenges in mobilising international military responses. These relate to issues of the legitimacy and capacity of the intervening organisations and the paucity of the political will of their members. Only a handful of organisations have both the political and military capacity to lead military operations that fall outside of the norms of self-defence, while of those that do, including the UN, NATO, EU, AU and ECOWAS, none have effective operational-level concepts for civilian protection *per se*.

Other actors are also poorly placed. Humanitarian agencies frequently lack the capacity to operate in the more volatile environments in conditions of chronic insecurity, while the UN system itself is ill-equipped either to coordinate or to deliver protection activities on behalf of (particularly) internally displaced persons (IDPs). Finally, the weak reach and jurisdiction of the International Criminal Court (ICC) limits the deterrent effect of its powers.

In November 2002 Kofi Annan, then secretary-general of the UN, was perhaps more specific about the problems, highlighting weaknesses in three *critical* areas:

- securing humanitarian access;
- separating clearly civilians and combatants; and
- swiftly re-establishing the rule of law, justice and reconciliation during post-conflict transitions.[8]

It is perhaps in these three areas, but particularly in terms of the principle of 'distinction' that underlies the first two, that we see the 'crisis' in contemporary IHL's capacity to provide civilian protection.

NO SUCH THING AS DISTINCTION?

The principle of 'distinction' is the cornerstone of contemporary concepts of 'civilian protection': establishing a critical prohibition against direct attacks upon civilians. As a principle it is not contested. The ICRC Customary Law Study records the principle as rooted in a wide variety of statements of national courts, national legislation and military manuals, the rulings of the ICJ and state practice more generally.[9] Even a cursory perusal of legal instruments reveals its centrality: Articles 48, 51(2) and 52(2) of Additional Protocol I,[10] Protocol II, Amended Protocol II and the Protocol III to the Convention on Certain Conventional Weapons as well as the Ottawa Convention all make explicit reference to the principle, while the Rome Statute of the International Criminal Court specifies that

> intentionally directing attacks against the civilian population as such or against individual civilians not taking direct part in hostilities constitutes a war crime in the context of both international and non-international armed conflicts.[11]

While the principle is a central component of IHL it is also perhaps its Achilles' heel. It has evolved a considerable degree of complexity from the time of the Hague Rules' rather simple prohibition (Article 25, Hague Regulation)[12] of attacks upon undefended towns and villages, becoming a broader rule that only *military objectives* may be attacked. This implicitly necessitates a distinction being drawn between civilian and military objects. However, neither is defined in terms of their intrinsic characteristics; rather it is the purpose to which they are put by the belligerents that determines their status.[13] In effect, 'when an object is used in a way that it loses its civilian character and qualifies as a military objective, it is liable to attack'.[14] This lends the principle a degree of abstract ambiguity in the minds of belligerents, encouraging a sense that all objects could potentially confer an advantage and can therefore potentially be considered legitimate objectives.

Consequently, there have been significant efforts to constrain the scope for defining *all* objects as military objectives. These are enshrined most explicitly in the dual limits imposed by Article 52(2) of Protocol I (considered as reflecting customary law even by the US (which opposes other parts of Protocol I). This Article states that:

> Those objects which by their nature, location, purpose or use make an effective contribution to military action and whose total or partial destruction, capture or neutralization, in the circumstances ruling at the time, offers a definite military advantage. (Additional Protocol I, Art. 52)

Additional Protocol I establishes two sets of limiting criteria: firstly, that the objective should contribute effectively to the military action of the enemy, and secondly, that its 'destruction, capture or neutralisation' offers a definite advantage to the other side. Sassòli argues that this rules out attacks that offer '*indirect* contributions and *possible* advantages',[15] arguing further that both criteria should be fulfilled 'in the circumstances ruling at the time',[16] with the purpose being to limit and make material the types of objects that can be pursued.

However, in warfare, the imperative to prevail constantly encourages the search for targets that can force the enemy to capitulate at the lowest level of effort. Military doctrines such as Effects Based Operations or Counter Insurgency's emphasis on the will of the people as the centre of gravity of an insurgency potentially serve to stretch the target lists, particularly in situations where the list of specifically military targets is unlikely to exert leverage upon the enemy's leadership. However, IHL sets relatively clear limits upon these. The St Petersburg Declaration rules that 'the only legitimate object which States should endeavour to accomplish during war is to weaken the military forces of the enemy'.[17] The assumption underpinning this specifically and IHL generally is that violence against political, psychological or economic targets *may* represent more efficient ways of overcoming an enemy but 'are never necessary, because every enemy can be overcome by weakening sufficiently its military forces'.[18]

While warfare may be characterised by doubt, Additional Protocol I makes clear that

> in case of doubt whether an object which is normally dedicated to civilian purposes, such as a place of worship, a house or other dwelling or a school, is being used to make an effective contribution to military action, it shall be presumed not to be so used.[19]

Basing civilian protection on this approach to the principle of distinction is inevitable but also fragile. In effect the process of determining the status of an objective or an individual is performed by those engaged in the conflict – with the resulting regime being upheld by the twin pillars of non-combatants abiding by the principle of their non-participation in hostilities and combatants upholding the principle of civilian immunity from attack. This bargain presupposes that non-combatants are willing or able to refrain from direct participation in combat; and that combatants are able to draw distinctions and are prepared to forgo the potentially greater advantage from ignoring elements of the principle – respect to targeting both civil objects and civilians.

There are features of the 'new wars' that make this presupposition difficult both in terms of the complex wars within failed states and, significantly, conflicts involving states possessing advanced forms of technology. While both customary and treaty law remain crystal clear on the meaning of distinction and its central role in the regime of civilian protection, the regime faces three significant challenges that will be considered next: a process of 'decivilianisation' in the 'new wars'; the consequences of a failure to recognise the utilitarian nature of IHL and military ethics; and the consequences of an ambiguous crisis of humanitarian principles.

'DECIVILIANISATION' AND THE RATIONALITY OF ABUSE?

'Decivilianisation' is one consequence of a much broader trend in which the perceived strategic significance of civilian populations in conflict environments has increased. The fragmentation of weak states along ethnic, tribal or religious fracture lines and the weakening of the state in the face of globalisation's pressures have increasingly complicated the ways in which belligerents conceptualise conflict 'participants'. Conflicts between identity groups in particular raise a number of issues related to collective responsibility and perceived guilt, often leading to a practical dilution of the application of civilian status and distinction generally. This elision from what people *do* to who people *are* is particularly problematic, contributing to a sense that wars are no longer *between* peoples but are increasingly *among* them. This also serves to broaden the objectives of warfare, increasingly defining them more in terms of the control of populations as another form of resource.

In addition to direct and traditional military advantages the selective application of violence, or simply its threat, potentially offers a range of direct and indirect benefits at a number of levels. It may be perceived to offer a violent means for conflict resolution in the absence or breakdown of more peaceful processes. It can be seen to serve as a means for transferring essential or desirable resources (land, water, oil, drugs) or for establishing control of economic or political institutions or simply delivering political benefits in terms of the breakdown of the relationship between a population and its government. To some it can also provide personal gratification at a number of levels – prestige, status, sexual gratification, etc.

State failure also offers significant opportunities for individuals to gain or to lose resources – encouraging the creation, solidification and arming of social networks in order to protect existing or to secure new investments or even to influence the outcome of the conflict. In effect the heady mixture of state fragmentation and the ready availability of weapons can strongly encourage the defensive arming of tribal and other social networks, causing the transaction costs of security to be borne by much smaller social groups than the state itself.

However, building a capacity to defend a social network and its asset base also involves arming the group with attitudes that have the potential to breed more acquisitive aspirations that paradoxically militarise and dilute the civilian status of the community as a whole. This may lead to a tribally (or, more broadly 'identity group') based crystallization of formal and informal economic and security networks. This is perhaps most obvious in Afghanistan's northern Helmand province where inter-tribal frictions and competition for power and resources, particularly related to the drugs trade, have become the dominant dynamics of the renewed insurgency. The Pashtun Itzakzai and Noorzai tribes in particular have been key Taliban supporters, principally because they have felt excluded from both provincial power structures and the province's lucrative illicit drugs trade since 2001. The Taliban have offered an alternative and attractive route to satisfying political and economic aspirations.

While 'decivilianisation' has confused the applicability of 'distinction' in a practical sense, there is significant evidence that 'rational' or 'utilitarian' choices have also undermined restraint in the application of IHL. Jessica Stanton[20] for one explores what incentives exist for governments and opposition groups to abide by key IHL norms, particularly with regard to the protection of civilians. Utilising quantitative analysis of an impressively broad array of 82 case studies, she concludes that a key factor in decisions to target civilians is a strategy of obtaining legitimacy from domestic and international communities with an expectation that this will translate into material and diplomatic support.

Stanton's findings parallel the thinking of the legal realists of the 1920s.[21] A key element of their approach was a belief that in a domestic context people's expectations of the law were based more upon utilitarian calculations as to the likely punishments that courts would deliver rather than more deeply held ethical or natural law traditions. In effect people's behaviour was conditioned by a predictive exercise rooted in the probabilities of particular punishments and, in Stanton's paradigm, in rewards. The implication of both legal realism and Stanton's research is that the active maintenance of the declaratory normative regime surrounding the conduct of warfare is just as significant as the specific legal regime and that *both* define the political costs of non-compliance.

CHANGING ASSUMPTIONS AND THE PURPOSE OF LAW?

Perhaps the observation that upholding IHL is in part a product of a utilitarian calculation is to miss the point that IHL was never intended to be an open-ended commitment to humanitarian norms and justice; rather it was itself a form of enlightened self-interest on the part of states. While 'humanitarian norms' undoubtedly played a significant part in mobilising political support for the process of creating the laws, this role was largely catalytic, hastening states' identification and then codification of interests rather than broader norms and aspirations. In effect IHL emerged as a mechanism that codified reciprocal entitlements and interests that were difficult to create through less regulated forms of cooperative behaviour. IHL has provided a framework that enshrines a somewhat perverse and almost invisible paradox: cooperative behaviour between belligerent states in times of an armed conflict between them.

The basis of the shared interests is, however, both limited and fragile. Wars are times of profound uncertainty in which belligerents seek to preserve combat power for the point at which it may contribute 'decisively' to the defeat of an enemy. A critical consideration, therefore, is ensuring its application against objectives that provide a direct military advantage. A presumption is thus that the military obtain advantages from targeting only combatants and military objectives. The corollary of this is that targeting civilians and civil objects rarely provides military advantages or, if they do, the longer-term consequences largely negate the short-term benefits.

Sassòli argues that while

> Acts of violence against persons or objects of political, economic
> or psychological importance may sometimes be more efficient
> to overcome the enemy' they are 'never necessary, because
> every enemy can be overcome by weakening sufficiently its
> military forces. Once its military forces are neutralized, even the
> politically, psychologically or economically strongest enemy can
> no longer resist.[22]

Hence it could be argued that the principle of *distinction*, perhaps
the central organising principle of IHL, is based on an essentially
utilitarian calculation – that irrespective of any moral calculations it
is practical to preserve combat power and to exercise it only against
the enemy combatants. A key and perhaps rather unpalatable
conclusion is that Geneva Convention IV, and the core principle of
civilian distinctiveness is based as much on a particular perception
of military rationality, preferences and benefits in warfare as it is an
adherence to any particular moral compass.[23] A further worry, and
one that may be central to the contemporary crisis in IHL, is that
belligerents no longer share an interest in codifying these original
reciprocal entitlements and interests.

VIRTUE VERSUS UTILITARIAN ETHICS?

This shift towards a new *utilitarianism* is visible even within armies
that pride themselves on what could be described as *virtue*-based
ethics. The utilitarian nature of modern military morality resonates
powerfully in the dominant military philosophies of this age: the
'Manoeuvrist Approach to Operations (MoD (Army) 2005)' and
'Effects Based Operations'. Both emphasise a willingness to reduce
military reliance on brute force, underlining precision, precaution
and distinction in targeting but for essentially utilitarian reasons.
Each is pursued in order to bring about the disintegration of the
enemy 'system' by eroding his will to fight as well as his physical
integrity. The dominance of utilitarian ethics is also echoed in the
received wisdom of counter-insurgency doctrine. Patrick Mileham
quotes General Kiszely's[24] argument that in the space between
intense combat and passive forms of peace support operations it has
been recognised that 'in the eyes of the warrior, counter insurgency
calls for some decidedly un-warrior like qualities, such as emotional
intelligence, empathy, subtlety, sophistication, nuance and political

adroitness'. Mileham argues that 'A *fortiori*, these are acute moral sensitivities', but perhaps misses the point that these 'virtues' are instrumental in the achievement of military efficiency.

Many soldiers would be uncomfortable with the suggestion that their morality was essentially, if not wholly, utilitarian. Developed militaries in particular invest significantly in the codification of an 'ethos' (a word originating from the Greek 'ethikos' (ἠθικός), and meaning 'moral, or showing moral character') or framework of individual and collective morality and moral standards. While 'ethos' can be constructed by different armies in overtly different ways, at a more fundamental level they remain rooted in largely *utilitarian* rather than *virtue* ethics. The British example is illustrative in this regard, with the British Military Doctrine pamphlet (MoD 1989),[25] for example, placing morality as one of the three so-called components of fighting power: 'physical', 'intellectual' (formerly 'conceptual') and 'moral'. The Military Ethos paper echoes this, producing a statement of ethos that represents a complex amalgam of legal liabilities relating to equal opportunities, employment law and health and safety with those behaviours that are necessary in order to achieve operational effectiveness.[26]

The 'Values and Standards Policy Statement' takes this logic further; arguing that the

> Standards underpin the ethos of the British Army and that ethos supports the moral component of fighting power. Although the attempting to seize the moral high ground per se, without moral standards are about maintaining combat effectiveness, rather than validity, the standards are useless and bankrupt.[27]

This creates what Mileham suggests to be a moment of moral ambiguity in which the Army is unclear whether its ethical concepts are rooted in underlying and more fundamental 'virtues' or more utilitarian calculations of benefit – the identification of values that are necessary to achieve organisational cohesion and military efficiency.[28] However, the latter approach has the potential to render armies excessively vulnerable to operationally defined imperatives, and perhaps leaving them predisposed to favour ethical and legal deregulation in circumstances where these norms do not obviously and directly contribute to military effectiveness. Such predispositions are likely to be more compelling in the circumstance of war, where lives potentially hang by the thread of every decision. However, other factors are also likely to be significant: contexts where the armed groups are unfamiliar with IHL; where an enemy has been strongly 'demonised' or where perceptions of the overwhelming morality of the *jus ad bellum* legitimise or excuse what are then perceived to be more minor abuses of *jus in bello*.

COMPROMISES: HARNESSING MILITARY AND HUMANITARIAN POWER TO POLITICAL EFFECT

The tendency to favor ethical deregulation in the application of 'distinction' can be seen even in developed militaries that are drawn from societies with strong moral traditions. A useful example can be seen in the prosecution by General Wesley Clark (former NATO Supreme Allied Commander in Europe (SACEUR)) of the 1999 air campaign against Slobodan Milošević, and particularly his much-publicised desire to deploy Apache AH-64 attack helicopters to Albania.[29]

Clark requested the deployment of the helicopters shortly before the Kosovo air campaign began, announcing their deployment on 4 April 1999. It was anticipated that this would take only ten days but in reality it lasted over three weeks and became extremely controversial in the process.[30] This controversy stemmed mainly from its potential to contradict President Clinton's desire to avoid committing ground troops to Kosovo. But a second and far less visible controversy stemmed from the potential for the helicopters to inflict collateral damage.

The mountainous terrain of the Albanian/Kosovo border promised to channel the aircraft through valleys in which the Serbs were able to place high densities of surface-to-air missiles. US Army doctrine envisaged using massive missile barrages from ground-based (in Albania) Multiple Launch Rocket Systems (MLRS) and Army Tactical Missile Systems (ATACMS) in order to suppress these – promising the indiscriminate use of literally tens of thousands of sub-munitions. Such a tactic was out of the question given NATO's determination to avoid collateral damage,[31] but created tensions within the US military that were reflected in Richard Betts's observation that:

> Once the Apaches were finally deployed to the region, they could not even rehearse their mission because they lacked the legal authorization for the supporting artillery and rocket fires that would have been needed to suppress enemy defenses in

the path of the helicopter attacks. Without understanding the operational problems that made such requirements impractical, NATO lawyers insisted that all targets had to be directly observed shortly before firing. Carried to this extreme, NATO's lawyers thus became, in effect, its tactical commanders.[32]

Betts describes this as 'hyperlegalism', implicitly dismissing the precautionary principle that requires targets to be observed immediately prior to being engaged. In this case the political opposition to a ground offensive and antipathy towards collateral damage imposed limitations that, arguably, would not have been applied to the same degree by US forces operating in more remote theatres of operation. However, while this is a case of calculations of political costs restricting military proclivities and options in a way that accords with IHL, harnessing military power to political effects may also have an entirely negative effect on the civil population.

The 2006 Israeli invasion of Lebanon provides a useful example in this regard. Following the capture of two Israeli soldiers by Hezbollah, between 12 July and 14 August 2006 Israel launched thousands of attacks against what it described as Hezbollah targets in Lebanon. The Israeli Air Force conducted attacks on approximately 7,000 targets while the Navy conducted 2,500 bombardments.[33] These attacks caused an estimated 1,183 fatalities[34] and displaced over 970,000 people[35] (or 25 per cent of the entire population, with over half a million in Beirut alone). Hezbollah rocket attacks killed 40 Israeli civilians.[36]

The attacks had a catastrophic impact on the civilian population and infrastructure of Lebanon. Official Israeli statements insisted that the Israeli military were targeting only Hezbollah positions and that the damage to the Lebanese civilian infrastructure was an incidental consequence of attacks on military objectives or resulted from their use by Hezbollah fighters. Amnesty International disagreed, arguing instead that the

> evidence strongly suggests that the extensive destruction of public works, power systems, civilian homes and industry was deliberate and an integral part of the military strategy, rather than 'collateral damage' – incidental damage to civilians or civilian property resulting from targeting military objectives.[37]

AI also recorded the Lebanese government's own estimates of damage:

> 31 'vital points' (such as airports, ports, water and sewage treatment plants, electrical facilities) have been completely or partially destroyed, as have around 80 bridges and 94 roads. More than 25 fuel stations and around 900 commercial enterprises were hit. The number of residential properties, offices and shops completely destroyed exceeds 30,000. Two government hospitals – in Bint Jbeil and in Meis al-Jebel – were completely destroyed in Israeli attacks and three others were seriously damaged.[38]

Furthermore, the Israelis created a *de facto* blockade of most of southern Lebanon, hermetically sealing the area for a period of weeks. Air attacks against the arterial routes and bridges, ports and airports, the imposition of a naval blockade and an Israeli Government statement threatening to bomb vehicles using roads south of the Litani river prevented much of the civilian population from moving out of harm's way[39] and curtailed both humanitarian and media access. The bombing of the electricity grid system forced healthcare centres into reliance on diesel generators – but the blockade paralysed the fuel distribution network, making useless much of the medical equipment and also impacting on the water and sanitation systems. While blockades are not prohibited by the laws of war, preventing the supply of items indispensable to the survival of the civilian population is.[40] Article 23 of Geneva Conventions IV, for example, states the necessity for 'Free passage for consignments of certain objects necessary for the survival to the survival of the civilian population.'[41]

While Hezbollah undoubtedly did use civilian objects for military purposes the scale of the damage inflicted by Israel raised the question of whether the targeting of the infrastructure was intended as the principal aim of the attacks. Amnesty concluded that the

> widespread destruction of apartments, houses, electricity and water services, roads, bridges, factories and ports, in addition to several statements by Israeli officials, suggests a policy of punishing both the Lebanese government and the civilian population in an effort to get them to turn against Hizbullah. Israeli attacks did not diminish, nor did their pattern appear to change, even when it became clear that the victims of the bombardment were

predominantly civilians, which was the case from the first days of the conflict.

Arguably this was a case of politically driven ethical deregulation, Israeli perceptions of the *jus ad bellum* trumping *jus in bello* and, consequently, legitimising the effect on the Lebanese civilian population. It was also a direct and powerful consequence of Hezbollah's adoption of asymmetric tactics, leading directly to an intermingling of guerrilla groups and the civilian population.

Both the Kosovo and Lebanese cases highlight the importance of reasserting the continued applicability and relevance of the law in order to create essentially political incentives for all armed groups to apply it. Arguably the international focus on collateral damage during the 1999 Kosovo bombing campaign was a significant factor in preventing the assertion of the US Army's preferred model for employing a critical war fighting asset, its attack helicopters. In the case of the Israeli invasion of Lebanon the failure of the international community to gain traction over *both* Hezbollah and the Israeli military undoubtedly increased the range and scale of abuses perpetrated by both sides.

Perhaps what this analysis suggests is that international civil society groups are invaluable in holding the moral line in defining the essential illegality of violence perpetrated against civilians and reinforcing the sense that the context of warfare does not imply a lesser, unique and separate framework for human rights and international humanitarian law. It requires the active drawing of international human rights law (IHRL) standards into the very heart of war and a strong articulation and reassertion of the rights of victim groups. This is in effect implying the need to more effectively operationalise a range of legal instruments – particularly the 1951 Convention relating to the Status of Refugees, the 1979 Convention on the Elimination of All Forms of Discrimination against Women, the 1984 Convention against Torture, and the 1989 Convention on the Rights of the Child.[42]

This also implies that one purpose of IHL is to provide a valuable *mobilising norm* for action in the face of egregious breaches. In effect, 'advocacy' on the part of international civil society establishes for the belligerents the new benefits for compliance and the costs for failure now that the old forms of reciprocal benefits are breaking down. If this is the case, the monitoring of belligerent compliance with IHL is a critical part of ensuring that utilitarian ethics do not lead to ethical deregulation. Perhaps one component of the 'crisis' in civilian protection is more that IHL is not built on virtue ethics but a constant process of defining political benefits for compliance. This also hints at a much more limited range of objectives for IHL – halting *injustice* rather than the creation of *justice*.

DIFFERENCES OVER THE MEANING OF PROTECTION

However, the above model risks placing civil society groups and states in a dangerously adversarial relationship, raising also the danger that the thresholds for compliance between armed groups in the same conflict would be unequal. Arguably the more developed militaries would face greater pressure to apply a more expansive interpretation of IHL largely because they were more vulnerable to pressure from a broad range of field actors – human rights and humanitarian organisations, networks of media, etc. – who share an immediate and direct link with the 'victim' populations. The consequence is that the external policing of IHL standards is, in the long term, likely to be less efficient than internal forms of policing.

The implication of this is that armed groups of all types need to adopt a broader and common understanding of civilian protection, although there are clearly challenges in effecting this. For example, conventional armies tend to define civilian protection in extremely limited terms – characterising it as refraining from attacking directly civilians and civil objects and certain quite limited positive obligations towards sustaining civilian populations in times of belligerent occupation. Militaries also tend to be more comfortable with civilian protection when it is defined in largely logistical terms, such as the response to the Pakistan earthquake or the Asian tsunami. It becomes far more challenging when protection strategies are to be defined in opposition to the direct targeting of civilians by other armed groups, particularly non-state actors.

Conventional militaries also tend to portray civilian protection as a set of discrete and reactive tasks – such as the provision of framework security and patrolling, the collection of tasks known as 'IDP Operations', the employment of 'public order' tactics – rather than an operational concept or strategy. Furthermore, conceptualising civilian protection as being achieved largely through abiding by the principle of 'distinction' and the limited obligations of GCIV largely misses the point of how wars kill civilians – combat-related deaths are only a small percentage of the overall deaths. By far the greatest percentage of deaths arises from the unintended consequences of the fragmentation of the state and its socioeconomic foundations increasing the vulnerability of the civilian population.

Unsurprisingly, therefore, humanitarian and human rights communities are far more expansive and nuanced in their approaches to civilian protection. ICRC, for example, defines protection as

> all activities aimed at ensuring full respect for the rights of the individual in accordance with the letter and the spirit of the relevant bodies of law (i.e. human rights law, international humanitarian law and refugee law).[43]

Françoise Bouchet-Saulnier, legal adviser to Médecins Sans Frontières, defines it in terms of

> recognising that individuals have rights and that the authorities who exercise power over them have obligations. The notion of protection reflects all the concrete measures that enable individuals at risk to enjoy the rights and assistance foreseen for them under international humanitarian law. When providing relief in times of conflict, humanitarian organisations must not separate the provision of assistance from protection, since protection is part of realising these rights.[44]

These definitions also tend to result in an internally coherent operational strategy for establishing a physical presence, negotiating humanitarian access, deterring breaches of IHL and potentially providing evidence to legal bodies. It also creates a layered response from one of immediate action through to efforts designed to facilitate broader aspects of social and economic recovery.

It is unclear what the precise military role is in relation to these broader aims and even whether militaries *per se* (as opposed to other branches of government) should take a more active role in their delivery. It is also apparent that expanding the approach of states to encompass these broader conceptualisations of civilian protection involves multiple tasks that cross national governments' departmental boundaries (between defence, diplomatic and development ministries), and national governments tend to lack the capacity to effectively formulate policies when they fall outside single departmental frameworks. This would entail reforming elements of governmental crisis response machinery around different norms and objectives.

The development of the UK Stabilisation Unit (formerly the Post Conflict Reconstruction Unit) as well as Canadian, US and German equivalents may facilitate the emergence of cross-departmental strategy setting particularly if they more actively seek to establish mechanisms for civilian protection as conscious policy choices in a stabilisation strategy. However, this approach does contain dangers: while it may fill a gap in terms of upholding the practice of IHL and widen the set of possible policy choices it may also represent the ultimate securitisation of aid policy. However, the point remains that conventional state militaries must expand their understanding of civilian protection even if they do not assume direct responsibilities for its delivery.

But to what extent does this analysis apply to encouraging more developed civilian protection strategies among non-state actors? Louise Fréchette implies that addressing their abuses is perhaps more critical:

> Wars today are often fought not between sovereign countries or with regular armies, but between different religious, ethnic and political groups and irregular armed groups. In these conditions, civil defence forces, vigilante groups and militias often prey on civilians for their own private and destabilizing purposes, and in some cases specifically target them.[45]

Arguably insufficient attention has been focused on the 'supply side' of civilian abuse, with too little lavished on the role and applicability of IHL to non-state armed actors. A particular weakness is that most rules of IHL are 'still exclusively addressed to States' while its 'implementation mechanisms are even more state centred'. Marco Sassòli argues that even 'when rules apply to non-State actors or are claimed to apply to them, in most cases no international forum exists in which the individual victim, the injured State, an international intergovernmental or non-governmental organization or a third State could invoke the responsibility of a non-State actor and obtain relief'.[46]

Liesbeth Zegveld argues that international law can be enforced against non-state actors in three ways – firstly, holding a sponsoring or host state to be accountable for their actions (either because it controls the group or lacked due diligence in controlling it); secondly, for some of the most egregious crimes (such as war crimes, crimes against humanity and genocide) international criminal law can be enforced directly against individuals through mechanisms such as international criminal tribunals;[47] thirdly, and, according to Sassòli, perhaps the most innovative,[48] enforcing the law directly against the armed group itself. Zegveld suggests that this approach has a number of practical advantages. In particular where states have lost control of the armed groups, proving attribution to the state can be extremely difficult. Consequently, in some situations seeking to create mechanisms for encouraging the group *itself* to punish its own members is likely to be a more effective deterrent than international attempts to punish the individual within the group.

Sassòli develops Zegveld's argument further by suggesting that

> individual criminal responsibility exists only for the most egregious violations and may only be enforced through a fair trial in which the facts and their individual attribution have to be proven beyond reasonable doubt. Such standards of evidence are not necessary towards the group itself.[49]

Perhaps a further component of the crisis in contemporary IHL is that while wars have become 'federalised and privatised', its guardians have not focused sufficiently on the mechanisms for encouraging compliance among the newly dominant actors.

DECONSTRUCTING PROTECTION

A starting point for developing more effectively the mechanisms for civilian protection would be to define more appropriately the contexts in which it is operationalised. Victoria Holt's typology is particularly useful in this regard. While there is little that is explicitly new within any of the categories that she uses, the categorisation into the following six layers of protection is potentially extremely helpful in terms of encouraging actors to think through the modalities for each.[50]

1. *Protection as an obligation within the conduct of war* – Holt argues that these are the minimum responsibilities of the belligerents and the occupying powers during armed conflict. This largely involves obligations to ensure minimum standards of civilian welfare and to avoid targeting and collateral damage. IHL effectively seeks to reduce the occurrence of situations in which civilians are displaced or civilian infrastructure is damaged through the triple principles of distinction, proportionality and precaution. It could be argued that this is best delivered through

a combination of the armed groups accepting the bulk of the norms of civilian protection but with their acceptance being reinforced by international civil society, creating a matrix of political costs and benefits for non-compliance.

2. *Protection as a military mission to prevent mass killings* – this largely reflects the type of intervention envisaged by the ICISS – a protection mission deployed to prevent large-scale violence against a civilian population.

3. *Protection as a task within UN-mandated peace operations* – this form of protection is envisaged as being one of a group of tasks rather than *the* central organising concept of a UN operation. It may include protecting a civilian convoy, IDP camp or compound. These tasks tend to be fairly straightforward, particularly where the military can define the task in fairly limited geographic terms – e.g., the protection of a finite location such as an IDP camp. Holt argues that the language used in Security Council resolutions has been somewhat limited in this regard, with a tendency to 'refer to protecting civilians "under imminent threat," "within capabilities" and "within areas of responsibility"'.[51] A particular challenge with this approach is that many soldiers characterise these roles as essentially 'rule of law' functions and therefore as lying outside of the sphere of military competence.[52] This approach can be very manpower-intensive and tends to 'fix' troops in static locations – an approach that, while sometimes necessary, tends to be resisted by commanders.

4. *Protection as providing area security for humanitarian action* – this involves the provision of a framework of security in which humanitarian action can take place and the civilian population can exist with an enhanced degree of security. There is some disagreement over whether 'security' is the same thing as protection *per se* – with protection being seen by some as a much broader concept that includes political and humanitarian responses and upholding legal rights. This approach is also very manpower-intensive, and manpower is one resource that the international community tends to lack.

5. *Protection through assistance/operational design* – in this form, protection is afforded through well-designed relief programmes and projects – for example, situating IDP camps, etc., in locations that minimise threats to their inhabitants.

6. *Protection as the use of traditional force* – civilians are provided with improved levels of protection once a particular enemy

has been defeated. The military defeat of a threat creates the conditions for improvements in civilian protection.

Arguably, additional work would need to be dedicated to creating integrated civilian/military operational-level strategy-setting structures and also determining how force might be used, against whom and in what circumstances. The latter is not simply a question of rules of engagement, but of strategising the use of force in the service of short-term civilian protection. It presents what is perhaps the most challenging of problems in Holt's categories 2 and 6 – that of reconciling the short-term and immediate demands for operational civilian protection with the imperatives of combat and the objective of defeating a particular armed actor.

HUMANITARIAN ACTION AS A THREAT TO CIVILIAN PROTECTION?

While much of the preceding analysis clearly advocates encouraging a range of actors to hold belligerents to account and create frameworks of costs for non-compliance with IHL/IHRL, paradoxically this is itself not necessarily without costs in terms of civilian protection. The expansion of the concept and particularly the growth in humanitarian organisations' involvement in extending its scope may blur dangerously the boundaries between humanitarian and political action. This may have negative implications particularly when states back away from situations in which humanitarian imperatives are less clear and there is a paucity of policing (or military) capacity to ensure the physical protection of the civilian population. Such contexts can lead to the overstretching of humanitarian mandates, responsibilities and abilities as humanitarians seek to identify patterns of violence imposed upon civilian populations, place pressure on belligerents to open up humanitarian space and access, and, where this does not progress, seek to trigger other political or military mechanisms for providing protection. Humanitarianism cannot easily fill these vacuums without comprising its core principles.

Some authors, including David Rieff,[53] are extremely critical of this approach, arguing that 'humanitarianism' has portrayed itself as 'a saving idea that cannot save'. Rieff describes how frustration with their inability to change the political conditions that produce humanitarian crises has led the humanitarian community to sacrifice its integrity and independence to become a part of larger political and military operations – 'a catchall for the thwarted aspirations of our age' – and concludes that humanitarianism is ill equipped to resolve the issues it increasingly has portrayed itself as capable of dealing with. He argues that humanitarianism has sacrificed itself in order to get into the much bigger business of 'armed protection of threatened civilians and neo-liberal state construction'. The bargain involved attaching contemporary humanitarianism to an interventionist or containment agenda of the Western powers, echoing, says Hugo Slim,[54] the process through which European missionary philanthropy became a component of nineteenth-century colonialism. For Rieff, contemporary humanitarianism has arrived at its 'Constantine moment' – passing from a movement based on private faith to becoming a state-based orthodoxy leading to what he describes as 'state humanitarianism'.[55]

This has had profoundly negative consequences. Tracing the history of humanitarian action and, particularly its recent failures in Bosnia, Rwanda, Kosovo and Afghanistan, Rieff highlights an intellectual and moral crisis. 'Instead of political action backed by the credible threat of military force,' Rieff writes, 'the Western powers would substitute a massive humanitarian effort to alleviate the worst consequences of a conflict they wanted to contain.' They did so by enabling politicians to use humanitarianism as a 'humanitarian alibi' for doing little but containing the war in Bosnia and the genocide in Rwanda[56] (creating a 'cruel deception' that something was being done) and then through employing the 'humanitarian ideal' as a 'warrant for war' in its invasions of Kosovo and Iraq.[57] Rieff suggests that the underlying purpose humanitarianism served was 'as a pretext for what was essentially a political decision '… to put an end militarily once and for all to Slobodan Milošević's fascist rebellion in the European backlands' and, similarly, using humanitarianism to legitimise military operations in Afghanistan.

This process, Rieff argues, creates two problems – excusing the international community from a need to act meaningfully while compromising humanitarian principles and creating an inappropriate sense that something effective was being done, thereby weakening the humanitarian movement. He also argues that the extension of traditional humanitarian mandates into prevention activities has placed agencies in the uncomfortable position of lobbying governments to take action, potentially including military action. Rieff asks whether 'an ideal based on both universal values and unbending neutrality can be politicized successfully', suggesting that the 'price for such a transformation would seem to be very high – perhaps too high'.

Rieff offers a potent critique of contemporary humanitarianism but goes too far. His critique of NGO rights-based approaches as being largely irrelevant in the context of conflict – a form of political posturing – ignores the capacity of such language to engage other actors, to establish the price of 'abuses' and to enable the victims themselves to develop a voice. Furthermore, the focus on politicisation through 'integration' with statist objectives ignores the challenge of moving beyond a humanitarian moment in which only limited symptoms are addressed.

There may also be a threat to civilian protection from another unlikely quarter. The 'Responsibility to Protect' (R2P)[58] principle contains potential pitfalls if extended too far or, particularly, when elided with concepts such as the 'duty to prevent'.[59] The 'duty to prevent', or more specifically, anticipatory forms of self-defence, involves the extension of existing rules – particularly Article 51 and Chapter VII of the Charter – that may be profoundly unhelpful in obtaining consensus on the R2P. Furthermore, the means for determining the triggers and means for intervention present significantly more challenges, are more subject to manipulation and distortion, and potentially throw wide open the gates for intervention. In contrast, the R2P concept was subject to extremely careful formulation, its authors seeking to create a mechanism in which the responsibilities to the civilian population lie with the states themselves and only in cases of gross abdication or failure of responsibility would the responsibility shift to the wider community of states.

CONCLUSIONS

So where does this analysis leave us? It began with the observation that international law is at the vanishing point of law and IHL itself at the vanishing point of international law. In this regard IHL has always been in crisis. However, the chapter has charted challenges that are becoming critical. The *utilitarian* rather than *virtue* basis of military morality is a source of profound vulnerability, particularly as the benefits and assumptions upon which the Conventions were constructed are no longer as attractive to armed groups as they once were. This has the potential to threaten the application of IHL more generally.

Furthermore, while we have witnessed a commendable growth in the norms and institutions dedicated to civilian protection, Victoria Holt's[60] conclusion that the operationalisation of civilian protection by conventional militaries has lagged behind the emergence of policies and norms is worrying – as is the growth in the range of operational challenges and imperatives stemming from changes in the typology of warfare. Perhaps the only conclusion that can be drawn is that the crisis of civilian protection continues to mature.

NOTES

1. H. Lauterpacht, *International Law, Collected Papers*, Volume 2 (Cambridge: Cambridge University Press, 1975), p. 37.
2. Report of the International Commission on Intervention and State Sovereignty, available at: http://www.iciss-ciise.gc.ca/menu-en.asp.
3. HPG Research Briefing No. 22 (March 2006), 'The Military and Civilian Protection: Developing Roles and Capacities', p. 2.
4. *Ibid.*
5. Gilbert Burnham, Riyadh Lafta, Shannon Doocy and Les Roberts, 'Mortality after the 2003 Invasion of Iraq: A Cross-sectional Cluster Sample Survey', *The Lancet*, 11 October 2006. See also Gilbert Burnham, Shannon Doocy, Elizabeth Dzeng, Riyadh Lafta and Les Roberts, 'The Human Cost of the War in Iraq: A Mortality Study, 2002–2006', a supplement to the October 2006 *Lancet* study.
6. Deputy Secretary-General of the UN Statement to the Security Council meeting on the protection of civilians in armed conflict, New York, 23 April, DSG/SM/129 or SC/7051, dated 24 April 2001.
7. HPG Briefing Note, 'Humanitarian Issues in Ituri, Eastern DRC', dated June 2003, available at: http://www.odi.org.uk/hpg/.
8. He also highlighted the emergence of three new challenges for the protection of civilians in conflict – sexual exploitation and gender-based exploitation; commercial exploitation; and the escalating threats posed by global terrorism. See OCHA, 'Special Report: Civilian Protection in Armed Conflict', available at: http://www.irinnews.org/webspecials/civilprotect/IntElissaGolberg11.asp, p. 9.
9. Jean Marie Henckaerts and Louise Doswald-Beck (eds), *Customary International Humanitarian Law*, Volume 1 (Cambridge: Cambridge University Press, 2006), pp. 3–24.
10. *Ibid.*, pp. 3–4.
11. ICC Statute, Art. 8(2) (b) (i).
12. Article 25 prohibits the 'attack or bombardment, by whatever means, of towns, villages, dwellings, or buildings which are undefended'.
13. Even specially protected objects, such as hospitals and dams may, under some circumstances, become military objectives if they are used for military purposes. See Art. 56(2) of Protocol I and Art. 19 of Convention IV. Protocol I, Arts 52(2) and 52(3), provides a definition and a list of examples of objects that are commonly presumed to be civil objects rather than military objectives.
14. Henckaerts and Doswald-Beck, *Customary International Humanitarian* Law, 1, p. 34.
15. Marco Sassòli, 'Legitimate Targets of Attacks under International Humanitarian Law', background paper prepared for the Informal High-Level Expert Meeting on the Reaffirmation and Development of International Humanitarian Law, Cambridge, 27–29 January 2003, pp. 2–3.

16. *Ibid.*
17. St Petersburg Declaration, preamble, Para. 2.
18. Sassòli, 'Legitimate Targets', p. 3.
19. Additional Protocol I, Art. 52(3), Para.719.
20. Jessica Stanton, 'The Rationale of Restraint: Compliance with International Laws of War During Civil War', paper presented at the annual meeting of the International Studies Association, Hilton Hawaiian Village, Honolulu, Hawaii, 2005, unpublished mimeo.
21. Brian R. Leiter, *American Legal Realism*, University of Texas Law, Public Law Research Paper No. 42, available at: http://ssrn.com/abstract=339562; Michael Steven, 'Legal Realism as Theory of Law', *William & Mary Law Review* 46 (2005), pp. 1915–2000, available at: http://ssrn.com/abstract=761007.
22. Sassòli, 'Legitimate Targets', p. 3.
23. This logic can be extended to other parts of IHL (Geneva Conventions III – protection provided to prisoners of war on the basis of a reasonable expectation of reciprocal treatment) and international law more broadly (the regulation of the use of force, for example, is essentially about preserving systemic order).
24. J. Kiszely, 'Learning about Counter Insurgency', *Journal of the Royal United Services Institute* 151, no. 6 (2006), pp. 16–21.
25. MoD, *British Military Doctrine*, A.C. 71451 (1989).
26. MoD (Army), *The Military Ethos (The Maintenance of Standards)* (1993).
27. See MoD, Army Training and Recruiting Agency, 2000 and 2006.
28. Patrick Mileham, 'Teaching Military Ethics in the British Armed Forces', in *Ethics Education in the Military*, ed. Paul Robinson, Nigel de Lee and Don Carrick (Aldershot: Ashgate, 2008), p. 68.
29. W.K. Clark, *Waging Modern War: Bosnia, Kosovo, and the Future of Combat* (New York: HarperCollins, 2002).
30. Paul E. Gallis, *Kosovo: Lessons Learned from Operation Allied Force*, Report for Congress, 19 November 1999.
31. Benjamin S. Lambeth, *NATO's Air War for Kosovo: A Strategic and Operational Assessment* (Santa Monica, CA: Rand, 2001). See also Gallis, *Kosovo*, p. 22.
32. Richard K. Betts, 'Compromised Command', available at: http://www.foreignaffairs.org/20010701fareviewessay4999?richard-k-betts/compromised-command.html.
33. See Israel Defence Force website, http://www1.idf.il/DOVER/site/mainpage.asp?sl=EN&id=7&docid=56765.EN.
34. *Middle East Crisis*, UNICEF Situation Report No. 26, available at: http://www.reliefweb.int/rw/rwb.nsf/db900SID/HMYT-6SSLUF?OpenDocument&rc=3&emid=SODA-6RT2S7.
35. Figures from Lebanese Higher Relief Council: http://www.reliefweb.int/rw/rwb.nsf/db900SID/EKOI-6ST5ZM?OpenDocument. Within hours of the ceasefire, thousands of Lebanese began returning to their homes: according to UNHCR, as of the evening of 15 August, around 522,000 remained displaced.
36. Amnesty International, 'Israel/Lebanon: Deliberate Destruction or "Collateral Damage"? Israeli Attacks on Civilian Infrastructure', available at: http://www.amnesty.org/en/report/info/MDE18/007/2006.
37. *Ibid.*
38. *Ibid.*
39. This is a potential breach of API, Art. 58, which requires that civilians should be allowed to leave besieged areas.

40. Amnesty argues that 'The parties to the conflict may not deny consent to relief operations on arbitrary grounds, and can only control the content and delivery of humanitarian aid to the extent necessary to ensure that aid convoys are not being used, for example, for military purposes.' Amnesty International, 'Israel/ Lebanon'.

41. See also Arts 55 and 59 of Geneva Convention IV and Arts 69 and 70 of Additional Protocol I.

42. See Claude Bruderlein and Jennifer Leaning, 'New Challenges for Humanitarian Protection', available at: http://bmj.com/cgi/content/full/319/7207/4, p. 2.

43. R. Williamson, *Protection of Civilians: Bridging the Protection Gap*, Report on Wilton Park Conference 766 (May 2005).

44. Françoise Bouchet-Saulnier, *The Practical Guide to Humanitarian Law* (Oxford: Rowman & Littlefield, 2002), p. 44.

45. UN Document DSG/SM/129 or SC/7051, 24 April 2001.

46. Marco Sassòli, 'Possible Legal Mechanisms to Improve Compliance by Armed Groups with International Humanitarian Law and International Human Rights Law', paper presented to the Armed Groups Conference, Vancouver, 13–15 November 2003.

47. Liesbeth Zegveld, *Accountability of Armed Opposition Groups in International Law* (Cambridge: Cambridge University Press, 2002), pp. 97–228.

48. Sassòli, 'Possible Legal Mechanisms'.

49. *Ibid.*

50. HPG Research Briefing No. 22, 'The Military and Civilian Protection: Developing Roles and Capacities' (March 2006), p. 2.

51. *Ibid.*, p. 2.

52. *Ibid.*

53. David Rieff, *A Bed for the Night: Humanitarianism in Crisis* (New York: Simon & Schuster, 2002), pp. 1–33.

54. Hugo Slim, 'Is Humanitarianism Being Politicised? A Reply to David Rieff', The Dutch Red Cross Symposium on Ethics in Aid, The Hague, 8 October 2003, Centre for Humanitarian Dialogue, Geneva.

55. *Ibid.*, p. 1.

56. *Ibid.*

57. *Ibid.*

58. Report of the International Commission on Intervention and State Sovereignty, available at: http://www.iciss-ciise.gc.ca/menu-en.asp.

59. Lee Feinstein and Anne-Marie Slaughter, 'A Duty to Prevent', *Foreign Affairs* 83, no. 1 (Jan./Feb. 2004), pp. 136–50.

60. Victoria Holt, 'The Military and Civilian Protection: Developing Roles and Capacities', in *Resetting the Rules of Engagement: Trends and Issues in Military–Humanitarian Relations*, ed. Victoria Wheeler and Adele Harmer, HPG Report No. 21, Overseas Development Institute, London (March 2006).

5
The Protection of Detainees in International Humanitarian Law

Keiichiro Okimoto[1]

INTRODUCTION

So long as armed conflicts exist, the respect or non-respect of international humanitarian law (hereafter IHL) inevitably comes into question. It is an endless process of applying and interpreting IHL according to the situation, and on some occasions the application and interpretation can be more controversial than in others. Moreover, some areas of IHL might cause more controversies in their application and interpretation than others. At times, the adequacy of the law itself might be called into question and a proposal for additional rules might be raised.

In the course of applying and interpreting IHL, there is a general tendency to put more emphasis on the non-respect of IHL than the respect of it. It could be that the respect of IHL is often more subtle than non-respect. Clearly, the non-respect should be addressed appropriately but the respect of IHL should also be recognised when a conflicting party is trying to apply it. It is easy simply to criticise non-respect, but to find ways to encourage the conflicting parties to act in accordance with the rules should also be thought through. One case of respect by a conflicting party does not mean that it will comply throughout an armed conflict. A party can still fall back to non-respect of IHL at any time. In this sense, the application and interpretation of IHL is a constant process. The respect of IHL should be recognised, but in the event of non-respect the rules should be stressed and possible ways to comply with IHL should be discussed with the appropriate authorities. In some cases, the authorities might have to refer cases to national or international courts.

It is against this background that the treatment of detainees in IHL should be understood. It is worth emphasising at this point that the very reason why IHL contains so many rules relating to the treatment of detainees is that the power relation between the detaining authorities and the detainees is clearly unequal and places of detention are normally a restricted area where outsiders cannot easily enter. Hence, IHL provides various safeguards to ensure humane conditions of detention for the detainees.

The number of rules of IHL relating to the treatment of detainees is large, especially with regard to prisoners of war and internees in international armed conflict. It can be assumed that there could be various practical complications in the course of application, especially when there are many different people supervising places of detention. These people can be privates in an army or fighters in an armed group, or an interrogator from the investigation branch of an established military or a child soldier not at all trained in interrogation. Making all these people involved in the supervision of a place of detention conducted according to the rules of IHL is a major challenge, but is an important role of the superior who is responsible for that place. It is important to recognise any instances of respect, but in the event of non-respect, facts should be established and the person responsible for the detention centre should be encouraged to take necessary measures to halt and prevent the non-respect.[2]

Keeping in mind the above background relating to the treatment of detainees in IHL, this chapter will show that no one detained in an armed conflict is out of the legal framework of IHL. It will also describe various safeguards at all stages of detention, starting from the beginning of captivity to release. Finally, the ICRC's role in protecting detainees will be discussed.

I. APPLICABLE LAW

IHL consists of numerous treaties and customary rules, but the rules relating to the treatment of detainees are found in Geneva Conventions III and IV, Additional Protocols I and II, and customary rules. However, the rules relating to the treatment of detainees are different in international and non-international armed conflict.

In international armed conflict, there are several categories of detainees and the protection afforded differs for each category. There are at least four categories: (1) prisoners of war; (2) civilian internees; (3) civilians directly participating in hostilities; and (4) spies and mercenaries. Prisoners of war are protected by Geneva Convention III and Additional Protocol I, civilian internees are protected by Geneva Convention IV, civilians directly participating in hostilities and spies/mercenaries are protected by Article 5 of Geneva Convention IV and Article 75 of Additional Protocol I. To all these categories of persons, one may add the customary rules of IHL.

In non-international armed conflict, there are no categories of detainees and all persons in the hands of an adversary are protected by common Article 3 of the Geneva Conventions, Additional Protocol II, and customary rules of IHL.

Specific provisions or rules will be examined in more detail in the subsequent sections. The first section will discuss the rules relating to the treatment of detainees in international and non-international armed conflict from the beginning to the end of captivity. It will then discuss the issues relating to internment and administrative detention. The final section will discuss the ICRC's role in ensuring humane conditions of detention.

II. BEGINNING OF CAPTIVITY AND STATUS DETERMINATION[3]

Detention begins with captivity. In peacetime, deprivation of liberty is an exception to the right of liberty and as such it can only be carried out 'in accordance with such procedures as are established by law'.[4] Normally, the penal procedure code sets out various safeguards to prevent abuse of state power, namely by law enforcement officials.

In wartime, so far as those participating directly in hostilities are concerned, deprivation of liberty is not an exception but rather presumed as permitted. Nowhere in IHL does it provide that those participating directly in hostilities have the right to liberty and that the deprivation of their liberty is an exception. On the other hand, once captured, there are detailed rules governing the treatment of detainees.

This section discusses the various safeguards that ensure that no one captured during an armed conflict falls out of the protection of IHL.

A. International Armed Conflict

1. General

Once a person is captured during an international armed conflict, his/her status under IHL should be determined in order to define the protection afforded to the person.

It is important to clarify that the question of the status determination of detainees only occurs in an international armed conflict where there are two statuses, combatants and civilians.[5] There is no combatant/civilian distinction under the law of non-international armed conflict. Thus, the first condition is that the situation should be an international armed conflict as defined in common Article 2 of the Geneva Conventions.[6]

2. Prisoners of War

When a person who has participated directly in hostilities is captured, the status of the person under IHL might not be evident. In this case, the detainees are presumed as prisoners of war at the time of capture and the whole of Geneva Convention III applies.[7] This continues until a 'competent tribunal' determines the status of the detainees.[8]

Even if the detainees are *prima facie* held as not being prisoners of war, those detainees still have the 'right to assert [their] entitlement to prisoner-of-war status before a judicial tribunal and to have that question adjudicated',[9] before any trial for an offence arising out of the hostilities takes place. Until their status is determined, they benefit from the protection in Geneva Convention III and Additional Protocol I.[10]

The criteria to determine whether a detainee is a prisoner of war or not are set out in Article 4 of Geneva Convention III[11] and Articles 43 and 44 of Additional Protocol I. Anyone who meets the criteria set out in these provisions is considered as a prisoner of war (or as an equivalent) and thus benefits from the protection of Geneva Convention III and Additional Protocol I.

First, members of the armed forces are *prima facie* prisoners of war when they are captured by the adversary's armed forces. Article 4(A)(1) of Geneva Convention III provides that the following persons are prisoners of war:

> Members of the armed forces of a Party to the conflict as well as members of militias or volunteer corps forming part of such armed forces.

Article 43(1) of Additional Protocol I defines armed forces as follows:

> The armed forces of a Party to a conflict consist of all organized armed forces, groups and units which are under a command

responsible to that Party for the conduct of its subordinates, even if that Party is represented by a government or an authority not recognized by an adverse Party. Such armed forces shall be subject to an internal disciplinary system which, *inter alia*, shall enforce compliance with the rules of international law applicable in armed conflict.

Article 4(A)(3) of Geneva Convention III further provides as follows:

Members of regular armed forces who profess allegiance to a government or an authority not recognized by the Detaining Power.

An important point with the latter two provisions above is that government recognition by an adversary is not required for armed forces to qualify as 'armed forces' within the meaning of the provisions.[12] Thus, even if one conflicting party has not recognised the government of the adversary, the armed forces of the latter still qualify as 'armed forces' within the meaning of the above provisions, if they meet the standard set out therein. As a consequence, members of these armed forces will be considered *prima facie* as prisoners of war when captured.

Second, members of the armed forces who do not distinguish themselves from civilians are not prisoners of war. This loss of prisoner of war status occurs only when the members of the armed forces fail to meet the standard of distinguishing themselves from civilians as set out in Article 44(3) of Additional Protocol I:

… he [a combatant] carries his arms openly:
(a) During each military engagement, and
(b) During such time as he is visible to the adversary while he is engaged in a military deployment preceding the launching of an attack in which he is to participate.

However, even if they fail to meet these standards, they still benefit from the protection in Geneva Convention III and Additional Protocol I in accordance with Article 44(4) of Additional Protocol I. Thus, in practice, the scope of protection is the same as ordinary prisoners of war. However, the difference is that those combatants who do not comply with the above standards can be prosecuted for such failure. Their direct participation in hostilities will likewise be regarded as unlawful if they do not meet the above standards. On the other hand, prisoners of war will not be prosecuted for their mere participation in hostilities.[13]

Third, religious and medical personnel in the armed forces are exceptions, who are not considered as prisoners of war when captured but will benefit from the protection provided in Geneva Convention III.[14]

Fourth, even if a person is not a member of the armed forces, one is considered as a prisoner of war if one meets certain criteria. Article 4(A)(2) of Geneva Convention III provides as follows:

> Members of other militias and members of other volunteer corps, including those of organized resistance movements, belonging to a Party to the conflict and operating in or outside their own territory, even if this territory is occupied, provided that such militias or volunteer corps, including such organized resistance movements, fulfil the following conditions:
>
> (a) That of being commanded by a person responsible for his subordinates;
> (b) That of having a fixed distinctive sign recognizable at a distance;
> (c) That of carrying arms openly;
> (d) That of conducting their operations in accordance with the laws and customs of war.

Fifth, certain persons accompanying armed forces with no combat role in armed conflict and crews and pilots of merchant ships and civil aircrafts are also considered as prisoners of war when captured.[15]

Finally, certain persons resisting invading forces,[16] persons who belong to the armed forces of the occupied country,[17] and persons qualifying as prisoners of war under Article 4 of Geneva Convention III received in neutral or non-belligerent power[18] are also considered as prisoners of war.

Persons who qualify under the above provisions are all considered as prisoners of war (or equivalent) and thus, benefit from the protection of Geneva Convention III and Additional Protocol I.

As can be seen, combatants and associated persons are automatically liable for being deprived of their liberty for the mere fact of their status. However, there are various safeguards to avoid arbitrary determinations, namely Article 5 of Geneva Convention III and Article 45 of Additional Protocol I.

Those who do not qualify under the above provisions do not benefit from the protection of Geneva Convention III and Additional Protocol I as prisoners of war. There are several categories of persons who fall out of the category of prisoners of war and thus, entitled to do different protection.

3. Detained/Interned Civilians

Civilians are the corollary of combatants. As such, they are defined as follows in Article 50(1) of Additional Protocol I:

> A civilian is any person who does not belong to one of the categories of persons referred to in Article 4 A(1), (2), (3) and (6) of the Third Convention and in Article 43 of this Protocol.

In principle, civilians 'shall enjoy general protection against dangers arising from military operations'.[19] 'Military operations' are understood as 'all the movements and activities carried out by armed forces related to hostilities',[20] which may well include detention of civilians.

As Article 50(1) of Additional Protocol I further provides, '[i]n case of doubt whether a person is a civilian, that person shall be considered to be a civilian'. This seems to conflict with Article 5 of Geneva Convention III, which provides that a person should benefit from Geneva Convention III if the status of the person is doubtful. However, the drafters clarified that

> [i]n the case of the Third Geneva Convention the persons concerned have committed a belligerent act and claim the status of combatants, and therefore ask to be treated as prisoners of war. Article 50 of the Protocol concerns persons who have not committed hostile acts, but whose status seems doubtful because of the circumstances. They should be considered to be civilians until further information is available ...[21]

In other words, Article 5 of Geneva Convention III assumes that the captured person has participated directly in hostilities and claims prisoners of war status whereas Article 50(1) of Additional Protocol I assumes that the person has not participated directly in hostilities and is a civilian. Thus, as a matter of law, there is no conflict between the two.

However, once further information is available and a belligerent state considers detention of civilians, there are various steps that need to be taken into account.

First, one should know if the person is a protected person within the meaning of Article 4 of Geneva Convention IV. This provision basically excludes foreign nationals in the territory of a belligerent state who can be protected by their diplomatic representations (in practice, embassies and consulates).[22] Otherwise, protected persons within the meaning of Article 4 are 'those who ... find themselves, in case of a conflict or occupation, in the hands of a Party to the conflict or Occupying Power of which they are not nationals'. The conditions of nationality and diplomatic representation in Article 4 are commonly referred to as 'nationality criteria'.

Once the nationality criteria are met and it is established that a person is a protected person, the person can only be interned on the basis of Articles 41, 42, 43, 68 and 78 of Geneva Convention IV, as provided in Article 79 of the Convention. Articles 41, 42 and 43 are applicable to 'aliens in the territory of a party to the conflict'. Protected persons can be interned or placed in assigned residence 'only if the security of the Detaining Power makes it absolutely necessary'.[23] Although the meaning of 'the security of the Detaining Power' is admittedly unspecified, the words 'only if' and 'absolutely necessary' are enough to emphasise the exceptional character of the internment and assigned residence.[24]

Second, Articles 68 and 78 are only applicable in an occupied territory. Article 78 provides that the protected persons may be interned or placed under assigned residence '[i]f the Occupying Power considers it necessary, for imperative reasons of security, to take safety measures'. Again, the exceptional character is emphasised by the words 'necessary' and 'imperative'.[25]

Article 68 envisages internment or imprisonment in a more restricted situation:

> Protected persons who commit an offence which is solely intended to harm the Occupying Power, but which does not constitute an attempt on the life or limb of members of the occupying forces or administration, nor a grave collective danger, nor seriously damage the property of the occupying forces or administration or the installations used by them, shall be liable to internment or simple imprisonment, provided the duration of such internment or imprisonment is proportionate to the offence committed.

As in the earlier provisions, this also emphasises the exceptional character of internment. Hence, civilians in an international armed conflict can only be deprived of liberty in very limited circumstances, and once this is put into effect, the detailed rules on the treatment of civilian internees in Geneva Convention IV apply.

Those who pose more serious threats to the belligerent state are dealt with under a special regime under Article 5 of Geneva Convention IV, which provides as follows:

> Where, in the territory of a Party to the conflict, the latter is satisfied that an individual protected person is definitely suspected of or engaged in activities hostile to the security of the State, such individual person shall not be entitled to claim such rights and privileges under the present Convention as would, if exercised in the favour of such individual person, be prejudicial to the security of such State.
>
> Where in occupied territory an individual protected person is detained as a spy or saboteur, or as a person under definite suspicion of activity hostile to the security of the Occupying Power, such person shall, in those cases where absolute military security so requires, be regarded as having forfeited rights of communication under the present Convention.
>
> In each case, such persons shall nevertheless be treated with humanity, and in case of trial, shall not be deprived of the rights of fair and regular trial prescribed by the present Convention ...

What is probably different from the earlier provisions is that this article deals with persons who not only pose a threat to the security of the state in general, but also those who have in fact engaged in hostile activities, such as 'seriously damag[ing] the property of the occupying forces or administration or the installations used by them'.[26]

It is worth noting at this point that civilians directly participating in hostilities lose the protection accorded to civilians, pursuant to Article 51(3) of Additional Protocol I.[27] However, they are still entitled to the fundamental guarantees in Article 5 of Geneva Convention IV and Article 75 of Additional Protocol I.

Finally, it is worth noting that spies[28] and mercenaries,[29] despite their disadvantaged position in IHL, benefit from the fundamental guarantees provided in Article 5 of Geneva Convention IV and Article 75 of Additional Protocol I.

As can be seen from the above, deprivation of liberty of civilians in international armed conflict is an exceptional measure strictly regulated by Geneva Convention IV. However, once they participate directly in hostilities, civilians lose their protection as civilians and are automatically liable for being captured, but still benefit from the fundamental guarantees provided in Article 5 of Geneva Convention IV and Article 75 of Additional Protocol I. Owing to the growing acceptance of Article 75 of Additional Protocol I as customary international law, even where Additional Protocol I does not apply, the persons who come under Article 5 of Geneva Convention IV may be protected by Article 75 of Additional Protocol I as a matter of customary law.[30]

As noted, the status determination procedure has a number of safeguards so that no one captured during an armed conflict, regardless of whether they are combatants or civilians directly participating in hostilities, falls out of the protection of IHL. The status determination heavily depends on the facts of each case, but the application of the above procedure to the facts is an obligation of states and none of the steps can be circumvented.

B. Non-international Armed Conflict

As noted earlier, there is no combatant /civilian distinction under the law of non-international armed conflict and hence the status determination of a person does not arise. Once a person is deprived of freedom, that person is equally entitled to the protection of common Article 3 of the Geneva Conventions, Additional Protocol II and customary rules of IHL. However, their status under IHL and domestic law may potentially be in conflict.

In non-international armed conflict, the equilibrium between armed groups and government forces is inherently uneven under domestic law, where the former are criminal groups and the latter are entitled to enforce domestic law against the armed groups to restore law and order, including the prosecution of the members of the armed groups.[31] The state's right to maintain law and order is recognised in Article 3(1) of 1977 Additional Protocol II:

> Nothing in this Protocol shall be invoked for the purpose of affecting the sovereignty of a State or the responsibility of the government, by all legitimate means, to maintain or re-establish law and order in the State or to defend the national unity and territorial integrity of the State.[32]

However, it is equally clear that the unequal legal status under domestic law does not affect the equal application of IHL. A commentary confirms this point as follows:

These rules [in the law of non-international armed conflict] grant the same rights and impose the same duties on both the established government and the insurgent party, and all such rights and duties have a purely humanitarian character.[33]

Although this conflict between domestic law and IHL might not affect the treatment of detainees during captivity, it might have certain consequences after the armed conflict, which will be dealt with later in this chapter.

III. TREATMENT OF DETAINEES DURING CAPTIVITY

A. International Armed Conflict

The status determination of a captured person has significant practical implications for the detaining power, namely the scope of obligations. First, if captured persons are determined to be prisoners of war, the whole of Geneva Convention III applies, which contains 143 articles. Likewise, civilian internees are protected by Geneva Convention IV, which contains 159 articles. With regard to civilians who have participated directly in hostilities, they are protected by a much narrower protection provided in Article 5 of Geneva Convention IV and Article 75 of Additional Protocol I. In general, the various obligations can be separated into those involving financial and non-financial considerations.

1. Prisoners of War

First, with regard to prisoners of war, their maintenance involves massive financial, material and human resources. The maintenance of prisoners of war is a general obligation of the detaining power as provided in Article 15 of Geneva Convention III:

The Power detaining prisoners of war shall be bound to provide free of charge for their maintenance and for the medical attention required by their state of health.

Even when the detaining power may fall short of adequately maintaining prisoners of war, they are still expected to endeavour to do as much as possible in good faith. Article 26 of the 1969 Vienna Convention on the Law of Treaties provides the fundamental principle of treaty compliance or *pacta sunt servanda*: Every treaty in force is binding upon the parties to it and must be performed by them in good faith.[34] Article 55 of the draft Vienna Convention specifies the meaning of 'good faith' as follows: 'Good faith, inter alia, requires that a party to a treaty shall refrain from any acts calculated to prevent the due execution of the treaty or otherwise to frustrate its objects.'[35]

Article 18 of the Vienna Convention also prohibits acts that would defeat the object and purpose of the treaty, once it is signed or ratified.[36] The comment of the Eritrea–Ethiopia Claims Commission in relation to the treatment of prisoners of war during the Eritrea–Ethiopia War is instructive in this regard:

> Neither Party has sought to avoid liability by arguing that its limited resources and the difficult environmental and logistical conditions confronting those charged with establishing and administering POW camps could justify any condition within them that did in fact endanger the health of prisoners.[37]

This is an important indication that limited resources do not release the detaining power from the obligation to maintain prisoners of war but rather oblige it to take all necessary measures to fulfil that obligation within the given circumstances.

The financial implications of the maintenance of prisoners of war should be foreseen before an international armed conflict begins. Some of the important areas include transportation, infrastructure, daily products and medical care. First, the evacuation of prisoners of war from combat zones (Article 19 of Geneva Convention III) requires, in practice, trucks, petrol, drivers and armed escorts to ensure their safety (Article 20). Second, prisoner-of-war camps should be set up, which in practice requires tents and blocks for prisoners of war, buildings for the detaining authorities, watch towers, water supply system, latrines, showers, kitchens and fences (Articles 21–25, 28, 29). Third, various daily products should be supplied to maintain the health of prisoners of war such as sleeping materials (Article 25), food (Article 26), water, firewood for cooking, clothing (Article 27) and soap (Article 29). Fourth, medical care should be provided (Articles 30–32), which requires medical personnel, infirmaries, wards, medical equipment and medicines. To fulfil these obligations, good preparation is required, namely securing sufficient funds, reliable suppliers, and allocating enough personnel and transportation.

However, other obligations do not necessarily require budgetary considerations but rather relate to the behaviour of the camp authorities. Two examples can be cited: humane treatment of prisoners of war and the ICRC's right to visit them. First, Article 13 of Geneva Convention III provides the obligation to treat prisoners of war humanely.[38] It prohibits:

- Any unlawful act or omission causing death or seriously endangering the health of a prisoner of war;
- Physical mutilation and medical or scientific experiments;
- Acts of violence, intimidation, insults, exposure to public curiosity; and
- Reprisals.

Compliance with these obligations requires awareness of the prohibitions by all camp staff and close supervision by the person responsible of the camp. Article 12 of Geneva Convention III provides as follows:

Prisoners of war are in the hands of the enemy Power, but not of the individuals or military units who have captured them. Irrespective of the individual responsibilities that may exist, the Detaining Power is responsible for the treatment given them.

Thus, the role of the person responsible for a prisoner of war camp is important. It is this person who is in a position to influence, and is responsible for influencing, the behaviour of the camp staff to treat prisoners of war humanely.

Likewise, the right of the ICRC to visit prisoners of war pursuant to Article 126 of Geneva Convention III depends on the awareness of this right at all levels of the detaining authority, ranging from government officials to camp commanders. For example, even if the ICRC's right to visit is known at the ministry level, if the camp commanders are not aware of it, there could be problems with access upon ICRC's visit. Thus, the role of the higher officials in keeping their subordinates at all levels informed of the ICRC's right to visit is important in implementing Article 126.

It may be said that changing the behaviour of people is more difficult than improving material conditions. In some instances, a 'quick fix' of material conditions is possible. For example, in

Rwanda, the ICRC set up tents and supplied food in prisons shortly after the genocide in 1994, when the prison system was at a breaking point owing to severe overpopulation. However, ill treatment by the staff of a prisoner-of-war camp cannot be eradicated just by replacing them with new staff. A more targeted approach is necessary, namely by ensuring that the camp commander exerts stricter control over the staff, organising awareness-raising sessions for camp staff, and punishing the camp staff and camp commander for their failure to comply with IHL. However, for this to materialise, it normally requires a significant amount of time and effort, since it requires a shift in the mindset from considering the detainees as people they can control as they wish, to people who are entitled to humane treatment under the law, namely IHL.

2. Civilian Internees

The treatment of civilian internees during internment as provided for in Geneva Convention IV is almost identical to that of prisoners of war as provided for in Geneva Convention III, hence this section will not repeat what has been said above.

3. Civilians who have Directly Participated in Hostilities

Leaving aside the complexity of the notion of 'direct participation in hostilities',[39] civilians who have directly participated in hostilities are protected by a significantly reduced form by Article 5 of 1949 Geneva Convention IV and Article 75 of 1977 Additional Protocol I.

Article 5(3) of Convention IV and Article 75(1) of Protocol I provides for the humane treatment of persons in the power of a conflicting party in the most general terms. Article 75(2) specifies prohibited acts.[40]

There is no provision in Article 5 of Convention IV nor Article 75 of Protocol I on the material conditions of persons once they are detained. However, Article 5(3) of Convention IV provides as follows:

> They [persons not protected by Convention IV according to Article 5(1)] shall also be granted the full rights and privileges of a protected person under the present Convention at the earliest date consistent with the security of the State or Occupying Power, as the case may be.

Hence, although civilians who have directly participated in hostilities do not benefit from the protection of Convention IV, if the security of the state or occupying power permits, the material conditions afforded to civilian internees should also be accorded to them.

On material conditions, Article 5 of Convention IV and Article 75 of Protocol I are complemented by customary rules of IHL that regulate most aspects of material conditions of detention.[41] They provide rules relating to detention facility[42] and daily basic needs (food, water, clothing, shelter, medical attention).[43] In addition, they go so far as to regulate aspects such as registration of detainees,[44] ICRC visits to detainees,[45] correspondence with families,[46] family visits[47] and freedom of belief.[48]

B. Non-international Armed Conflict

The law of non-international armed conflict also contains rules on material conditions of detention and behaviour of the detaining party, albeit in a significantly reduced form compared to the law of international armed conflict.

First, common Article 3(1) and (2) of the 1949 Geneva Conventions[49] and Article 4(1) and (2) of the 1977 Additional Protocol II[50] prohibit certain acts against persons not taking direct part in hostilities.

Second, although common Article 3 is silent on the material conditions of detention, Article 5 of the 1977 Additional Protocol II provides rules relating to the treatment of wounded and sick persons deprived of liberty, detention facilities, daily basic needs (food, water, hygiene, shelter, medical attention), individual and collective relief, freedom of belief, conditions of labour and corre-spondence. Most of them are customary rules of IHL,[51] and where there is a gap, Protocol II and customary rules complement each other.

As can be seen from the above, in international and non-inter-national armed conflict, and for all categories of persons deprived of their liberty, IHL provides for rules on the treatment of persons deprived of their liberty during their captivity, particularly material conditions of detention and prohibitions on certain acts against persons deprived of their liberty by the detaining party.

IV. RELEASE AND REPATRIATION

The final stage of captivity is the release, which is also regulated by IHL in both international and non-international armed conflict.

A. International Armed Conflict

1. Prisoners of War

The release and repatriation of prisoners of war is provided in Article 118 of the 1949 Geneva Convention III as follows:

> Prisoners of war shall be released and repatriated without delay after the cessation of active hostilities.

From the provision, the release and repatriation of prisoners of war seems straightforward, but its application is considerably more delicate, particularly when they might face dangers to their physical and mental well-being once they are repatriated, owing to political changes in the home state.

In international law, when a person within the effective control of a state is going to be transferred to another state, the overriding principle that must be taken into account is the obligation of *non-refoulement*. This obligation requires that a person within the effective control of a state shall not be transferred into a situation where they would face the risk of arbitrary deprivation of life, torture or other forms of cruel, inhuman or degrading treatment or punishment.[52]

This principle also applies to prisoners of war at the time of their release and repatriation. Whenever a prisoner of war fears that he or she might face dangers to their physical and mental well-being, they should be given an opportunity to express this fear to the appropriate authorities, such as the detaining power, the Protecting Power or the ICRC. The detaining power should also carry out its own assessment by an independent body whether the concerned prisoner of war's fear is well founded. Such assessment should be done on an individual basis, in other words, for each prisoner of war and not for a certain group of prisoners of war. If such fear is well founded, the prisoner of war should not be repatriated but should rather be resettled in the detaining power's country or a third country.

Apart from the principle of *non-refoulement*, consideration should be given to whether the prisoner of war is still in the course of criminal proceedings or has been convicted and serving the sentence. Article 119 of 1949 Geneva Convention III provides as follows:

> Prisoners of war against whom criminal proceedings for an indictable offence are pending may be detained until the end of

such proceedings, and, if necessary, until the completion of the punishment. The same shall apply to prisoners of war already convicted for an indictable offence.

Such prisoners of war remain protected by 1949 Geneva Convention III until release and repatriation, even if after the 'cessation of active hostilities'. Article 3(b) of 1977 Additional Protocol I confirms this point:

> [T]he application of the Conventions [1949 Geneva Conventions] and of this Protocol shall cease, in the territory of Parties to the conflict, on the general close of military operations ... except ... for those persons whose final release, repatriation or re-establishment takes place thereafter. These persons shall continue to benefit from the relevant provisions of the Conventions and of this Protocol until their final release, repatriation or re-establishment.

2. Civilian Internees

The release and repatriation of civilian internees is set out in two categories: during hostilities and occupation, and after the close of hostilities. The former is provided for in Article 132 of 1949 Geneva Convention IV:

> Each interned person shall be released by the Detaining Power as soon as the reasons which necessitated his internment no longer exist.

The latter is provided for in Article 133 of the same Convention:

> Internment shall cease as soon as possible after the close of hostilities.

The reason for setting out two provisions for the release of civilian internees can be understood by comparing the nature of the deprivation of liberty between civilian internees and prisoners of war. Prisoners of war are held by the detaining power until the 'cessation of active hostilities' precisely to prevent them from rejoining their own armed forces and continuing the fighting. In an international armed conflict, the internment of prisoners of war is a rule rather than an exception. On the other hand, civilian internees are held 'only if the security of the Detaining Power makes it absolutely necessary' or for 'imperative reasons of security'. They are interned on an ad hoc basis and as an exception rather than a rule in an international armed conflict.

Therefore, it is a logical consequence that prisoners of war are only released after the 'cessation of active hostilities' but civilian internees are released not only after the 'close of hostilities' but also during the hostilities and occupation. Indeed, the reason to intern prisoners of war invariably remains until the end of an international armed conflict while the reason to intern civilians can cease even during an international armed conflict as the threat to security ceases to exist.

As similar to prisoners of war, civilian internees can continue to be detained if they are still in the course of criminal proceedings or have been convicted and are serving the sentence.[53] They remain entitled to the protection of 1949 Geneva Convention IV.

3. Civilians who have Directly Participated in Hostilities

Civilians who have directly participated in hostilities, although only entitled to a reduced form of protection of Article 5 of 1949 Geneva Convention IV and Article 75 of 1977 Additional Protocol I, are treated in a similar manner as civilian internees, so far as their release is concerned.[54] Article 75(3) of 1977 Additional Protocol I provides as follows:

> Except in cases of arrest or detention for penal offences, such persons shall be released with the minimum delay possible and in any event as soon as the circumstances justifying the arrest, detention or internment have ceased to exist.

Moreover, Article 75(6) provides as follows:

> Persons who are arrested, detained or interned for reasons related to the armed conflict shall enjoy the protection provided by this Article until their final release, repatriation or re-establishment, even after the end of the armed conflict.

The two provisions make it clear that civilians who have directly participated in hostilities should be released once the reason for their deprivation of liberty ceases to exist, except when criminal proceedings are ongoing or when they are convicted, in which case they continue to be entitled to the protection of Article 5 of Geneva Convention IV and Article 75 of 1977 Additional Protocol I.

B. Non-international Armed Conflict

Although the timing of the release of persons deprived of their liberty in non-international armed conflict was not expressly included in either common Article 3 of the 1949 Geneva Conventions or 1977 Additional Protocol II, customary law establishes that they must be released as soon as the reason for the deprivation of their liberty ceases to exist, which may be either during hostilities or after the end of hostilities.[55]

However, such release in non-international armed conflict often takes place in a context significantly different from international armed conflict since it is often linked to a broader issue of the tension between punishment of the members of the defeated party and post-conflict national reconciliation.[56] The problem stems from the fact that domestic law and IHL do not operate on the same basis. On one hand, domestic law creates an unequal status between armed groups and government forces, of which the members of the former are criminals and can be punished by maximum sentence in many countries while the latter can lawfully use force to maintain law and order.[57] On the other hand, under IHL, the conduct of hostilities by armed groups and government forces is equally lawful so long as it does not violate IHL. Because of this underlying assumption, Article 6(5) of 1977 Additional Protocol II even provides that 'the authorities in power shall endeavour to grant the broadest possible amnesty to persons who have participated in the armed conflict'.[58] Thus, the court of a state is faced with two opposing legal obligations: domestic law obliges it to hand down maximum sentence against the members of armed groups while IHL instructs it to grant amnesty to them. In addition, the court is asked to try war crimes committed by the members of both armed groups and government forces equally. Faced with such a situation, it may be the case that the court will choose domestic law and hand down maximum sentence as well as be stricter with the prosecution of war crimes committed by the members of armed groups, while being lenient to those committed by the members of government forces.[59]

The choice between punishment based on domestic law or amnesty is a policy question for the government, and this chapter is not the place to discuss this issue further.[60] However, it is worth noting that the release of persons deprived of their liberty in non-international armed conflict also has an important bearing on the relationship between punishment of the members of the defeated party and post-conflict national reconciliation.[61]

Finally, it merits mention that, similar to the case of persons deprived of their liberty in international armed conflict, those undergoing criminal proceedings or who have been convicted can continue to be detained even after the end of hostilities, and they remain under the protection of the law of non-international armed conflict.[62]

V. PARTICULAR PROBLEMS WITH INTERNMENT/ADMINISTRATIVE DETENTION[63]

Internment or administrative detention during international and non-international armed conflicts has been highlighted in many contexts in recent years, and they merit a separate discussion. Internment or administrative detention generally means 'deprivation of liberty ordered by the executive authorities when no specific criminal charge is made against the individual concerned'.[64] It is distinguished from regular pre-trial detention and detention of prisoners of war. Regular pre-trial detention normally requires an arrest by a judicial order and a charge against specific crimes. On the other hand, detention of prisoners of war is regulated specifically by 1949 Geneva Convention III. The problem is often that regular pre-trial detention and detention of prisoners of war are normally regulated in detail by either criminal procedure code or 1949 Geneva Convention IV, whereas the procedural principles and safeguards for internment or administrative detention do exist but are not well codified. This section clarifies that while internment/administrative detention *per se* are not unlawful, it should be carried out according to the procedural principles and safeguards established by international law. This section will first discuss the procedural principles and safeguards for internees in international armed conflict and then internees in non-international armed conflict.

A. Internees in International Armed Conflict

In international armed conflict, the procedures for the deprivation of liberty are defined by the nature of the deprivation of liberty. Civilian internees, as opposed to prisoners of war, can only be held so long as there are reasons that necessitate their internment, particularly for the 'security of the Detaining Power' (Article 42) or for 'imperative reasons of security' (Article 78).[65] Otherwise, they must be released. On the other hand, prisoners of war can be held until the 'cessation of active hostilities'.[66] The difference between the two kinds of detention is logical since the primary aim of holding prisoners of war is to prevent them from rejoining their armed forces whereas that of civilian internees is for security reasons. The latter is an exceptional measure, which is regulated by the safeguards in 1949 Geneva Convention IV.[67]

Once a civilian is interned according to Article 42 or 78 of Convention IV, they are entitled to the safeguards provided for in Article 43 and 78. Article 78, first and foremost, provides that internment 'shall be made according to a regular procedure to be prescribed by the Occupying Power in accordance with the provisions of the present Convention'. Thus, an occupying power should establish a procedure before it can carry out any internment. Such procedure will inevitably vary from one context to another, and it is for the occupying power to decide the detailed rules of procedures. However, the minimum standard that must be met in the procedure is provided for in Convention IV itself.

First, the reasons that necessitate internment, namely 'security of the Detaining Power' (Article 42) or for 'imperative reasons of security' (Article 78), are already limits on the conflicting parties upon internment. No other reasons can serve as bases of internment. Hence, the interning authority is required to justify, for each and every internee, that the person poses a threat to the security of the interning authority.

What 'security of the Detaining Power' or 'imperative reasons of security' means depends on the specific context of each internment. However, in any case, the threat should be directed towards the security of the detaining or occupying power, and not towards the security of other states. When the detaining or occupying power is a coalition of forces, the threat directed against the security of any of the members of the coalition forces can be regarded as security of the detaining or occupying power. But internment can be carried out only if it is 'absolutely necessary' or for 'imperative' reasons of security. These phrases make it clear that the standard of proof to justify the internment is extremely high.

Beyond this, a commentary on Convention IV provides that 'the person concerned, by his activities, knowledge or qualifications' should represent 'a real threat to its [the detaining or occupying power's] present or future security'. Examples given in the commentary are as follows:

- Subversive activity carried on inside the territory of a Party to the conflict;
- Actions which are of direct assistance to an enemy Power;

- Serious and legitimate reasons to think that members of organisations whose object is to cause disturbances; and
- Other acts by such members which may seriously prejudice the security of the detaining or occupying power, such as sabotage or espionage.[68]

On the other hand, the commentary notes that

the mere fact that a person is a subject of an enemy Power cannot be considered as threatening the security of the country where he is living.[69]

Once a civilian is interned, they are entitled to have the decision of internment reviewed. Article 43 of 1949 Geneva Convention IV provides that such review should take place 'as soon as possible' after the internment, and if the continued internment is upheld, the review should take place 'at least twice yearly ... with a view to the favourable amendment of the initial decision, if circumstances permit'.

Likewise, Article 78 provides that an internee has the right to appeal against the decision of internment. The appeals should be decided 'with the least possible delay' and if the continued internment is upheld, the review should take place 'if possible every six months'. These are important procedural safeguards to prevent arbitrary deprivation of liberty and prolonged internment without justification, and preserve the exceptional character of internment.

Such review should be undertaken by a 'court or administrative board designated by the Detaining Power' (Article 43) or a 'competent body set up by the said [Occupying] Power' (Article 78). A commentary on Convention IV seems to use the terms in Articles 43 and 78 interchangeably, emphasising that the important elements are that the decisions for continued internment must not be left to one individual but should be a joint decision,[70] which would offer 'the necessary guarantees of independence and impartiality'[71] and 'a better guarantee of fair treatment'.[72]

In international armed conflict, the failure to comply with these procedural safeguards could constitute 'unlawful confinement', which is a grave breach of Geneva Convention IV under Article 147. This triggers the exercise of universal jurisdiction, which would enable any state party to the Geneva Conventions to try the suspects involved in unlawful confinement.[73]

So far as civilians who have directly participated in hostilities are concerned, Article 75(3) of 1977 Additional Protocol I provides as follows:

> Any person arrested, detained or interned for actions related to the armed conflict … shall be released with the minimum delay possible and in any event as soon as the circumstances justifying the arrest, detention or internment have ceased to exist.

As a commentary notes, this provision is based on Article 43 of 1949 Geneva Convention IV, which provides for the periodic review of internment decisions and Article 132, which provides that internees should be released 'as soon as the reasons which necessitated his internment no longer exists'. This has been discussed earlier.

B. Internees in Non-international Armed Conflict

International humanitarian law, particularly common Article 3 of the 1949 Geneva Conventions and 1977 Additional Protocol II, is silent on the procedural safeguards for persons interned during non-international armed conflict. It is thus complemented by IRHL.[74]

The principle and the exception of the deprivation of liberty is provided for in Article 9(1) of the International Covenant on Civil and Political Rights (ICCPR):

> Everyone has the right to liberty and security of person. No one shall be subjected to arbitrary arrest or detention. No one shall be deprived of his liberty except on such grounds and in accordance with such procedure as are established by law.

The principle here is that everyone is free and has the right to liberty. The deprivation of liberty is the exception. Its exceptional character is reflected in the fact that the deprivation of liberty can only take place on grounds and procedure established by law. This applies also to internment during non-international armed conflict and, in this sense, the exceptional character of internment is a common principle in international and non-international armed conflict.

In international human rights law (IHRL) there are two types of deprivation of liberty: (1) regular pre-trial detention requiring judicial order for arrest and criminal charges; and (2) internment/ administrative detention ordered by the executive branch and not aimed at bringing criminal charges. Both are lawful so long as they are carried out on grounds and procedure established by law.

However, the law that establishes the grounds and procedure of internment should include the minimum standards in IHRL.

Among the procedural safeguards in the ICCPR, two of them are particularly important:[75] (1) the right to be informed of the reasons of arrest; and (2) the right to challenge the lawfulness of detention. Article 9(2) provides that '[a]nyone who is arrested shall be informed, at the time of arrest, of the reasons of his arrest'. In the case of internment, the interning party should inform on the reasons of internment. The reasons should include sufficient information on the facts and legal basis so that the internee can challenge the lawfulness of the internment at the earliest possible occasion.

The right to challenge the lawfulness of detention is provided for in Article 9(4) of the ICCPR:

> Anyone who is deprived of his liberty by arrest or detention shall be entitled to take proceedings before a court, in order that that court may decide without delay on the lawfulness of his detention and order his release if the detention is not lawful.

Similar to international armed conflict, the exceptional character of internment is reinforced by this right to challenge the lawfulness of detention. In other words, in IHRL, internment itself is already an exceptional measure and, in addition to it, whenever such an exceptional measure is effectuated, its lawfulness is subject to review, with a view to granting release to the concerned internee.

Any internment that does not comply with the procedural safeguards in IHRL would be an arbitrary deprivation of liberty, unless the state has officially derogated from the relevant provisions. The conditions for derogation in Article 4 of the ICCPR are strict. First, the situation must be a 'public emergency which threatens the life of the nation' and its existence should be officially proclaimed. Second, certain provisions can never be derogated from, such as the right to life, prohibition on torture and other forms of ill treatment, and prohibition on punishment not based on law. Third, the measures taken for derogation should be proportionate to the 'exigencies of the situation', should be consistent with other obligations under international law, and should not be discriminatory. Fourth, the derogated provision and the reasons for derogation must be communicated to other states parties through the UN Secretary-General, and the date the derogation will terminate should also be communicated through the same channel. Hence, any derogation from Article 9 of the ICCPR on the right to liberty can only be lawful after all these conditions are met.

As can be seen from the above, internees in both international and non-international armed conflict are protected by certain procedural safeguards. In particular, internment is considered as an exceptional measure, which should only be carried out according to grounds and procedures established by law, and the review of internment decision should take place periodically.

VI. ROLE OF THE ICRC

A. Background and Purpose of ICRC Visits to Places of Detention

As noted at the beginning, detainees are in a vulnerable position owing to the unequal power relations between the detaining authorities and the detainees, and because places of detention are normally a restricted area where outsiders cannot easily enter.

There are various ways to ensure humane conditions and treatment of detainees. The primary responsibility to ensure humane conditions and treatment lies with the detaining authority. In case of inhumane treatment or lack of respect for judicial guarantees, investigation should be carried out against the detaining authority and the perpetrator should be brought to justice. In exceptional cases, recourse to international bodies might be available, such as international and regional human rights committees, courts and international criminal courts and tribunals. Among these bodies, the European Committee for the Prevention of Torture and Inhuman or Degrading Treatment or Punishment is unique in the sense that it can directly carry out visits to places of detention.[76]

In this context, the ICRC is not the sole institution working towards the humane conditions and treatment of detainees, but is one of many. However, the ICRC's role in ensuring human conditions and treatment of detainees during and after an armed conflict is distinct in several respects. First, the ICRC has a solid legal basis in international instruments, which will be further discussed in section B following, 'Legal Basis'. Second, it has the longest history in visiting detainees (since 1915) during and after armed conflict. Third, it employs rigorous modalities when conducting visits to detainees. Finally, it tries to influence the behaviour of the detaining authorities through confidential dialogue, meaning that the ICRC does not systematically publish its findings from the visits. These points will be discussed further in the following sections.

B. Legal Basis

1. Statutes of the International Red Cross and Red Crescent Movement

The Statutes of the International Red Cross and Red Crescent Movement provide the legal basis for the ICRC to ensure humane conditions and treatment of detainees during and after international and non-international armed conflict as well as internal disturbances and tensions. The Statutes were adopted by the International Conference of the Red Cross and Red Crescent, composed of the states party to the 1949 Geneva Conventions, ICRC, International Federation of Red Cross and Red Crescent Societies, and National Red Cross and Red Crescent Societies, and hence is binding on all of these members.[77]

First, Article 5(2)(c) of the Statutes provides as follows:

> The role of the International Committee [of the Red Cross], in accordance with its Statutes, is in particular ... to undertake the tasks incumbent upon it under the Geneva Conventions, to work for the faithful application of international humanitarian law applicable in armed conflicts and to take cognizance of any complaints based on alleged breaches of that law ...

As will be seen later, the ICRC is specifically mandated by 1949 Geneva Conventions III and IV to ensure humane conditions and treatment of prisoners of war and civilian internees. The provision, however, mentions that the ICRC should 'work for the faithful application of international humanitarian law', which includes the rules applicable in non-international armed conflict protecting detainees. In this sense, the ICRC is also mandated to ensure humane conditions and treatment of detainees in non-international armed conflict.

However, Article 5(2)(d) extends the ICRC's mandate beyond armed conflict:

> The role of the International Committee [of the Red Cross], in accordance with its Statutes, is in particular ... to endeavour at all times – as a neutral institution whose humanitarian work is carried out particularly *in time of international and other armed conflicts* or *internal strife* – to ensure the protection of and assistance to military and civilian victims of such events and of *their direct results*...[78]

First, this confirms that the ICRC is mandated to ensure humane conditions and treatment for detainees in international and non-international armed conflict. However, this scope is extended to two additional situations: (1) internal strife; and (2) direct results of an armed conflict or internal strife.

As mentioned earlier, IHL does not apply to 'situations of internal disturbances and tensions' pursuant to Article 1(2) of 1977 Additional Protocol II and hence, persons held in these situations are not protected by IHL. However, according to the Statutes, the ICRC can act to ensure the humane conditions and treatment of detainees held in times of internal disturbances and tensions.

Second, even where IHL has no applicability or upon its cessation, the ICRC can continue to act on behalf of persons held as direct results of international or non-international armed conflict, or internal disturbances and tensions.

Finally, Article 5(3) provides basis to act on behalf of any detainee whom the ICRC considers requiring protection:

> The International Committee may take any humanitarian initiative which comes within its role as a specifically neutral and independent institution and intermediary, and may consider any question requiring examination by such an institution.

2. International Armed Conflict

Besides the Statutes, 1949 Geneva Convention III and IV specifically mandate ICRC delegates to visit prisoners of war and civilian internees. Article 126 of 1949 Geneva Convention III (prisoners of war) and Article 143 of 1949 Geneva Convention IV (civilian internees) provide the ICRC delegates with the same right to visit prisoners of war and civilians as for the delegates of the Protecting Power. The modalities of the visit are specified in this provision, which can be summarised as follows:

(1) Delegates shall have permission to go to all places where prisoners of war/civilian internees may be and shall have access to all premises occupied by them;

(2) Delegates shall be able to interview the prisoners of war/civilian internees without witnesses;

(3) Delegates shall have full liberty to select the places they wish to visit;

(4) The duration and frequency of the visits shall not be restricted; and

(5) Visits may not be prohibited except for reasons of imperative
     military necessity, and then only as an exceptional and
     temporary measure.

Hence, in international armed conflict, the states parties to the
1949 Geneva Conventions have the obligation to accept visits to
prisoners of war and civilian internees by the ICRC delegates. The
ICRC has also adopted these modalities of visits for non-international armed conflict and internal disturbances and tensions. The
ICRC's modalities of visits are discussed in greater detail in many
earlier works and hence will not be discussed further here.[79]

3. Non-international Armed Conflict

In non-international armed conflict, there are no rules of IHL
obliging states to accept visits by the ICRC delegates to detainees.
As noted earlier, the ICRC is mandated by the Statutes of the
International Red Cross and Red Crescent Movement to ensure
humane conditions and treatment of detainees, albeit in general
terms. Common Article 3(2) of the 1949 Geneva Conventions,
applicable in non-international armed conflict, only goes so far
as to allow the ICRC to 'offer its services to the Parties to the
conflict'. Hence, the ICRC will have to obtain the permission of
the conflicting parties in order to visit the detainees held by them.
However, as noted above, when obtaining permission, the ICRC
endeavours to ensure that its visits can be conducted according to
the modalities of visits adopted in international armed conflict.

C. Confidentiality

Contrary to common understanding, the ICRC published its
findings from its visits to detainees during armed conflict until
the end of the Second World War.[80] During the First World War,
these ICRC reports were widely published and were available in
bookshops.[81] During the Second World War, regular publication
of the reports was terminated but extracts were still published in
the *International Review of the Red Cross*.[82] Since the end of the
Second World War, the ICRC has not published any of its reports
as it saw the use of its reports for political ends, which jeopardised
its humanitarian work.[83]

Since then, time and again, the ICRC has been criticised for its
confidentiality regarding its findings on vulnerable people during
and after armed conflict, and time and again, the ICRC has clarified
the misunderstandings about its confidentiality.[84] This shows that it

is not an easy concept to grasp. This is particularly the case with the proliferation of non-governmental organisations denouncing human rights violations publicly, which, at first sight, appears more straightforward and robust than the ICRC's confidential approach. For this reason, more frequent clarification is required for the ICRC's confidentiality. Indeed, it is not a straightforward concept for it is neither an end in itself nor a synonym for not making the ICRC findings public in any circumstances.

First, confidentiality is a means and not an end. It is a means that serves to gain the trust of the authorities, gain access to the vulnerable people affected by armed conflict, and to positively influence the behaviour of authorities towards IHL. Hence, whenever confidentiality is debated, it should not be forgotten that it is a means to achieve the above ends.

The functioning of confidentiality in practice is an art rather than science, which ICRC delegates learn on the job. However, in the most general sense, confidentiality can be explained as a general principle that applies at all times to all aspects of the dialogue with the authorities, whether it be governmental authorities or armed groups, and which binds both the ICRC and the authorities. First, it not only applies to dialogue relating to conditions and treatment of detainees but also to other areas such as violations of IHL concerning civilians and the civilian population. Second, it applies to both written and oral interactions with the authorities. Third, it also covers all stages of the dialogue with the authorities, be it before or after the written or oral intervention. Fourth, it applies not only to where IHL is applicable, in other words international and non-international armed conflict, but also to other situations the ICRC is mandated to work in, namely internal disturbances and tensions, and other situations that come under the consideration of the ICRC. Finally, it binds both the ICRC and the authorities, and once either side divulges any part of the confidential dialogue the other side would no longer be bound by the confidentiality.[85]

The confidentiality principle also extends to the vulnerable people affected by armed conflict and ICRC staff members. First, ICRC delegates are bound to keep the information collected from a vulnerable person confidential if the person wishes not to be disclosed to the authorities. Second, all ICRC staff members are bound not to divulge any confidential information outside the ICRC. Providing testimony before national or international courts and tribunals is not only prohibited but is also an immunity recognised as customary international law.

Confidentiality is not a synonym for not making the ICRC findings public in any circumstances. The ICRC in fact reserves the right to disclose confidential information but only if strict conditions are met. It has already been mentioned that when any of the authorities divulge any part of the confidential dialogue, the ICRC is no longer bound by the confidentiality principle and may publish the whole report to 'put the facts straight'.[86] Beyond such clear situations, the ICRC has adopted an institutional guideline regulating the disclosure of confidential information in the event of violations of IHL and other fundamental rules protecting persons in situations of violence.[87] It first stresses that '[b]ilateral confidential representations to the parties to a conflict remain the ICRC's preferred mode of action'. Three exceptions to this principle are envisaged: (1) mobilisation of third parties; (2) public declaration on the quality of the bilateral dialogue; and (3) public condemnation.

First, the institutional guideline envisages the sharing of confidential information with third parties, such as governments of third parties and international or regional organisations, in the hope that they would take measures to 'ensure respect' of IHL by the conflicting parties, an obligation provided for in Article 1 of the 1949 Geneva Conventions. Second, the ICRC may make a public declaration when the dialogue with the authorities 'is not having the desired results on the issues raised in the ICRC's representations', in the hope of 'strengthening the impact of the ICRC's bilateral and confidential dialogue'.[88] However, this declaration only relates to the quality of the dialogue with the authorities and not to the contents of the dialogue.

The third exception is the most extreme, where the ICRC would 'issue a public condemnation of specific violations of international humanitarian law'. However, four cumulative conditions must be met:

(1) the violations are major and repeated or likely to be repeated;
(2) delegates have witnessed the violations with their own eyes, or the existence and extent of those violations have been established on the basis of reliable and verifiable sources;
(3) bilateral confidential representations and, when attempted, humanitarian mobilisation efforts have failed to put an end to the violations;
(4) such publicity is in the interest of the persons or populations affected or threatened.

As can be seen from above, confidentiality is a wider concept than merely keeping information on the conditions and treatment of detainees away from the public eye. However, since visits to places of detention are one of the most frequent and sensitive activities of the ICRC, the principle of confidentiality is most pertinent. As one writer depicted concisely, '[a] place of detention is by definition a closed area; any information gathered there is to some extent confidential', which shows the highly sensitive nature of visits to places of detention, especially in times of armed conflict and other situations of violence, and the relevance of the principle of confidentiality. In this sense, resort to exceptional measures to disclose confidential information would require extra caution.

VII. CONCLUSIONS

The above discussions lead to the conclusion that all persons deprived of liberty in an armed conflict, international or non-international, are protected by IHL throughout their captivity, beginning from the time of their capture to their release and repatriation. While internment or administrative detention for security reasons can be carried out in international or non-international armed conflict, it should be done so only if there are procedures established by law, and international law imposes certain minimum procedural principles and safeguards protecting internees. Any internment or administrative detention falling short of these minimum procedural principles and safeguards would amount to an arbitrary deprivation of liberty. The ICRC is mandated by IHL and the Statutes of the International Red Cross and Red Crescent Movement to ensure that persons deprived of liberty in armed conflict and other situations of violence are treated according to IHL and other applicable rules of international law. Its modalities of visits to places of detention/internment and confidential dialogue with the authorities concerned have been tried and tested for decades, and the ICRC believes that they are still valid today.

The apparent disregard for the rules protecting persons deprived of liberty in recent years, in particular on the basis of struggle against 'terrorism', is a concerning trend towards the breakdown of the rule of law in armed conflict situations. There might be various reasons for such disregard such as simple ignorance of the rules of IHL by the members of armed forces or armed groups, or a deliberate policy to circumvent the constraints of the rules.

While armed conflicts are admittedly exceptional situations, IHL imposes limits, and any security concerns of military necessity were already taken into consideration during the negotiations of the rules of IHL. Hence, once these rules of IHL are accepted by states as binding on them, security reasons and military necessity are not available as reasons for disregarding the rules contained therein, including the rules protecting persons deprived of liberty. The current trend is a strange paradox where the very states that agreed to abide by the rules of IHL are trying to ignore them. From both humanitarian and legal points of view, this is deeply concerning, particularly where the lives and well-being of those deprived of their liberty are involved.

NOTES

1. This chapter reflects the views of the author and not necessarily the views of the ICRC.
2. For an overview of the ICRC activities relating to the protection of detainees, see ICRC, *Deprived of Freedom* (Geneva: ICRC, 2002); F. Bugnion, *The International Committee of the Red Cross and the Protection of War Victims* (Geneva: ICRC, 2003), from p. 545; A. Aeschlimann, 'Protection of Detainees: The ICRC's Action Behind Bars', *International Review of the Red Cross* 857 (2005), p. 83; A. Aeschlimann and N. Roggo, 'Visits to Persons Deprived of Their Freedom: The Experience of the ICRC', available at: http://www.icrc.org/web/eng/siteeng0.nsf/html/detention-visits.article-300906.
3. See the following for discussion: G. Aldrich, 'The Taliban, Al Qaeda, and the Determination of Illegal Combatants', *American Journal of International Law* 96 (2002), p. 891; Y. Arai-Takahashi, 'Disentangling Legal Quagmires: The Legal Characterisation of the Armed Conflicts in Afghanistan since 6/7 October 2001 and the Question of Prisoner of War Status', *Yearbook of International Humanitarian Law* 5 (2002), p. 61; F. King and O. Swaak-Goldman, 'The Applicability of International Humanitarian Law to the "War against Terrorism"', *Hague Yearbook of International Law* 15 (2002), p. 39; Y. Naqvi, 'Doubtful Prisoner-of-War Status', *International Review of the Red Cross* 847 (2002), p. 571; R. Wolfrum and C. Philipp, 'The Status of the Taliban: Their Obligations and Rights under International Law', *Max Planck Yearbook of United Nations Law* 6 (2002), p. 559; K. Dörmann, 'The Legal Situation of 'Unlawful/Unprivileged Combatants', *International Review of the Red Cross* 849 (2003), p. 45; M. Sassòli, '"Unlawful Combatants": The Law and Whether it Needs to be Revised', *American Society of International Law Proceedings* (2003), p. 196; R. Wolfrum, 'The Attack of September 11, 2001, the Wars against the Taliban and Iraq: Is There a Need to Reconsider International Law on the Recourse to Force and the Rules in Armed Conflict?', *Max Planck Yearbook of United Nations Law* 7 (2003), p. 36; M. Sassòli, 'The Status of Persons Held in Guantanamo under International Humanitarian Law', *Journal of International Criminal Justice* 2 (2004), p. 96; J. Yoo, 'The Status of Soldiers and Terrorists under the Geneva Conventions', *Chinese Journal of International*

Law 3 (2004), p. 135; S. Borelli, 'Casting Light on the Legal Black Hole: International Law and Detentions Abroad in the "War on Terror"',*International Review of the Red Cross* 857 (2005), p. 39; H. Duffy, *The 'War on Terror' and the Framework of International Law* (Cambridge: Cambridge University Press, 2005).

4. See Article 9 of the International Covenant on Civil and Political Rights.
5. See Articles 43 and 51, as well as Article 48, of Additional Protocol I.
6. International armed conflict also includes wars of national liberation, stipulated in Article 1(4) of Additional Protocol I.
7. Second sentence, Article 5 of Geneva Convention III and Article 45(1) of Additional Protocol I.
8. *Ibid.*
9. Article 45(2) of Additional Protocol I.
10. Second sentence, Article 5 of Geneva Convention III and Article 45(1) of Additional Protocol I.
11. For similar provisions, see Article 13 of Geneva Conventions I and II.
12. For government recognition, see generally S. Talmon, *Recognition of Governments in International Law with Particular Reference to Governments in Exile* (Oxford: Clarendon Press, 1998).
13. Article 43(2) of Additional Protocol I.
14. Articles 4(C) and 33 of Geneva Convention III.
15. Article 4(A)(4) and (5) of Geneva Convention III.
16. Article 4(A)(6) of Geneva Convention III.
17. Article 4(B)(1) of Geneva Convention III.
18. Article 4(B)(2) of Geneva Convention III.
19. Article 51(1) of Additional Protocol I.
20. Y. Sandoz et al. (eds), *Commentary on the Additional Protocols of 8 June 1977 to the Geneva Conventions of 12 August 1949* (1987), at para. 1936.
21. *Ibid.*, at para. 1920.
22. For a more detailed explanation, see O. Uhler and H. Coursier et al., *Commentary on the Geneva Conventions of 12 August 1949*, Vol. IV (1958), at p. 45.
23. Article 42 of Geneva Convention IV.
24. Uhler, Coursier et al., *Commentary on the Geneva Conventions of 12 August 1949*, Vol. IV, p. 258.
25. *Ibid.*, p. 368.
26. See Article 68 of Geneva Convention IV.
27. See generally ICRC, 'Direct Participation in Hostilities under International Humanitarian Law' (2003 and 2004), available at: http://www.icrc.org/Web/Eng/siteeng0.nsf/iwpList74/459B0FF70176F4E5C1256DDE00572DAA.
28. Article 46 of Additional Protocol I.
29. Article 47 of Additional Protocol I.
30. Rules 87–108 in J.-M. Henckaerts and L. Doswald-Beck, *Customary International Humanitarian Law*, Vol. I: *Rules* (Cambridge: Cambridge University Press and Geneva: ICRC, 2005).
31. See, for example, Article 77 of the Japanese Criminal Code, which provides that those who were directly involved in the destruction of the territorial integrity will face the death penalty or a life sentence. Article 412(6) of the French Criminal Code also provides that leading or organising an insurrectional movement is punished by a life sentence.

32. See also Sandoz et al. (eds), *Commentary on the Additional Protocols*, at para. 4441.
33. *Ibid.*, at para. 4442. See also J. Pictet et al., *Commentary on the Geneva Conventions of 12 August 1949*, Vol. I (1952), at pp. 60–1.
34. For the applicability of international law to the UN, see above section C.2.
35. R. Wetzel and D. Rauschning, *The Vienna Convention on the Law of Treaties: Travaux Preparatoires* (1978), at p. 209.
36. Article 18 of the 1969 Vienna Convention on the Law of Treaties provides as follows:

> A state is obliged to refrain from acts which would defeat the object and purpose of a treaty when: (a) it has signed the treaty or has exchanged instruments constituting the treaty subject to ratification, acceptance or approval, until it shall have made its intention clear not to become a party to the treaty; or (b) it has expressed its consent to be bound by the treaty, pending the entry into force of the treaty and provided that such entry into force is not unduly delayed.

37. Eritrea–Ethiopia Claims Commission, *Partial Award: Prisoners of War, Eritrea's Claim 17*, 1 July 2003, at para. 89 and *Partial Award: Prisoners of War, Ethiopia's Claim 4*, 1 July 2003, at para. 89.
38. See also Articles 16, 17, 87, 88, 89 and 92 of Geneva Convention III.
39. See above, note 27.
40. Article 75(2) of 1977 Additional Protocol I provides as follows:

> The following acts are and shall remain prohibited at any time and in any place whatsoever, whether committed by civilian or by military agents: (a) violence to the life, health, or physical or mental well-being of persons, in particular: murder; torture of all kinds, whether physical or mental; corporal punishment; and mutilation; (b) outrages upon personal dignity, in particular humiliating and degrading treatment, enforced prostitution and any form of indecent assault; (c) the taking of hostages; (d) collective punishments; and (e) threats to commit any of the foregoing acts.

41. For a suggestion of customary rules of IHL, see Henckaerts and Doswald-Beck, *Customary International Humanitarian Law*, Volume I: *Rules*. See also J.-M. Henckaerts and L. Doswald-Beck (eds), *Customary International Humanitarian Law*, Volume II: *Practice* (Cambridge: Cambridge University Press, 2005). For a useful list of customary rules of IHL, see J. Henckaerts, 'Study on Customary International Humanitarian Law: A Contribution to the Understanding and Respect for the Rule of Law in Armed Conflict', *International Review of the Red Cross* 857 (2005) from p. 98.
42. Rules 119–21 in Henckaerts and Doswald-Beck, *Customary International Humanitarian Law*, Volume I: *Rules*.
43. Rule 118, in *ibid.*
44. Rule 123, in *ibid.*
45. Rule 124, in *ibid.*
46. Rule 125, in *ibid.*
47. Rule 126, in *ibid.*
48. Rule 127, in *ibid.*
49. Common Article 3 of the 1949 Geneva Conventions provides as follows, in part:

> (1) Persons taking no active part in the hostilities, including members of armed forces who have laid down their arms and those placed 'hors de combat' by

sickness, wounds, detention, or any other cause, shall in all circumstances be treated humanely, without any adverse distinction founded on race, colour, religion or faith, sex, birth or wealth, or any other similar criteria. To this end, the following acts are and shall remain prohibited at any time and in any place whatsoever with respect to the above-mentioned persons:

> a) violence to life and person, in particular murder of all kinds, mutilation, cruel treatment and torture; b) taking of hostages; c) outrages upon personal dignity, in particular humiliating and degrading treatment; d) the passing of sentences and the carrying out of executions without previous judgment pronounced by a regularly constituted court, affording all the judicial guarantees which are recognized as indispensable by civilized peoples.

(2) The wounded and sick shall be collected and cared for.

50. Article 4(1) and (2) of the 1977 Additional Protocol II provides as follows:

(1) All persons who do not take a direct part or who have ceased to take part in hostilities, whether or not their liberty has been restricted, are entitled to respect for their person, honour and convictions and religious practices. They shall in all circumstances be treated humanely, without any adverse distinction. It is prohibited to order that there shall be no survivors.

(2) Without prejudice to the generality of the foregoing, the following acts against the persons referred to in paragraph 1 are and shall remain prohibited at any time and in any place whatsoever: a) violence to the life, health and physical or mental well-being of persons, in particular murder as well as cruel treatment such as torture, mutilation or any form of corporal punishment; b) collective punishments; c) taking of hostages; d) acts of terrorism; e) outrages upon personal dignity, in particular humiliating and degrading treatment, rape, enforced prostitution and any form of indecent assault; f) slavery and the slave trade in all their forms; g) pillage; h) threats to commit any of the foregoing acts.

51. These customary rules of IHL are applicable in both international and non-international armed conflict.

52. See Article 3 of the Convention against Torture and Other Cruel, Inhuman or Degrading Treatment or Punishment; Articles 6 and 7 of the International Covenant on Civil and Political Rights; and Human Rights Committee General Comment No. 31, *Nature of the General Legal Obligation Imposed on States Parties to the Covenant*, UN Doc CCPR/C/21/Rev.1/Add 13, 26 May 2004, para. 12.

53. Article 133 of Geneva Convention IV.

54. A commentary notes that the second sentence of Article 75(3) of 1977 Additional Protocol I was 'based on Articles 43 and 132 of the fourth Convention', which relates to the review of internment and release of civilian internees. Sandoz et al. (eds), *Commentary on the Additional Protocols*, at para. 3076.

55. Rule 128 (C) in Henckaerts and Doswald-Beck, *Customary International Humanitarian Law*, Volume I: *Rules*.

56. ICRC, *Improving Compliance with International Humanitarian Law, ICRC Expert Seminars* (2003), at pp. 22–3.

57. F. Bugnion, '*Jus ad Bellum, Jus in Bello* and Non-International Armed Conflicts', *Yearbook of International Humanitarian Law* 6 (2003), pp. 168 and 170.

58. See also Rule 159 in Henckaerts and Doswald-Beck, *Customary International Humanitarian Law*, Volume I: *Rules*.

59. See, for example, Bugnion, '*Jus ad Bellum*'; J. Pejic, 'Terrorist Acts and Groups: A Role for International Law?, *British Yearbook of International Law* 71 (2004), pp.75–6.
60. For a recent case on amnesty for members of armed groups, see Chapter 9 of the Lusaka Ceasefire Agreement, 10 July 1999, available at: http://www.monuc. org/downloads/Lusaka_Ceasefire_Agreement.pdf. Signed by Angola, DRC, Namibia, Rwanda, Uganda, Zimbabwe, Congolese Rally for Democracy, and Movement for the Liberation of the Congo.
61. For further discussions, see generally, L. Zegveld, *Accountability of Armed Opposition Groups in International Law* (Cambridge: Cambridge University Press, 2002); L. Olson, 'Provoking the Dragon on the Patio – Matters of Transitional Justice: Penal Repression vs. Amnesty', *International review of the Red Cross* 862 (2006), p. 275.
62. See Henckaerts and Doswald-Beck, *Customary International Humanitarian Law*, Volume I: *Rules*; and Article 2(2) of 1977 Additional Protocol II.
63. See generally, J. Pejic, 'Procedural Principles and Safeguards for Internment/ Administrative Detention in Armed Conflict and Other Situations of Violence', *International Review of the Red Cross* 858 (2005), p. 375.
64. Sandoz et al. (eds), *Commentary on the Additional Protocols*, at para. 3063.
65. Article 132 of 1949 Geneva Convention IV.
66. Article 118 of 1949 Geneva Convention III.
67. Uhler, Coursier et al., *Commentary on the Geneva Conventions of 12 August 1949*, Vol. IV, at 258 and 368.
68. *Ibid.*, at 258.
69. *Ibid.*
70. *Ibid.*, at 260 and 369.
71. *Ibid.*, at 260.
72. *Ibid.*, at 369.
73. Article 146 of 1949 Geneva Convention IV. For grave breaches and universal jurisdiction in other Geneva Conventions, see Articles 49, 50 of Convention I; Articles 50, 51 of Convention II; Articles 129, 130 of Convention III. See also Article 85 of 1977 Additional Protocol I. 'Grave breaches' of IHL are considered as war crimes in Article 2 of the ICTY Statute (Article 2(g) on unlawful confinement) and Article 8(2) (a) of the Statute of the International Criminal Court (Article 8(2)(a)(vii) on unlawful confinement). For an excellent summary of universal jurisdiction, see Separate Opinion of Judge Guillaume in the *Case Concerning the Arrest Warrant of 11 April 2000*, available at: http:// www.icj-cij.org/.
74. The complementarity between IHL and IHRL is well established in international law and hence will not be discussed here. See ICJ, *Legality of the Threat or Use of Nuclear Weapons* (Advisory Opinion), at para. 25, and *Legal Consequences of the Construction of a Wall in the Occupied Palestinian Territory* (Advisory Opinion), at para. 106.
75. For a full list of procedural safeguards in international law, see Pejic, 'Procedural Principles and Safeguards for Internment/Administrative Detention'.
76. See European Convention for the Prevention of Torture and Inhuman or Degrading Treatment or Punishment.
77. Bugnion, *The International Committee of the Red Cross and the Protection of War Victims*.
78. Emphasis added.

79. See note 2 above.

80. Bugnion, *The International Committee of the Red Cross and the Protection of War Victims*, from p. 609.

81. *Ibid.*

82. *Ibid.*

83. For a recent case of the misuse of ICRC reports, see, for example, ICRC, 'Sri Lanka: ICRC Deplores Misleading Public Use of its Confidential Findings on Disappearances', News Release 08/50, 19 March 2008, at: http://www.icrc. org/web/eng/siteeng0.nsf/htmlall/sri-lanka-news-190308?opendocument. See also ICRC, 'Clarification of ICRC Procedures for Visiting Places of Detention', News Release 08/40, 4 March 2008, at: http://www.icrc.org/web/eng/siteeng0. nsf/htmlall/chad-news-040308?opendocument.

84. See J. Kellenberger, 'Speaking Out or Remaining Silent in Humanitarian Work', *International Review of the Red Cross* 855 (2004), p. 593. At the time of writing, Jakob Kellenberger is the President of the ICRC and Dominik Stillhart is the Deputy Director of Operations of the ICRC.

85. Bugnion, *The International Committee of the Red Cross and the Protection of War Victims*, p. 615.

86. *Ibid.*

87. ICRC, 'Action by the International Committee of the Red Cross in the Event of Violations of International Humanitarian Law or of Other Fundamental Rules Protecting Persons in Situations of Violence', *International Review of the Red Cross* 858 (2005), p. 393.

88. *Ibid.*, p. 397.

6
Non-Lethal Weapons:
A Rose by any Other Name

Nick Lewer

INTRODUCTION

With the rapid advances in new weapons technologies over the last few decades there has been an intense debate concerning their impact on international humanitarian law and other legal treaties and arms control conventions. In this chapter we will focus on one set of new weapons – those that have also been referred to as non-lethal or less-lethal weapons[1] – and examine their operational relationship with international humanitarian law. There is already a literature associated with this,[2] and this chapter will draw considerably from these sources.

The first section will summarise non-lethal technologies, highlighting their physical and psychological effects, and describe the types of conflict in which they could be used, including international armed conflict, internal civil wars, anti-terrorist operations, civil police actions (riots, restraint, dissuasion), UN operations, and operations other than war. The second section will discuss the problems associated with the very term 'non-lethal' and how some analysts would prefer them to be subsumed under the generic terminological heading of 'new weapons'. The third section will locate these weapons within the context of the historical agreements and precedents that define the limits that states should adhere to (see Table 6.2), which demonstrate that combatants do not have the legal right or ethical legitimacy to use unlimited means and methods of warfare. As part of these agreements international humanitarian law, the 1949 Geneva Conventions and the 1977 Additional Protocols provide an important codification of the importance and legitimacy for states to review new weapons technologies and for diligent oversight of their operational deployment.

NON-LETHAL TECHNOLOGIES

Non-lethal weapons have been defined as:

[S]pecifically designed to incapacitate people or disable equipment, with minimal collateral damage to buildings and the environment; they should be discriminate and not cause unnecessary suffering; their effects should be temporary and reversible; and they should provide alternatives to, or raise the threshold for, use of lethal force.[3]

Table 6.1 summarises the main categories of non-lethal weapons.

Table 6.1   Examples of Non-Lethal Technologies[4]

Technology	Type
Electrical	stun guns and batons, electrified shields and nets, electrified water cannon and adhesive projectiles, 'landmines', grenades; systems to interfere with the electronics of vehicles; impulses to impede brain activity;
Acoustic	infrasound, ultrasound, stun grenades, long-range acoustic devices (LRAD); vortex generators;
Kinetic Energy	impact projectiles including: plastic and rubber bullets; lead shot-filled beanbags; water cannon;
Chemical	riot control agents including irritant agents such as CS, CN and CR (tear gases) and OC pepper spray; malodorants – foul-smelling chemicals; anti-traction materials – slippery agents preventing passage of people and vehicles; obscurants – smokes and underwater dyes; foams – rigid, sticky or aqueous as barriers to people; anti-material – embrittling agents, super-adhesives and corrosives; fuel contaminants; defoliants and herbicides;
Biological	anti-material micro-organisms; anti-crop agents;
Directed Energy	high power microwave (HPM); millimetre wave such as the Active Denial System (ADS); low energy laser dazzlers; high energy pulsed chemical lasers, which produce a 'shock wave';
Barriers and Entanglements	spikes and caltrops to stop vehicles; nets for snaring people, catching vehicles or tangling boat propellers; rigid foams to block doorways and passageways;
Combined Technologies	'multi-sensory grenade' combining acoustic–optical and chemical; modified water cannon delivering kinetic energy, electrical and chemical stunning and incapacitating stimuli; laser-delivered 'wireless' electrical weapons;
Delivery Methods	mortar shells; unmanned aerial vehicles (UAVs); encapsulation such as paintball type projectiles; micro-encapsulation for rapid skin absorption; shotguns; sprays and aerosols; grenades; aircraft

Like all weapons, non-lethal weapons are designed to cause pain but, as we have noted in the definition at the beginning of this section, they should not inflict permanent injury. However, non-lethal weapons do have physical and psychological impacts on people, and there are serious concerns both with respect to their safety and opportunities for misuse. So, before we can make a judgment as to whether these weapons do cause unnecessary pain and suffering, within the context of 'military necessity' and international humanitarian law, we need to look a little more closely at some of their characteristics.[5]

Non-lethal weapons are required to perform a variety of functions. For example, NATO policy[6] states that non-lethal weapons should enhance the capability of NATO forces to achieve objectives such as:

- accomplish military missions and tasks in situations and conditions where the use of lethal force, although not prohibited, may not be necessary or desired;
- discourage, delay, prevent or respond to hostile activities;
- limit or control escalation;
- improve force protection;
- repel or temporarily incapacitate personnel;
- disable equipment or facilities;
- help decrease the post-conflict costs of reconstruction.

Perhaps the best known of the electrical weapons is the Taser electric shock weapon, which fires out two barbed darts attached to fine wires that attach to the skin or clothing. Upon impact a 50,000-volt electric shock is rapidly discharged into the victim. While the barbs remain attached this shock can be administered repeatedly. Critics have argued that electrical incapacitating weapons are being used too soon in arrest situations, such as when people refuse immediately to obey a police command, or when there are still opportunities for resolution using negotiation and communication skills. As we will see later, the potential for abuse of these weapons is worrying.

Acoustic weapons emit either audible sound, infrasound or ultrasound and represent a maturing technology.[7] In the audible range, one company has developed High Intensity Directed Acoustic (HIDA) devices such as the Long Range Acoustic Device (LRAD), which is designed to deliver audible warning messages over long ranges of up to 1 km. However, at closer distances it is considerably more incapacitating and produces a high audible decibel level that can cause hearing damage. In addition to ear pain, some HIDA devices can cause side effects such as loss of equilibrium, vomiting and migraines. A hand-held acoustic weapon, the 'directed stick radiator' is being developed to fire high-intensity 'sonic bullets' or pulses of sound with the intention of knocking people off their feet. Weapons that utilise infrasonic frequencies can cause nausea, disorientation and bowel spasms.

Kinetic energy (KE) weapons such as plastic and rubber bullets, truncheons, shot-filled beanbags, small rubber balls and water cannons have been used by police and military forces for many years. There are many documented cases of serious injury as a result of being struck by KE projectiles, especially plastic and rubber bullets.

Riot control agents (RCAs), also known as incapacitants and harassing agents, include synthetic chemicals such as CS, CN and CR sprays and gases, as well as Oleoresin Capsicum (OC) or 'pepper spray', which is biological in origin. PAVA, a more potent synthetic version of OC, has also been developed. Under the terms of the 1993 Chemical Weapons Convention (Article 1) toxic chemicals, such as RCAs, cannot be used for war fighting, but may be used in domestic riot control situations. Prior to the war in Iraq, alarm was raised in weapons control circles when US Secretary of Defense Donald Rumsfeld indicated that the US was attempting to 'fashion rules of engagement' to enable their use in war. President Bush authorised their use in Iraq in certain circumstances, and CS and pepper spray were deployed. In US law this is legal under Executive Order 11850, which was signed by President Ford in 1975 and permits the use of RCAs under specific conditions such as in 'riot control situations in areas under direct and distinct US military control, to include controlling rioting prisoners of war' and in 'situations in which civilians are used to mask or screen attacks and civilian casualties can be reduced or avoided'.[8]

A new generation of RCAs is now being used – malodorants or 'skunk shots' – which are foul-smelling chemicals sprayed over rioters. First seen in action when used by the Israeli Army against Palestinian protestors in August 2008, these are claimed to be safer than using plastic bullets or tear gas. They are organic and even drinkable, according to an Israeli spokesman,[9] and cause less injury than traditional kinetic energy weapons.

Other incapacitating agents, classified as biochemical, are known more familiarly as calmatives, knock-out gases or immobilising agents. They differ from RCAs in that whereas RCAs are chemicals that cause local irritation to the eyes and other mucous membranes, biochemical agents work on the central nervous system, causing sedation, disorientation, unconsciousness and even death.[10] As we will see later, the use of one of these – fentanyl – which was used by Russian special forces in rescuing hostages from a siege, sparked an intense debate over the legality and ethics of use of such weapons.[11]

Non-lethal directed energy (DE) weapons include millimetre wave weapons, high-power microwave, low-power diode lasers and high-energy chemical lasers. Such weapons have a rheostatic function, that is, of being tunable. An example of a DE weapon is the Active Denial System (ADS), which uses millimetre wave energy in the 95 GHz range to heat up water molecules in the subcutaneous layers of the skin, causing a painful and intolerable burning sensation. High-power microwave (HPM) weapons deliver a burst of radio-frequency energy designed to degrade or destroy the circuits of military electronic hardware such as missile and artillery launch and targeting systems. A collateral effect, of course, is that non-military electronic infrastructure and individuals, such as hospital equipment or patients fitted with pacemakers, could also be affected.

Laser weapons include low- and high-power systems. Devices called 'illuminators' or 'dazzlers' use a low-power diode laser to temporarily blind or obscure vision. For example, the US Marine Corps has deployed a non-lethal laser called the Green Beam Designator, which, on hitting a vehicle's windscreen, lights up the interior with an intense glaring green light that temporarily blinds the occupants. The weapon is also used to target a vehicle or individual, warning them that they are approaching a roadblock or military area. Some health concerns have been expressed regarding targeting people at too close a distance or exposing eyes to the beam for an extended period. But military proponents argue that it is an extremely useful device in the escalation of force or use of force continuum concepts.

Some non-lethal technologies are being combined into one weapon. For example, a water cannon producing water under high pressure may combine an electrical current and a RCA agent, or an aqueous foam barrier may be impregnated with irritant chemical agents. A multi-sensory grenade can combine light, sound and a malodorant chemical, and flash-bang devices emit bright light and painful sound levels.

One final set of technologies with enormous non-lethal potential is robots (incorporating 'intelligent' capabilities) armed with either lethal or incapacitating technologies, and nanotechnology.[12] We need to ask the question: how will international humanitarian law regulate the behaviour of autonomous non-human coercive machines?

Torture

Unfortunately, non-lethal weapons can be misused to torture people, and it is necessary to review this abhorrent practice within the context of these new weapons. There have been attempts to 'redefine' torture and justify its use in obtaining information from terrorists and terrorist suspects. For example, Allhoff has argued that:

> [T]orture is, under some circumstances, morally permissible. In doing so, I have not presupposed utilitarianism to be correct, but have argued that even other normative approaches would be able to accommodate this conclusion. The conditions that I have suggested to be met in order to allow torture are: pursuit of information, reasonable expectation that captive has the information, reasonable expectation that the information corresponds to an imminent and significant threat, and reasonable expectation that the information can be used to disarm the threat. There are, of course, substantive issues as to what constitutes reasonable expectation, but I think that we could settle these ostensively, or else be confident that we have made progress on the formal account. I have also stressed that, though I would support torture if these conditions were met, we should still be prudent to administer the minimum amount of torture necessary (measured both in terms of intensity and quality) that is necessary to achieve the desired goal. Hopefully this moderate position has both intuitive appeal and is theoretically attractive.[13]

Dershowitz has even advocated the issuing of 'torture warrants' to help with the war on terror,[14] and the use of non-lethal weapons for the torture of prisoners in Iraq by US soldiers has been reported:

> According to Sabbar, U.S. soldiers used Taser guns and rubber bullets to control detainees. 'They had another kind of torture using electrical shocks, pointing a hand gun towards you that shocks you and causes you to lose consciousness for a while,' he said. 'That was one of the methods at the airport [jail]. Or use rubber bullets that end up hurting or burning the area where it hits you, and very painful ones.'[15]

Civil law enforcement officers have used electric shock weapons for punishment and torture, and detainees have received multiple shocks while handcuffed and under restraint,[16] despite warnings from manufacturers that such use may impair breathing and respiration.[17] For the period 1990–2003 Amnesty documented electro-shock torture in 87 countries and urged

> governments to recognise their responsibilities under international conventions prohibiting torture, and adopt measures to halt the production of and trade in electro-shock stun weapons until a rigorous and independent investigation has been conducted into their effects.[18]

In June 2005 the European Council passed the Council Regulation (EC) No. 1236/2005 concerning trade in certain goods which could be used for capital punishment, torture or other cruel, inhuman or degrading treatment or punishment.[19] Under Articles 3 and 4 of the legislation all equipment with no practical use apart from capital punishment, torture and cruel, inhuman or degrading treatment or punishment will be banned for export or import from the European Community. Equipment covered (Annex II) includes electric-shock restraint belts. Under Article 5, Annex III, portable electric-shock devices and chemical irritant sprays will require a licence for export from the EU, and Article 7 allows member states to '... adopt or maintain a prohibition on the export or import of leg irons, gang chains and portable electric shock devices'.

NON-LETHAL WEAPONS: A ROSE BY ANY OTHER NAME

For some the development of 'non-lethal' technologies promised a new era in war fighting, the possibility of bloodless and 'humane' conflicts in which both combatants and non-combatants were neither killed nor mutilated. But the very term 'non-lethal' provoked a vigorous debate.

Robin Coupland, a surgeon working with the International Committee of the Red Cross, highlighted definitional problems associated in calling a weapon lethal or non-lethal, arguing that from the perspective of international humanitarian law they should just be considered as any other weapon,[20] a view supported by Lewer and Schofield.[21] Non-lethal weapons have also been referred to as less-than-lethal, sub-lethal, disabling, soft-kill, pre-lethal and even worse than lethal.[22] Coupland argues that while such terms imply that conventional weapons are 'lethal' the reality is that conventional weapons such as a Kalashnikov rifles kill (only) 20–25 per cent of casualties, anti-personnel mines designed to maim rarely kill victims, and the mortality associated with a hand grenade in open areas is about 10 per cent.[23] He asks the question: does this make them non-lethal weapons? It is not clear what a lethal weapon is.

Further, exploring the characteristic proponents associated with non-lethal weapons, that they 'disable' their victims, Coupland notes that this is more acceptable than talking about inflicting disability and does not ask for how long a victim will be disabled and whether there will be any permanent effects – either physical or psychological. In their definition Lewer and Davison state that effects should be temporary and reversible.[24] The medical effects of many new weapons, such as those that result from being hit by non-lethal technologies, are still not fully understood, and Coupland stresses the importance of making a distinction between weapons that 'injure by explosive and projectile force and weapons which injure by other means'.[25] If these effects are not understood, how can judgments be made with respect to whether a new weapon causes superfluous injury or unnecessary suffering?

We have already noted that non-lethal weapons have also been referred to as pre-lethal. By this we mean that both 'incapacitated' or 'disabled' combatants and non-combatants in war zones would be easier to kill either deliberately or during the chaotic fog of war. So, attacking soldiers may not know how long an opponent may be out of action as a result of a non-lethal effect, or even if an effect is being feigned. It may be prudent from a combat soldier's perspective not to take a chance and shoot to kill. Some critics of non-lethal weapons have also noted that this could be a deliberate act, as an incapacitated and stationary target is easier to hit – hence the pre-lethal name.

Coupland supports this potential scenario, noting that 'non-lethal weapons could cause increased mortality because of increased vulnerability'.[26] This has important implications because, as we will see in the next section, combatants considered *hors de combat* are protected under the Geneva Conventions. The definitional problem associated with deciding what a non-lethal weapon is compounded by weapons that have lethal-non-lethal capacities, as illustrated in the comment below:

In a sense, 'nonlethal weapons' is a misnomer. ... And there is no requirement that NLW be incapable of killing or of causing permanent damage. Moreover, the ideal NLW would be a system with continuously visible intensity and influence, ranging from a warning tap to a stunning blow to a lethal effect.[27]

The problem with such 'dual use' weapons, which have a rheostatic function from 'gentle' to 'lethal', means that opponents would find it difficult to know what degree of force is to be used against them. It also makes designing conventions very difficult. NATO defines non-lethal weapons as:

weapons which are explicitly designed and developed to incapacitate or repel personnel, with a low probability of fatality or permanent injury, or to disable equipment, with minimal undesired damage or impact on the environment.[28]

According to NATO policy, while they are not required to have zero probability of causing fatalities or permanent injuries, such weapons should significantly reduce these effects when compared with the employment of conventional lethal weapons under the same circumstances. The pre-lethal function we noted earlier is implicitly acknowledged in NATO policy since non-lethal weapons

may be used in conjunction with lethal weapon systems to enhance the latter's effectiveness and efficiency across the full spectrum of military operations.[29]

So, as Fidler summarises:

For sceptics, the moniker [NLWs] was misleading because it gave moral status to weapons simply by virtue of their technology and not on the basis of legal and ethical analysis of why, how and where they are used.[30]

THE GENEVA CONVENTIONS AND OTHER AGREEMENTS

When assessing the legal impact of new weapons on the Geneva Conventions two important and overarching questions need to be considered: would their use be contrary to existing principles of humanitarian law regarding the use of conventional weapons, and is there a case for developing a new measure that would specifically regulate the use of these weapons on the battlefield?[31] Within these questions we need to ask: (a) do NLWs have functions that are particularly unacceptable?; (b) do NLWs weaken or strengthen existing treaties?;(c) do NLWs offer alternatives to existing lethal weaponry that allow states space to seriously consider forms of conventional disarmament?; and (d) do NLWs help to 'humanise' war, making it more acceptable?[32]

Table 6.2   Instruments Limiting the Use of Weapons

1863	Lieber Code
1868	Declaration of St Petersburg
1899	Hague Declaration (IV, 2) Concerning Asphyxiating Gases
	Hague Declaration (IV, 3) Concerning Expanding Bullets
1907	Hague Convention (IV) Respecting The Laws and Customs of War on Land
	Martens Clause (contained in the Preamble to the Hague Declaration IV, 1907)
1925	Protocol for the Prohibition of the use in War of Asphyxiating Poisonous or Other Gases, and of Bacteriological Methods of Warfare
1949	Geneva Conventions
1972	Convention on the Prohibition of the Development, Production and Stockpiling of Bacteriological (Biological) and Toxin Weapons and on their Destruction
1977	Geneva Conventions – Additional Protocols I and II
1977	Convention on The Prohibition of Military or Any Other Hostile Use of Environmental Modification Techniques
1980	Convention on Prohibition or Restrictions on the Use of Certain Conventional Weapons Which May be Deemed To Be Excessively Injurious or to Have Indiscriminate Effects – UN Inhumane Weapons Convention (UNWC)
	Especially Protocol IV concerning Blinding Laser Weapons
1993	Chemical Weapons Convention
1997	Ottawa Convention

These considerations are linked with the concept of *proportionality*, which accepts that while all weapons cause suffering, this should be weighed against military necessity. Thus they should not cause *unnecessary suffering*. New weapons should also be *discriminate* (as described in 1977 Protocol 1, Article 51, paras 4 and 5) and that they must be able to be directed at a specific military objective. A further principle relevant to the ethical and legal impact of new weapons is located in the Hague Convention 1907, Article 23(b), prohibiting the killing or wounding of individuals who belong to a hostile nation or army 'treacherously'. But what constitutes such a treacherous act is somewhat vague.

However, Article 37, paragraph 1, of Protocol 1 (1977) Additional to the Geneva Conventions of 1949 more closely defined an understanding of treachery and perfidy referred to in the Hague Conventions. These are:

> Acts inviting the confidence of an adversary to lead him to believe that he is entitled to, or is obliged to accord, protection under the rules of international law applicable in armed conflict, with intent to betray that confidence, shall constitute perfidy.

Article 23(c) of the Hague Convention also prohibits the killing or wounding of an individual who, 'having laid down his arms, or no longer having means of defence, has surrendered at his discretion'.[33] As will be noted later, the effects of some non-lethal weapons, which render combatants *hors de combat*, allow opportunities for abuse of this regulation.

With respect to weapons yet to be developed, the Preamble to the Hague Convention No. IV, 1907, contains what is known as the 'Martens clause', which states that:

> Until a more complete code of laws of war has been issued, the High Contracting Parties deem it expedient to declare that, in cases not included in the regulations adopted by them, the inhabitants remain under the protection and rule of the principles of the law of nations, as they result from the usages established among civilised peoples, from the laws of humanity, and the dictates of the public conscience.

This was an important statement with respect to the unregulated development of future weapons technologies, and was later backed up in the 1977 Geneva Conventions, Protocol 1, Article 1(2), which states that:

> In cases not covered by this protocol or by other international agreements, civilians and combatants remain under the protection and authority of the principles of international law derived from established custom, from the principles of humanity and from the dictates of public conscience.

Articles 35 and 36 of the 1977 Additional Protocol 1 go further by defining more clearly the limitations on new weapons deployment:

Article 35
1. In any armed conflict, the right of parties to the conflict to choose methods of warfare or means of warfare is not unlimited.
2. It is prohibited to employ weapons, projectiles and material and methods of warfare of a nature to cause superfluous injury or unnecessary suffering.
3. It is prohibited to employ methods of warfare which are intended, or may be expected, to cause widespread, long-term and severe damage to the natural environment.

Article 36
In the study, development, acquisition or adoption of a new weapon, means or method of warfare, a High Contracting Party is under an obligation to determine whether its employment would, in some or all circumstances, be prohibited by this Protocol or by any other rule of international law applicable to the High Contracting Party.

An increasing concern regarding rapid advances in new weapons led to the ICRC examining the topic at its 2003 International Conference, when the problem of ensuring the legality of new weapons under international law was discussed. The conference stated that all new weapons, means and methods of warfare and that a rigorous review 'should involve a multidisciplinary approach, including military, legal, environmental and health-related considerations'. The conference also urged states 'to review with particular scrutiny all new weapons, means and methods of warfare that cause health effects with which medical personnel are unfamiliar' and encouraged states 'to promote, wherever possible, exchange of information and transparency in relation to these mechanisms, procedures and evaluations'.[34]
As Lawand points out,[35] the scope of the Article 36 legal review recommended in the ICRC (2006) document above is broad, covering:

- weapons of all types – be they anti-personnel or anti-materiel, 'lethal', 'nonlethal' or 'less lethal' – and weapons systems;
- the ways in which these weapons are to be used pursuant to military doctrine, tactics, rules of engagement, operating procedures and countermeasures; all weapons to be acquired, be they procured further to research and development on the basis of military specifications, or purchased 'off-the shelf';

- a weapon which the State is intending to acquire for the first time, without necessarily being 'new' in a technical sense;
- an existing weapon that is modified in a way that alters its function, or a weapon that has already passed a legal review but that is subsequently modified; and
- an existing weapon where a State has joined a new international treaty which may affect the legality of the weapon.

CASE STUDIES

To illustrate how treaty law (Geneva Conventions) and customary law work with respect to non-lethal weapons, the following section will review the operational use of selected non-lethal weapons within the context of these legal regimes. According to NATO guidelines, and drawing from our previous discussions, legal reviews should include questions asking whether the weapon causes effects that are discriminate and proportionate. So, does the new weapon discriminate between combatants and non-combatants, and will it comply with Articles 35 and 36 of 1977 Additional Protocol 1 referring to causing 'unnecessary suffering and superfluous injury'?

While there is room for interpretation here, because the meaning of these terms is not clearly defined, it is generally agreed that disproportionate suffering in respect of achieving a military objective (military necessity) is unlawful. While weapons must be measured against international law they also fall within the remit of domestic laws, including those concerning the safety and protection of national workers. As noted previously, during operational use military commanders have the responsibility to check that the weapon has undergone a rigorous legal evaluation, that the target is legitimate, that all effort is taken to avoid non-combatant injuries and fatalities, and that potential damage to the environment is carefully considered.

Blinding Lasers

At the review conference of the 1980 UN Inhumane Weapons Convention a landmark event occurred in the history of arms control and prohibition, when Protocol IV was negotiated, banning the use of non-lethal blinding laser weapons. Prior to this the only weapon to have been banned before use on the battlefield was the explosive bullet, outlawed under the St Petersburg Declaration (1868). The arguments that led up to the ban on blinding lasers are summarised by Doswald-Beck[36] and Lewer and Schofield,[37] but in essence, the key argument by opponents centred on the principles of unnecessary suffering and superfluous injury. Under the discrimination benchmark the weapon would have passed the test since it was accurately targetable and could, depending of course on the skill and training of the operator, distinguish between combatant and non-combatant. While opponents to the weapons refuted the argument that it was better to be 'blind than dead', others pointed out that there were already battlefield weapons that could cause blindness, and that Protocol IV was only concerned with the technology of the weapon, rather than its effect on people. Thus, if a different technology could produce blindness, it would not be illegal under Protocol IV. However there is a case to be made for opposing future weapons arguing from the standpoint of customary law.

Dazzling Lasers

Since dazzlers and illuminators are not specifically designed to blind victims, they are not covered under Protocol IV, and are legal. They are discriminate, and when used correctly cause a temporary and reversible loss of vision. Their intended effect clearly does not cause unnecessary suffering or superfluous injury, and is appropriate for the military context where they raise the threshold before deadly force has to be used, and therefore have the effect of lowering civilian casualties. When used, for example at roadblocks, soldiers can give vehicle drivers early warning that they need to stop – vehicles that continue despite this evident warning can be assumed to have hostile intent. However, it should be noted that overexposure at close range could cause irreversible eye damage.

Incapacitating Chemicals – the Moscow Theatre Siege, October 2002

Fidler discusses in some depth the use of fentanyl (a 'non-lethal' chemical incapacitating agent) by Russian special forces during the rescue of hostages from a Moscow theatre in October 2002.[38] Immediately prior to storming the building to affect a rescue, fentanyl was rapidly pumped into it. All the terrorists were killed by the attacking soldiers, and about 130 hostages out of the 830 or so being held died as a result of the fentanyl. As Fidler notes, this is a 16 per cent fatality rate, which is twice that of lethal chemical weapons used during the First World War.

While the use of fentanyl in this case did not contravene the 1993 Chemical Weapons Convention, because this was a civil law enforcement and not a war fighting action, the episode raised some vital questions. First, the killing of the incapacitated terrorists highlighted the danger of non-lethal weapons being used in a pre-lethal manner. That is, it is easier to kill enemy combatants who are *hors de combat* – an act that is in violation of the Geneva Conventions. Second, the weapon was used in an indiscriminate manner. Third, because the dosage and quantities of the gas used could not possibly take into account individual's susceptibility to the agent, the manner in which it was used could cause unnecessary suffering and superfluous injury. Fourth, adequate antidotes to the chemical were apparently not available.

The question has to be asked: if fentanyl had not been used and the special forces had to make a 'conventional' attack, would more lives have been lost, and more people injured? This is a difficult calculation for authorities to make, and in a case like this international human rights law (IHRL) can also shed some light on the issue. This tells us that even in extreme situations authorities have an obligation to protect the right to life. In the above scenario the Russian authorities did not do this because of failure to provide adequate aftercare and an inability to control the dosage with respect to individuals in the theatre.[39] Under IHRL the use of fentanyl in this blanket approach could be said to have caused degrading, inhumane and cruel treatment of the hostages.

Riot Control Agents

Alarm bells rang for arms control experts when, just before the Iraq War, US Secretary of Defense Donald Rumsfeld argued before the US Congress House Armed Services Committee that there could be situations where the use of non-lethal riot control agents (RCAs) in warfare would be appropriate, stating that the US was thinking of 'fashioning rules of engagement' to enable their use in the event of a war with Iraq.[40] President Bush later authorised their use in Iraq if required in certain circumstances,[41] an act legal in US law under Executive Order 11850, which was signed by President Ford in 1975 and permits the use of RCAs under specific conditions, including riot control situations in areas under direct and distinct US military control, the protection of aid convoys, the control of rioting prisoners of war, and in situations where civilians are used to camouflage attacks by enemy combatants. While, as we have seen, Article I of the 1993 CWC clearly states that riot control agents cannot be used as a method of warfare, it is a moot point in contemporary conflicts deciding where war fighting (peace enforcement) ends and civil law enforcement or policing actions (peace-keeping) begin.

Non-lethal Landmines

The Ottawa Convention of 1997 banned anti-personnel mines – weapons that can kill, mutilate and incapacitate victims. Classified as weapons that cause unnecessary suffering and superfluous injury, they are mostly indiscriminate and can remain hidden for years before being stepped on. As a result, there has been increased interest in non-lethal anti-personnel mines, which could, for example, fire out sticky entanglement nets, electrical stunning wires, small rubber balls, chemical incapacitants, or a combination of these. Lawyers have questioned the legality of such non-lethal devices because technically they still incapacitate, and such an effect is prohibited under the Ottawa Convention.[42] However, versions are being developed that are operator-activated and can be located using tracking devices – this would mean that they are discriminate and designed to minimise injury and suffering of the victim.

CONCLUSION

This chapter has signposted some of the key dilemmas posed by new weapons – particularly non-lethal weapons – that confront international humanitarian law and arms control treaties When summarising the use of fentanyl in Moscow 2002, and its impact on the future implications of non-lethal weapons development for international law Fidler concluded:

> In short, the meaning of Moscow teaches that rapid technological change will continue to stress international law on the development and use of weaponry, but in ways more politically charged, legally complicated and ethically challenging than the application of international humanitarian law in the past to technologies specifically designed to kill and destroy.[43]

While such weapons will continually test arms control treaties, international humanitarian and international human rights law, they may also provide opportunities for war to be waged in a more humane manner. For some, such a suggestion is anathema – all war is wrong and should be condemned. But we live in the 'real' world – war and violent conflict is a constant part of the lives of millions of people. Surely we have an obligation to reduce the suffering of innocent people caught up in the chaos of war? Indeed, politicians and the military are expected now to reduce the number of body bags coming home, and to demonstrate a greater humanitarian commitment to civilian populations. *Jus in bello* directs us to conduct war as ethically and humanely as possible; it is vital that states put in place disciplined, stringent and coherent review mechanisms for new weapons to ensure that the Geneva Conventions are adhered to and kept up to date. This may require new Conventions to be written.

NOTES

1. M. Dando. *A New Form of Warfare: The Rise of Non-Lethal Weapons* (London: Brasseys, 1996); N. Lewer and S. Schofield, *Non-Lethal Weapons: A Fatal Attraction? Military Strategies and Technologies for 21st Century Conflict* (London: Zed Books, 1997); J. Alexander, *Future War: Non-Lethal Weapons in 21st Century Warfare* (New York: St Martin's Press, 1999); J. Alexander, *Winning the War: Advanced Weapons, Strategies, and Concepts for the Post-9/11 World* (New York: St Martin's Press, 2003); N. Lewer (ed.), *The Future of Non-Lethal Weapons: Technologies, Operations, Ethics and Law* (London: Frank Cass, 2002); B. Rappert, *Non-lethal Weapons as Legitimizing Forces?* (London: Frank Cass, 2003); National Research Council, *An Assessment of Non-lethal Weapons Science and Technology* (Washington, DC: National Academies Press, 2003). Also at: http://books.nap.edu/openbook/0309082889/html/index.html.
2. I. Daoust, R. Coupland and R. Ishoey, 'New Wars, New Weapons? The Obligation of States to Assess the Legality of Means and Methods of Warfare', *International Review of the Red Cross* 84, no. 846 (2002), pp. 345–62; R. Coupland and D. Loye, 'Legal and Health Issues: International Humanitarian Law and the Lethality of or Non-Lethality of Weapons', in: *Non-Lethal Weapons: Technological and Operational Prospects – Jane's Special Report*, ed. M. Dando (London: Jane's Information Group, 2000); D. Fidler, 'The International Legal Implications of "Non-Lethal" Weapons', *Michigan Journal of International Law* 21 (1999), pp. 51–100; D. Fidler, '"Non-Lethal" Weapons and International Law: Three Perspectives on the Future', *Medicine, Conflict and Survival* 17 (1999), pp. 194–206; D. Fidler, 'The Meaning of Moscow: "Non-Lethal" Weapons and International Law in the Early 21st Century', *International Review of the Red Cross* 87, no. 859 (2005), pp. 525–52; D. Koplow, 'Tangled Up In Khaki and Blue: Lethal and Non-Lethal Weapons in Recent Confrontations', *Georgetown Journal of International Law* 36, no. 3 (2005), pp. 703–808; K. Lawand, 'Reviewing the Legality of New Weapons, Means and Methods of Warfare', *International Review of the Red Cross* 88, no. 864 (2006), pp. 925–30; D. Loye, 'Non-Lethal Capabilities and International Humanitarian Law', *Proceedings of the 2nd European Symposium on Non-Lethal Weapons*, 13–14 May 2003, European Working Group on Non-Lethal Weapons, Germany.
3. N. Lewer and N. Davison, 'Non-lethal Technologies – An Overview', *Disarmament Forum*, no. 1 (2005), p. 37.
4. *Ibid.*, pp. 38–9.
5. For a fuller account of non-lethal weapons development and operational use, see N. Davison, *The Early History of 'Non-Lethal' Weapons*, Occasional

Paper No. 1, Bradford Non-Lethal Weapons Research Project, University of Bradford (December 2006); *The Development of 'Non-Lethal' Weapons During the 1990s*, Occasional Paper No. 2, Bradford Non-Lethal Weapons Research Project, University of Bradford (March 2007); *The Contemporary Development of 'Non-Lethal' Weapons*, Occasional Paper No. 3, Bradford Non-Lethal Weapons Research Project, University of Bradford (May 2007).

6. NATO, *Non-Lethal Weapons and Future Peace Enforcement Operations*, NATO Research and Technology Organisation TR-SAS-040, Neuilly-sur-Seine Cedex, France (November 2004).

7. J. Altmann, 'Acoustic Weapons – A Prospective Assessment', *Science & Global Security*, Volume 9 (2001), pp. 165–234; and 'Acoustic NLW Working in the Audio Range', *Proceedings of the 3rd European Symposium on Non-Lethal Weapons*, Ettlingen, Germany, 10–12 May 2005.

8. D. McGlinchey, 'United States: Rumsfeld Says Pentagon Wants Use of Nonlethal Gas', *Global Security Newswire*, 6 February 2003, available at: http://www.nti.org/d_newswire/issues/thisweek/2003_2_6_chmw.html#2; A. Hay, 'Out of the straitjacket', *Guardian*, 12 March 2003, available at: http://www.guardian.co.uk/analysis/story/0,3604,912338,00.html.

9. BBC News, http://news.bbc.co.uk/2/hi/middle_east/7653156.stm.

10. M. Wheelis, 'Biotechnology and Biochemical Weapons', *The Nonproliferation Review* 9, no. 1 (2002), available at: http://cns.miis.edu/pubs/npr/vol09/91/91whee.htm; and '"Nonlethal" Chemical Weapons: A Faustian Bargain', *Issues in Science and Technology* (Spring 2003), available November 2003 from: http://www.nap.edu/issues/19.3/wheelis.htm.

11. Fidler, 'The Meaning of Moscow'.

12. J. Altmann, *Military Nanotechnology* (London: Routledge, 2005).

13. F. Allhoff, 'Terrorism and Torture', *International Journal of Applied Philosophy* 17, no. 1 (2003), pp. 105–18.

14. T. McKelvey, 'Rogue Scholars', *The Nation* (December 2005). Available at: http://www.thenation.com/docprint.mhtml?i=20051226&s=mcelvey2.

15. ABC News, 'Former Iraqi Detainees Allege Torture by U.S. Troops', *ABC News*, 14 November 2005, available at: http://abcnews.go.com/WNT/story?id=1312282.

16. P. Gorman, 'Torture by Taser', *Fort Worth Weekly*, 22 June 2005, available at: http://www.fwweekly.com/content.asp?article=770.

17. C. Bottorff, 'Police Warned of Multiple Taser Hits', *Tennessean*, 28 September 2005; also see: *Taser Safety Warnings*, Taser.com, available at: http://www.taser.com/safety/.

18. Amnesty International, *The Pain Merchants: Security Equipment and its Use in Torture and other Ill Treatment* (London: Amnesty International, 2003), p. 38.

19. Available at: http://europa.eu/scadplus/leg/en/lvb/r12535.htm.

20. R. Coupland, Editorial: '"Non-lethal" Weapons: Precipitating a New Arms Race', *British Medical Journal* 315, no.72 (1997).

21. Lewer and Schofield, *Non-Lethal Weapons*, p. 134.

22. *Ibid.*, p. 5.

23. R. Coupland, '"Calmatives" and "Incapacitants": Questions for International Humanitarian Law Brought by New Means and Methods of Warfare with New Effects', paper presented at the 19th Workshop of the Pugwash Study Group on the Implementation of the Chemical and Biological Weapons Conventions, Oegstsgeest, Netherlands, 26–27 April 2003.

24. Lewer and Davison, 'Non-lethal Technologies – An Overview', p. 37.
25. Coupland, '"Calmatives" and "Incapacitants"', p. 2.
26. *Ibid.*, p. 4.
27. G. Allison, P. Kelley and R. Garwin, *Nonlethal Weapons and Capabilities*, Report of an Independent Task Force Sponsored by the Council on Foreign Relations (New York, 2004), p. 14. Available at: http://www.cfr.org/pdf/Nonlethal_TF.pdf.
28. NATO, *Non-Lethal Weapons*, p. 53.
29. *Ibid.*, p. 54.
30. Fidler, 'The Meaning of Moscow', p. 529.
31. L. Doswald-Beck (ed.), *Blinding Weapons: Reports of the Meetings of Experts Convened by the International Committee of the Red Cross on Battlefield Laser Weapons, 1989–1991* (Geneva: ICRC, 1993), pp. 71–82.
32. Lewer and Schofield, *Non-Lethal Weapons*, p. 82.
33. F. Kalshoven, *Constraints On The Waging of War* (Geneva: ICRC, 1987), p. 33; C. Greenwood in *Blinding Weapons*, ed. Doswald-Beck, pp. 72–3.
34. K. Lawand, 'A Guide to the Legal Review of New Weapons, Means and Methods of Warfare: Measures to Implement Article 36 of Additional Protocol 1 of 1977', *International Review of the Red Cross* 88, no.864 (2006), pp. 931–56.
35. *Ibid.*, p. 7.
36. Doswald-Beck, *Blinding Weapons*.
37. Lewer and Schofield, *Non-Lethal Weapons*.
38. Fidler, 'The Meaning of Moscow'.
39. *Ibid.*, p. 538.
40. McGlinchey, 'United States: Rumsfeld Says Pentagon Wants Use of Nonlethal Gas'.
41. N. Wade and E. Schmitt, 'U.S. Use of Tear Gas Could Violate Treaty, Critics Say', *New York Times*, 5 April 2003.
42. P. Kim, 'Between Principles and Absolutes: Non-Lethal Weapons and the Law of Armed Conflict', *Proceedings of the 2nd European Symposium on Non-Lethal Weapons*, 13–14 May 2003, European Working Group on Non-Lethal Weapons, Germany.
43. Fidler, 'The Meaning of Moscow', p. 552.

7
From 'Total War' to 'Total Operations' – Contemporary Doctrine and Adherence to IHL

Björn Müller-Wille

INSURGENTS BREACH INTERNATIONAL HUMANITARIAN LAW

Given the present military operational environment, concerns have been raised with regard to the 'increased artificiality and elasticity'[1] of international humanitarian law (IHL). While it is quite clear that the IHL has rarely been completely respected by all parties involved in armed conflicts,[2] breaches seem to be more noticeable today. Perhaps most obvious are violations committed by irregular armed forces that resort to terrorist tactics in their fight against intervening western forces. Insurgents in Iraq and the Taliban in Afghanistan can serve as prominent examples. Their frequent and systematic breaches of IHL have been well documented.

Take the principle of distinction as a case in point. Deliberate attacks on civilians are commonplace, and both groups actively seek to blend with, rather than trying to distinguish themselves from non-combatants.[3] Moreover, their own manuals sanction such breaches. Both the Taliban's *Labeya* and al-Qaeda's *Training Manual* encourage intentional targeting and killing of civilians.[4] This derogation is not limited to irregular forces. Human shields, for instance, were used against western forces by Saddam Hussein during both invasions and by Milošević during the Kosovo campaign.[5]

Nevertheless, compliance with IHL also appears to have deteriorated among regular (western) forces. They seem to have taken on new roles and adapted their doctrine to the changing environment in a manner that runs the risk of conflicting with IHL. This chapter seeks to assess to what extent modern doctrinal developments undermine IHL. It sets the *use of force* and the principles of *distinction* and *proportionality* at the centre as these are essential to the main purpose of IHL, namely the protection of victims of war and the limitation of the effects of armed conflict, thus avoiding unnecessary suffering. Disregarding these would consequently constitute most serious breaches, often with lethal consequences. Furthermore, they represent good examples by which changes in operational thinking can be demonstrated.

The first section sets out with a clarification of the approach contemporary doctrine has to IHL, asking 'Does the doctrine contest the application of IHL?' It outlines the provisions of IHL concerning targeting decisions, most notably the principles of distinction and proportionality, explains the term doctrine and explores how current doctrine relates to the two principles. It suggests that contemporary doctrine formally promotes the applicability of both distinction and proportionality.

However, the doctrine seems to have generated a reinterpretation of these provisions. The second part, therefore, asks 'How does contemporary doctrine affect the interpretation of IHL and what problems does this raise?' While it largely draws on British and US terminology, placing *Effects Based Operations* (EBO) and the *Comprehensive Approach* at the centre, this doctrine is also developed and applied by other western-oriented countries. Consequently, the conclusions are not limited to UK and US operations. It argues that the doctrine leads to a reinterpretation of the existing texts and that new strategic goals and a changing operational environment recalibrate the points of reference used when making judgments, for example, on what is proportional. The third and final section before the conclusion is devoted to the future, asking 'How can current trends influence the future adherence to IHL?' It outlines contradictory trends, one suggesting less and the other more compliance with IHL.

DOCTRINAL APPLICABILITY OF IHL

What Does IHL Say?

The purpose of IHL is to limit the effects of armed conflict[6] and to avoid unnecessary suffering.[7] This does not mean that it seeks to avoid all suffering. Rather it seeks to balance the necessities of war and humanitarian concerns.[8] To this end, basic IHL principles prescribe a four-step assessment for the use of force, the first and third of which stand at the centre of this study:

1) *Distinction* to ensure that an attack is not directed against a civilian target.

2) *Military necessity* to limit the use of force against the military objective to what the mission requires.
3) *Proportionality* to avoid excessive collateral damage.
4) *Humanity* to minimise collateral damage.

Distinction, outlined in the 1977 Additional Protocol I to the Geneva Conventions (API), is arguably the most important principle of IHL. The assumption that the military dimension in which combat takes place can be separated from the civilian one, detached from the fighting (API 48), constitutes the fundamental principle upon which IHL is based.[9]

Therefore, it contradicts Ludendorff's idea of a 'Total War' in which one society as a whole, including the home front, fights another. Discrimination between what is civilian and what is military makes little sense in 'Total Wars' as the concept presumes that the entire society is geared towards and all its members contribute to the war effort. Hence, with the exception of the incapable, nobody is left out of the war machinery. If the war aims are also regarded as absolute, IHL as such does not make any sense at all, since everything must be subjugated to the war effort and the ends justify any means.[10]

By distinguishing those engaged in hostilities from victims and bystanders IHL offers general protection to non-participants. Accordingly, attacks shall not be aimed at civilian persons and objects (API 48, 51(2), (4)a and 52(1)).[11] Note that civilian persons and objects are not defined. Instead, all persons and objects are by default civilian unless they take direct part in hostilities or are military objects (API 50(1), 51(3) and 52(1)). This stance is reinforced by the provision that a person or an object should be presumed to be civilian if there is any doubt about their status (API 5(1) and 52(3)).

According to API 52(2), the definition of military objectives comprises two elements. First, such objects have to make an effective contribution to military action by either their (a) 'nature', which includes all objects directly used by the armed forces, for example weapons, equipment, transports, fortification etc.;[12] or (b) their 'location', which refers to a geographic site that is not military by its nature but in the circumstances ruling at the time contributes to military action, for example a bridge, hill, landing site or other location of special importance for military operations;[13] or (c) their 'purpose', which relates to the intended future use of the object;[14] or 'use', which relates to the object's present function.[15]

Second, the 'total or partial destruction, capture or neutralization' of the object 'in the circumstances ruling at the time' must 'offer a definite military advantage'. Thus, if an attack only offers a potential, hypothetical, speculative or indeterminate advantage the object is not regarded as a military one.[16] Consequently, those ordering and executing an attack must be able to explain what definite military advantage is to be gained from it. The temporal requirement 'in the circumstances ruling at the time' is crucial as it suggests that the status of objects can change over time. A bridge, for instance, can become a military objective for a certain period only to become civilian again at a later stage. Furthermore, by setting the present as the point of reference, this requisite limits the extent to which an object's 'purpose' can be taken into account, that is, how far into the future an object's intended use can be anticipated to qualify as a military objective. Thus, the status of persons and objects needs continuous reconsideration. API 57(2)a(i) emphasises this responsibility by obliging those planning and deciding on an attack to 'do everything feasible to verify that the objectives to be attacked are neither civilians nor civilian objects'. Note that all these provisions also apply to members of the armed forces, even if some definitions literally are limited to objects.[17]

Once an object has been identified as a military one, it no longer falls under the general protection IHL grants civilian objects, thereby passing the first threshold to qualify as a legitimate target. The principles of military necessity now restricts the use of lawful force against military objects to what is required to accomplish the mission, for example to make the enemy submit.[18]

The principle of proportionality extends this consideration by taking into account the effects of an attack on surrounding non-military objects. API 51(5)b and 57(2)a(iii) and 2b) all prohibit an attack that 'may be expected to cause incidental loss of civilian life, injury to civilians, damage to civilian objects, or a combination thereof, which would be excessive in relation to the concrete and direct military advantage anticipated'.[19]

While rather straightforward at first glance, its practical application has to rely on a subjective evaluation to a larger extent than any of the above. There simply is no objective way of weighing and balancing two such disparate notions as collateral damage and military advantage against each other.[20] The assessment does not only require 'apples to be compared with oranges', it is also difficult to quantify and qualify each category on its own, for example what aspects are included and how far in time and space does the assessment stretch. The interpretation of how the military advantage is to be understood can serve as an indicator of the difficulties involved. It appears that the terms 'concrete and direct' are meant to specify and limit what is meant by military advantage so as to avoid a situation where the intended end, victory, can justify any level of collateral damage. According to the ICRC commentary, the expression

> was intended to show that the advantage concerned should be substantial and relatively close, and that advantages which are hardly perceptible and those which would only appear in the long term should be disregarded.[21]

Even if all conditions above are met, commanders are restrained in their use of force by a final principle, the one of humanity (or unnecessary suffering).[22] It holds those who plan and decide upon attacks to take all feasible precautions to minimise even proportional collateral damage. This principle should be taken into account when selecting targets, for example when the same military advantage can be achieved by attacking different military objectives (API 57(3)); and when selecting means and weapons for the attack, for example choice of weapon system, time or direction of an attack (API 57(2) a(ii)).[23] When circumstances permit, advanced warnings can also be given to achieve this aim (API 57(2)c).

What is Doctrine?

To start an argument about the influence of contemporary doctrine on the adherence to these IHL principles, one first needs to clarify the term doctrine. Here, doctrine is understood as 'what is taught'[24] and in that sense is distinct from practice – that is, everything that is done on operations. It is based on experience and reactive in the sense that militaries develop and adapt their activities to meet adversaries' changing tactics and to improve their performance in a broadening spectrum of missions assigned by political masters. Doctrine is also proactive and forward thinking in that it drives new approaches permitted by evolving technology and the resources committed to operations as well as in that it anticipates new challenges posed by changing operational environments.

As doctrine is based on lessons drawn, existing capabilities and expectations, 'what is taught' varies somewhat from country to country, despite intense cooperation and exchanges. Furthermore, different countries have different traditions of collecting and transferring military knowledge. Thus, 'how' it is taught varies, and with it the understanding of what doctrine is and what relevance is ascribed to complying with it.[25] The US, for instance, has a well-established centralised system and tradition of documenting experiences and conveying doctrine in written, conventional form. In contrast, the British approach, for instance, has relied on decentralised and less standardised regimental traditions for much longer. As a result, the two countries have a tendency to rate doctrine in different ways. Simplified, one could argue that doctrine is read more widely and is more commonly applied by Americans, whereas the British have a much more modest volume of codified doctrine to draw on and a more flexible relationship to it. This study is therefore confronted with two difficulties: (a) to establish what is actually taught, and (b) to establish a causality between doctrine and operational behaviour, that is, to what extent doctrine rather than any other influences effect operational decisions and thus the adherence to IHL.

To address the former, formalised written doctrinal documents such as field manuals and doctrine notes have been consulted. Even if they are probably used more widely in the US, while British training possibly allows for more variations, these documents provide a standardised view and give a good indication of current military thinking. Since there is a time lag between their distribution, incorporation into training and implementation on operations, they can also indicate future operational developments. Nevertheless, 'what is taught' encompasses more than these documents, which is why the concept of doctrine has been broadened to include other texts and statements by leading military, judicial and political authorities.

As for the impact of doctrine, there will always be a discrepancy between formalised doctrine and behaviour on operations, be it that doctrine is reactive and lags behind actual conduct or that it is proactive and proposes new procedures that have to be communicated, understood and accepted before they are actually applied. Moreover, doctrine will never be sufficiently comprehensive to cover all aspects of operational activities. Hence establishing a direct causal link between doctrine and the adherence to IHL entails some difficulties. It would not only require doctrine to be more detailed than it is and give clear guidance to operational decision-making, but also necessitate commanders and soldiers in the field to apply and implement 'what is taught' rather than to show initiative and adapt to the situation they find themselves in. Obviously, neither of the two conditions is likely to be met. However, even if formalised doctrine is to be seen as something evolving and therefore not prescriptive in nature, it is still intended to give guidance to decision-makers, thereby streamlining and improving the efficiency of the military apparatus. This makes an examination of the relationship between 'what is taught' and IHL worthwhile despite the described limitations. If the doctrine conflicts with IHL, it will most likely bring about breaches sooner or later.

How Relevant is IHL, and How Does Doctrine Relate to the Principles?

When reading the flood of literature on IHL breaches during recent operations in Iraq, Afghanistan or southern Lebanon, one could be led to believe that contemporary doctrine openly rejects many of IHL's provisions. This is reinforced by the discussions on the applicability of IHL, or merely parts thereof, to these operations, as well as by questioned practices such as the treatment of prisoners as 'unlawful combatants' and what has been labelled as targeted killings.[26] This chapter does not seek to add to the series of texts trying to clarify any of these issues or the relationship between *jus ad bellum* and *jus in bello*, which others have already done in a much better way than the author could ever achieve.[27] Rather it is concerned with tensions between the military craftsmanship currently taught and IHL, and in particular its principles of distinction and proportionality.

Of course, one will not find any doctrine documents in any western-style democracy outright rejecting IHL or instigating breaches. This would be illegal, most likely lead to judicial proceedings and the document being rewritten to conform with international law. However, current operational practice and some leaders' statements suggest that the principles of distinction and proportionality have not really been internalised by decision-makers. Take President George W. Bush's famous address to Congress on 20 September 2001 as an example:[28]

> Every nation, in every region, now has a decision to make. Either you are with us, or you are with the terrorists. From this day forward, any nation that continues to harbor or support terrorism will be regarded by the United States as a hostile regime.

By negating the status of neutrality, this statement not only contradicts a long-standing principle of IHL.[29] Indirectly it also conflicts with the principle of distinction, discriminating those taking part in hostilities from non-participants. While it is obvious that the speech was not intended to elaborate on IHL, it demonstrates that this basic principle was not considered by those formulating the address and that distinction does not seem to constitute a baseline and starting point for those deciding on and planning military operations. Equally, one could argue that the principle of proportionality has come in tension with modern doctrine. The so-called Powell doctrine, favouring the 'overwhelming use of force' in order to achieve decisive victory quickly and at minimum cost in terms of US casualties,[30] can serve as another example reinforcing the suspicion that IHL has not really had a paramount standing in military thinking for some time.

One does not have to be a lawyer, let alone an expert in IHL, to understand that the principles of distinction and proportionality are based on common decency. And being so basic, one could expect them to apply to all military operations at all times, irrespective of the particular legal setting within which they are conducted. Against this backdrop, the above position can seem thoughtless at best. Sceptics could even believe that the US, as a non-signatory to API, does not consider itself bound by the two principles. Fortunately, a quick survey of both US and British documents used in training and practice is somewhat reassuring in this respect at least.

To begin with, the US has accepted both principles as customary law. The *Operational Law Handbook 2004* makes direct reference to the API in relation to the principle of distinction and to FM 27-10,[31] which contains a formulation clearly drawing on, and with the same meaning as, the one in API with regard to the principle of proportionality.[32] Consequently, neither American nor British doctrine contests either of the two principles as such. In the UK, training goes even further, as army officers passing through Sandhurst are taught to apply these principles on all operations, including those other than war.[33] In the US this is also likely to be common practice. In a 2006 directive on the Law of War Programme the DoD states that it is its policy that 'Members of the DoD Components comply with the law of war during all armed conflicts, however such conflicts are characterized, and in all other military operations.'[34] Nevertheless, provision that members of the DoD Components should comply 'with the principles and spirit of the law of war during all other operations' contained in the replaced directive from 1998 was dropped.[35] To what extent this actually reflects new thinking on the two principles is debatable, in particular since the *2006 Operational Law Handbook* still makes reference to the older version as well as

FROM 'TOTAL WAR' TO 'TOTAL OPERATIONS'   163

a version of Chairman of Joint Chiefs of Staffs' Instruction (CJCSI) 5810.01, outdated in 1999, stating that the US 'will apply law of war principles during all operations that are categorized as Military Operations Other Than War'.[36]

Although arguments and practical examples can be found suggesting that the two principles are not consistently applied on all military operations, it seems inconceivable that non-discrimination and disproportionate use of force is taught anywhere. The most significant change from the perspective of doctrinal development is not necessarily that the principles as such are contested or even the formulations by which they are codified. They do not have to be. A real challenge is that the texts are reinterpreted. The Effects Based Approach (EBA) changes the meaning of the principles without having to question their applicability.

DOCTRINAL REINTERPRETATION OF IHL

Modern Developments – What is EBO and What is NEC?

Alterations of the political and strategic aims of operations constitute the main driver of recent changes in military doctrine. The development of EBO[37] and the so-called 'Comprehensive Approach' can be attributed to the new tasks and role the military are given. Technological developments have then been used to support these adaptations.

The post-Cold War period has not only resulted in new security challenges requiring military adaptation and response. It has also produced new options and opportunities for politicians to employ the military instrument. Today, it seems as if a much more ambitious political aim is pursued than in previous ventures. One can note a shift from a reactive towards a more proactive stance. Rather than striving to negate an undesired state (for example, stopping the expansion of other ideologies or hindering parties from waging war in classical peace-keeping operations), it appears that recent western military efforts have been aligned with a much more elaborate general aim, namely the establishment of sustainable, democratic political systems based on the rule of law in other countries.

One could argue that this is not a novelty at all. The British, for instance, have already had similar experiences in a number of counterinsurgency campaigns, ranging from Malaya to Northern Ireland. In fact, fighting rebellions is a common and one of the oldest military tasks. However, contemporary operations are significantly different in one central respect. In none of the operations in the Balkans, Iraq or Afghanistan have western forces attempted to reverse a deteriorated situation to regain control and re-establish the previous political order. Rather they deploy into an alien environment with the aim to instate a new political system. Western forces no longer find themselves on operations where they simply try to *win* hearts and minds, understood as winning sympathy or at least respect, with a view to prevent open hostilities and maintain a status quo. Rather the political aim of today's missions has become to *change* the 'hearts and minds' of the local population.

This change in ambition does not only apply to stability or counterinsurgency operations, where we seek to win the indigenous population over to our way of thinking and make them embrace, not just accept, democracy. The development from traditional peace-keeping missions to peace support operations that try to address root causes and solve the conflict reflects the same transformation. Altering the political objective of military operations has far-reaching implications as it changes the desirable end state and, thus, the rationale of missions – that is, what forces try to achieve and most importantly *how*. It is therefore not surprising that the changing ambition is paralleled by a development of methods and capabilities. The recent development of the EBA is thought to fundamentally transform western forces' approach to military operations, and the understanding of IHL.

The EBA can be interpreted as a development of Mission Command,[38] in that it sets the definition of the desired outcome at the centre, and as a more sophisticated version of the Manoeuvrist Approach,[39] as it seeks an even deeper understanding of the enemy's complexity that allows for a more meticulous identification and exploitation of his vulnerabilities. However, it is also very different, taking a more differentiated view on both the 'red' and the 'blue' side. Somewhat simplified, one could argue that armed forces traditionally had a very selective view of reality, mainly focusing on the military dimension, viewing the adversary's different units and instruments in isolation and dealing with them accordingly. This resulted in an approach that emphasised force ratios, annihilation and simple attrition.[40]

Today, however, military superiority is never really questioned and a victory against identified adversaries expected in a rather short period. Consequently, combat operations are conducted with the forthcoming reconstruction and state-building period in mind. In fact, these operations often take place in parallel in today's fragmented battlefield environment. The centrepiece of the EBA is to assess the various long- and short-term effects – that is, first-, second- and third-order effects that different coercive and supportive measures can have on a selected target itself and on the opposition at large. To do so, decision-making is based on a more holistic approach that rejects the idea of an isolated military dimension and attempts to produce a more accurate replication of reality than merely a military one.

In a first step, the EBA proposes that the enemy should be understood as a complex system of interrelated systems consisting of many relevant civilian and military actors/units linked to each other via a plethora of relationships. By identifying the system's relevant 'nodes', its functionality and efficiency could be paralysed without obliterating the actors and with minimum destruction. Rather than seeking to destroy menacing targets, the military may for instance focus on preventing the adversary from applying his assets as he desires. Thereby, armed forces would achieve the same effect without impeding subsequent reconstruction efforts during the state-building phase.[41]

In a second step, the EBA views the 'blue' side in a similar manner, stressing a multi-disciplinary and multi-agency 'holistic' response to crisis and security threats, which can involve both coercive and non-coercive measures. The inclusion of non-military instruments appears very sensible given that the strategic aim actually boils down to making the local population think differently. Hence, the EBA emphasises the accomplishment of strategic goals, while taking into account the full range of governmental instruments and their possible effects. In the UK the coordination of all governmental agencies' activities is labelled the 'Comprehensive Approach'.[42] Thus, the military is expected to see itself, and operate, as a part of a much broader and more effective effort to achieve a clearly defined and desired long-term outcome. Ideally, the military should not just focus on desired effects on existing adversaries, but also take into account how its actions affect the local population in order to avoid undesired effects, such as encouraging further recruitment into armed opposition groups.

In terms of technology, EBOs are supported by a move towards Network Enabled Capabilities (NEC),[43] which has already begun to transform military thinking.[44] The basic thought behind it is rather simple and cogent as it incorporates and seeks to ameliorate traditional elements of warfare. By enhancing communications between people and platforms, it is expected to improve situation awareness and increase the speed by which assets can be (re)directed and coordinated. Thus, at least in theory, it should make assets more accessible at the same time as it becomes easier to use them to best effect. Fashionably, NEC is described as the linking of sensors, networks and strike assets, aimed at improving the detect–decide–destroy cycle.

What effect do they have on the two principles?

This doctrine equals a renaissance of a central aspect of Ludendorff's 'Total War': the denial of the existence of an isolated military dimension. Furthermore, the emphasis EBOs put on the strategic objectives fits well with Clausewitz's idea that military aims and objectives cannot be separated from the political ones.[45] Both contradict cornerstones upon which IHL is based. Even if western countries are not really engaged in or think in terms of 'Total War,' the EBA risks turning modern operations into what one could label 'Total Operations'. This alters the interpretation of the principles of distinction and proportionality.

Distinction

The principle of distinction is rethought because what constitutes a military objective seems to have altered. There are several reasons for this. To begin with, the military has a broader range of tasks. As the focus has shifted from a defensive to an interventionist use of military force, aimed at stabilising or liberating countries, the war fighting machinery has increasingly transformed into a state-building apparatus. Now western forces pursue operational aims that stretch beyond the traditional military domain of neutralising the enemy and require the military to perform a large variety of tasks in parallel to combat. In addition to providing security, they also engage in the reconstruction and development of the host nation. The so-called 'three block war' is a good illustration of this.[46] Since the military has most manpower in theatre and resources for force protection, they often find themselves delivering humanitarian aid, supporting elections, building infrastructure, supplying transport or supporting other functions required by the state-building. This is supplemented by activities primarily aimed at winning the support of the local population, such as the painting of schools.[47] What initially was perceived as mission creep has now been accepted as standard. As the spectrum of tasks has expanded, the notion of 'what is military' and what makes 'an effective contribution to military action' is broadened.

Simultaneously, the traditional remit of what could be considered as 'military' is diluted by the increased use of civilian contractors for tasks previously performed by military personnel.[48] The distinction is further blurred as the Comprehensive Approach actively seeks to bring together rather than to separate what is military and what is civilian. The creation of Provisional Reconstruction Teams in Iraq and Afghanistan, which bring together soldiers, representatives from civilian agencies and possibly local advisors, exemplifies these efforts. If all governmental agencies' efforts are considered relevant and interdependent, and all of them are coordinated towards the same strategic aim, they all become part of the same machinery. This makes it difficult to comprehend why any opponent should make a distinction between military forces and civilian agencies handing out food, or between security forces and any foreign civilian staff working for the same political masters and pursuing the same objective. And why should opponents make any effort to make it easier for western forces to distinguish them from the civilian population when faced with militarily superior apparatus engaged in 'Total Operations'?

Furthermore, EBO's focus on the strategic aim, namely to alter peoples' thinking, has refocused attention to 'civil centres of gravity'[49] and a more traditional one – the will to fight. Accordingly, relevant 'nodes' are identified and targeted. As a result, civilian objects are increasingly targeted by non-kinetic means, for example to gain support from the general public and to influence fighters. The broadening of tasks outlined above can also be seen in this light.

From an IHL perspective, one could of course welcome Information Operations, if, for example, propaganda efforts replace carpet bombing. Furthermore, one could argue that the military's expansion of non-kinetic tasks is unproblematic as it should not influence western forces' ability to apply the principle of distinction when targeting opponents.

Unfortunately, it is not quite so simple. Commanders do not necessarily make a clear separation between kinetic and 'non-military' operations. This is not mainly because they conduct all tasks with military equipment, bringing weapons along for force protection. The major tensions arise when the full spectrum of activities is regarded as proper military tasks and this understanding of what is military is mirrored upon opponents. In this case, persons or facilities countering any of operation conducted by western forces run the risk of becoming targets and force may be used against them. This is all the more likely if the temporal requirement is expanded.

An increased focus on the strategic aim is likely to prolong the timescale taken into account in comparison to previous more immediate tactical considerations. The time in which an object's 'purpose' is considered may stretch further if the expression 'in the circumstances ruling at the time' is extended.

These changes become particularly evident when considering dual-use objects. Since IHL only separates between military and civilian objects, facilities with dual functions fall within the former category. Targeting is therefore not limited by the principle of distinction but by the principle of proportionality.[50] As a result, more objects are classified as military ones, because the scope of what is military has grown. NATO's attack on the Serbian TV and radio station in Belgrade on 23 April 1999, the transmitter of which allegedly was integrated in the military communications network, may serve as an example.[51]

Proportionality

The recalibration of the principle of proportionality is equally critical. If the meaning of what is military changes, what is viewed as a 'concrete and direct military advantage' changes as well. Furthermore, it is evident that different countries already set different points of reference when determining if an attack offers a 'concrete and direct military advantage'. The UK, for instance, has declared that in its view 'the military advantage anticipated from an attack is intended to refer to the advantage anticipated from the attack considered as a whole and not only from isolated or particular parts of the attack'.[52] The US has gone even further. The *Operational Law Handbook* explains that in the context of proportionality, military advantage

> is not restricted to tactical gains, but is linked to the full context of war strategy. Balancing between collateral damage to civilian objects and collateral civilian casualties may be done on a target-by-target basis [...] but also may be weighed in overall terms against campaign objectives.[53]

This is quite significant. If an attack is seen as part of the strategic rather than the tactical context, the military advantage that can reasonably be expected will appear much larger. Therefore the amount of collateral damage that is regarded as proportional will also increase.[54] This move away from the intention of IHL to judge a specific attack in isolation from the strategic and political context is supported by the EBA. It urges commanders always to consider what effects, both military and civilian, their actions have on the achievement of the strategic aim, for example to develop and hand over responsibility to a legitimate, capable, self-sustaining democratic government. Consequently, proportionality is more generously applied to a broader range of what is considered to be military objects. The targeting of electrical power grid in al-Nasiriyya on 22 and 23 March 2003 and the Ministry of Information in Baghdad on 28 March can serve as examples.[55]

This shift could take place quite comfortably given the difficulties involved in the assessment of what is proportional. The subjectivity involved has made it all the more difficult to bring about convictions. API article 85, which deals with the repression of breaches, requires that a person 'knew with certainty' that the collateral damage would be excessive to the concrete and direct military advantage.[56] Equally, the Rome Statute of the International Criminal Court 8(2)b(iv) requires collateral damage to be '*clearly* excessive' (emphasis added) in relation to the 'concrete and direct *overall* military advantage anticipated' (emphasis added), to qualify as a war crime and, thus, to fall within its jurisdiction.

To make things worse, the emphasis on the strategic aim seems to have twisted some targeting procedures to the extent that the threshold function of the principle of distinction is skipped altogether in practice. Hence the classification of a person or facility as a military object is no longer a prerequisite for targeting. Accordingly, the principle of military necessity is also dispensed with. The principle of distinction is then merely applied for the assessment of proportionality and possibly for the principle of humanity (in the sense described above for targeting procedures). Following this derogation from IHL, the ends have started to justify the means. A prominent example from the Kosovo war was the targeting of factories and properties belonging to political supporters of Milošević.[57] As planners identified the will to fight and the political support to the regime as a centre of gravity, they started identifying targets suitable to achieve the desired effect. Rather than being guided by the principle of distinction, they were completely focused on the aim.

Breaches committed during the Israeli campaigns in southern Lebanon can also serve as slightly different examples for this. The IDF still follows the traditional military aim of self-defence, rather than to establish legitimate democratic government, reconstruction and development or any other state-building objectives. Hence, a

Comprehensive Approach is neither needed nor applied in the way that coalition forces do in Iraq or Afghanistan. Consequently, the doctrine has not generated the same reinterpretation of 'what is military' and what constitutes a 'military advantage'. Note that a parallel can be drawn to the first invasion of Iraq.

Of course, Hezbullah is responsible for a blurring of military and civilian objectives on its side. Not only do they deliberately seek to blend with and use civilians as shields. Parts of the civilian population is also known to giving logistical support to Hezbullah and thereby actively involved in hostilities. Moreover, the attacks against Israel were clearly directed against civilian targets, which is a breach in itself.[58] However, this does not release Israel from its responsibility to distinguish military from civilian objects.[59] And from a doctrinal perspective, at least, one would rather expect the traditional interpretation of distinction to apply.

The point is that most targeting of public works, ports, airports, electrical facilities, commercial enterprises, residential properties and even hospitals[60] cannot be explained by an EBO-driven reinterpretation of the principle of distinction. Nor can the establishment of a 'free fire zone' as implied by messages explaining to civilians that any presence in certain areas will be regarded as subversive and risk being targeted.[61] Even the suspicion that the western reading of 'what is military' has simply been duplicated without copying the other changes induced by the EBA and Comprehensive Approach is not really convincing. If the EBO doctrine had any influence, it was not a reinterpretation of the principle of distinction, but the skipping of this step in the targeting procedure owing to the increased focus on the traditional strategic aim of national survival. They can therefore only partially serve as examples of how the EBA depreciates IHL.

However, rather than arguing that the effects based doctrine suggests that the principle of distinction should be set aside, one could contend that this is simply an example of EBO misinterpreted and wrongly applied. We will return to this in the section contemplating the future.

Technological Development NEC

The new technology has two main effects relating to IHL. The first is the trend towards better situational awareness counterbalanced by increased speed of decision-making and thus less time to distinguish military from civilian objects. The second relates to the improved precision of weapon systems combined with increased automatisation of fire.[62] It is difficult to give a general answer to how this will affect collateral damage. Clearly, the technological support to correctly identify military objects should be applauded as it supports the principle of distinction.[63] However, the increased accuracy could be neutralised by the time pressure decision-makers can find themselves under and suffer further from increased automatisation. Equally, greater precision increases the likelihood that the intended target is hit. It also means that smaller charges can be used and it limits the need for restrikes. Both appear to favour the application of the principle of humanity. On the other hand, it allows the targeting of objects that previously were off limits, for example in urban areas, as an attack would have caused excessive collateral damage and conflict with the principle of proportionality. This could result in a net increase in harm to the civilian population.[64] Whether the technology will result in more or less collateral damage will depend on the future application of the EBA.

FUTURE ADHERENCE TO IHL

It is quite obvious that the EBA and the move towards 'Total Operations' entails a risk that IHL is eroded. As the EBA does not set a preference for traditional military targets as such, one could, for instance, assume that facilities that can be regarded as 'dual-use' installations under the new reading of 'what is military' may be targeted to a much higher degree than previously. It is not only easier to hit fixed targets than mobile military ones. It is also effective as it can increase the pressure from the population on their government. By focusing on the achievement of the strategic aim and by using this as the guiding principle for any decisions, IHL is possibly even set aside altogether. The 'intensive interrogation' of prisoners and the creation of the detention facility at Guantánamo Bay could serve as an example for such a development.

The counterargument is that the EBA restrains decision-makers. Owing to the relatively certain outcome of the war they will take their subsequent responsibility to rebuild the infrastructure into account during the combat phase.[65] Evidence for this can be seen if one compares targeting procedures during Operation Desert Storm and with those of Operation Iraqi Freedom, which actually largely did avoid power plants, public water facilities, refineries, bridges and other civilian structures.[66] That nearly 70 per cent of all munitions used by the air component were precision-guided, while they accounted for less than 10 per cent of the tonnage during Operation Desert Storm will also have helped to reduce unintended damage.[67]

Consequently, they will choose targets and means with more care than Cold War doctrine taught them. Hence they would try to use non-kinetic means as far as possible, for example dropping carbon filaments on power lines rather bombing electrical power plants.[68] Moreover, if correctly applied, the effects of breaching IHL are taken into account in EBOs. Since operational success is dependent on consent among the local population, commanders will take great care not to jeopardise their approval. Violating IHL would be counterproductive, especially when trying to enforce law and order. Rather than winning hearts and minds troops would alienate natives and lose legitimacy. With no prospect of gaining local support, mission failure is unavoidable.

Again, the US treatment of prisoners can serve as an example. It seems obvious to observe that it has alienated supporters within the US and among allies, and functioned as a major recruitment sergeant for insurgencies.[69] Although breaches of IHL may provide immediate tactical advantages they have backfired and proven counterproductive at the strategic level. In other words, those who promote or even consider breaches of the law are short-sighted and have a poor understanding of what EBO really entails.

However, if the adherence to the law relies on the contribution it makes to operational effectiveness, IHL is in practice reduced from a set of universal values to an instrumental commodity within the EBA. Rather than representing unbendable law, IHL merely needs to be complied with insofar as the adherence serves the attainment of the operational aim. It is reduced to being just another variable weighed against others in a decision-making process. Not only can IHL be completely disregarded if compliance is considered to conflict with goal attainment. Whether the operation is expected to be followed by a state-building phase or nearly serves to liberate an invaded country will also be decisive. Equally dangerous, because less obvious, is that the creeping change in the interpretation of IHL actually means that the original humanitarian considerations are replaced as a guiding standard by the attainment of certain desired effects within the broadened scope of 'what is military'.

A closer look at public support suggests a further erosion of the standing of IHL. It has been established that public support at home, among allies and most importantly in theatre is essential for operational success. It also appears fair to assume that most people, anywhere in the world, are not particularly familiar with, nor particularly interested in, the details of IHL. Consequently, it is not a breach of IHL as such that will disaffect them. Rather it is a combination of much simpler yardsticks, such as 'how many innocent people where killed', mixed with a general opinion about the legitimacy of the war in the first place. Not only does the targeting of civilian facilities appear acceptable if nobody gets killed and this shortens the war. It also appears as if the acceptable level of collateral damage varies with the perceived legitimacy of the operation. This blurring of *jus in bello* and *jus ad bellum* is all the more understandable as politicians make little effort to separate the two when communicating with the media.

It seems likely that the doctrinal development will continue in this direction, particularly since the legal consequences of breaching IHL hardly seem threatening.

Having said that, the involvement of legal advisors in decision-making procedures has increased considerably since the Cold War. Although actively involved, it does not seem as if they have been able to enforce adherence to the traditional interpretation of IHL. If anything, they appear to have focused on making sure that their commanders do not make decisions that get them into legal trouble and they participate in the adaptation of the interpretation of IHL to provide for 'operational requirements'.

CONCLUSION

While the effects-based doctrine does not expressively promote breaches of IHL, it certainly generates new interpretations of IHL. It contributes to the blurring of what is military and what is civilian, and changes the points of reference for assessments of proportional use of force. The practical application of 'Total Operations' has also demonstrated that its focus on the strategic aim can generate outright violations and disregard the principle of distinction. However, it is important to note that the latter is the result of a particular understanding of EBA rather than a necessary consequence. In part, the outcome seems to hinge on the strategic aim – that is, if the war fighting is expected to be followed by a reconstruction phase or not. In addition, it depends on whether EBA is taught and understood on equal footing with IHL, or if the effects-based part of the doctrine is given supremacy over its legal part. At present, the tendency appears to lean towards the latter.

NOTES

1. Thomas Smith, 'The New Law of War: Legitimizing Hi-tech and Infrastructure Violence', *International Studies Quarterly* 46 (2002), pp. 355–74.
2. For a critical evaluation of the application and interpretation of IHL in earlier conflicts, see Chris Jochnik and Roger Normand, 'The Legitimation of Violence: A Critical History of the Laws of War', *Harvard International Law Journal* 35, no. 1 (1994), pp. 49–95.
3. Amnesty International, 'Secondary Afghanistan: Taleban Attacks against Civilians Increasing and Systematic' (2007), available at: http://web.amnesty.org/libery/index/engASA110022007?open&of=eng-AFG.
4. Urs Gehriger, 'Layeha (Regelbuch) für die Mudschaheddin', *Die Weltwoche* 2006. Available at: http://www.weltwoche.ch/artikel/default.asp?AssetID=1 5351&CategoryID=91. An English translation can be found at: http://www.signandsight.com/features/1071.html. For documents referred to as al-Qaeda's training manual, see: http://cryptome.org/alq-terr-man.htm#1 or www.usdoj.gov/ag/manualpart1_1.pdf.
5. For more examples and details, see Daniel P. Schoenekase, 'Targeting Decisions Regarding Human Shields', *Military Review* 84, no. 5 (2004), pp. 26–31.
6. ICRC, *What is International Humanitarian Law?*, Advisory Service on International Humanitarian Law (2004). Available from: http://www.icrc.org/Web/eng/siteeng0.nsf/htmlall/humanitarian-law-factsheet/$File/What_is_IHL.pdf.
7. Centre, Director-General Joint Doctrine and Concepts, 'The Joint Service Manual of the Law of Armed Conflict', in *JSP-383* (2004), p. 3. See also *Operational Law Handbook*, ed. Joseph B. Berger, Derek Grimes and Eric T. Jensen (Charlottesville, VA: The Judge Advocate General's Legal Center and School, 2004), p. 12.
8. Joseph Holland, 'Military Objective and Collateral Damage: Their Relationship and Dynamic', *Yearbook of International Humanitarian Law* 7 (2004), p. 37.
9. *Ibid.*, p. 39.
10. The label 'Total War' appeared during the First World War and is often attributed to General Erich Ludendorff and his book *Der Totale Krieg* (1935). The German doctrine of *Kriegsraison geht vor Kriegsmanier* corresponds well with this idea in that it argues that military necessity overrides all law.
11. ICRC, *Commentary Protocol Additional to Geneva Conventions of 12 August 1949, relating to the Protection of Victims of International Armed Conflicts* (1977).
12. *Ibid.*, para. 2020.
13. *Ibid.*, para. 2021.
14. *Ibid.*, para. 2022.
15. *Ibid.*, para. 2022.
16. *Ibid.*, para. 2024.
17. *Ibid.*, paras 1951 and 2017.
18. The principle of military necessity was codified at an early stage of the history of IHL. The 1863 Lieber Code Article 14 defines it as those measures that are indispensable for securing the ends of the war, and that are lawful according to the modern law and usages of war. It is also to be found in the Preamble to the 1868 St Petersburg Declaration and in 1907 Hague IV, Article 23, paragraph (g) of the Annex, which forbids a belligerent to destroy or seize the enemy's

property, unless such destruction or seizure be imperatively demanded by the necessities of war.

19. The identical wording can also be found in Article 3(3c) of the *Protocol on Prohibitions or Restrictions on the Use of Mines, Booby-Traps and Other Devices (Protocol II)*, Geneva, 10 October 1980.

20. Holland, 'Military Objective and Collateral Damage', p. 46.

21. *ICRC, Commentary Protocol Additional to Geneva Conventions of 12 August 1949, and Relating to the Protection of Victims of International Armed Conflicts* (1977), para. 2209.

22. While the term 'humanity' is used in the UK, the US manuals speak of 'unnecessary suffering'. See MoD, *Joint Service Manual on the Law of Armed Conflict* (Oxford: Oxford University Press, 2004), para 2.4. See also *Operational Law Handbook,* ed. Derek I. Grimes, John Rawcliffe and Jeannine Smith (Charlottesville, VA: The Judge Advocate General's Legal Center and School, 2006), p. 13.

23. Jean-François Quéguiner, 'Precautions Under the Law Governing the Conduct of Hostilities', *International Review of the Red Cross* 88, no. 864 (2006), pp. 793–821.

24. DoD, Joint Doctrine Development System, *Chairman of the Joint Chiefs of Staff Instruction (CJCSI)*, no. 5120.02 30 (2004), p. A-1, para. 1b. MoD, British Defence Doctrine, *Joint Warfare Publication*, no. 0-01 (1997), p. 1.2. Oliver Daddow, 'Facing the Future: History in the Writing of British Military Doctrine', *Defence Studies* 2, no. 1 (2002), pp. 157–64.

25. NATO's definition clarifies that doctrine is authoritative but requires judgment in application. NATO Standardisation Agency, NATO Glossary of Terms and Definitions, *Allied Administration Publications*, AAP-6 (2007).

26. *The Israeli Supreme Court Sitting as the High Court of Justice*, Ruling on Targeted Killings, 2006.

27. Derek Jinks, 'The Temporal Scope of Application of International Humanitarian Law in Contemporary Conflicts', paper read at the Informal High-Level Expert Meeting on the Reaffirmation and Development of International Humanitarian Law, at Cambridge, 27–29 June 2003; Enzo Cannizzaro, 'Contextualizing Proportionality: *jus ad bellum* and *jus in bello* in the Lebanese War', *International Review of the Red Cross* 88, no. 864 (2006), pp. 779–92; Avril McDonald, 'Terrorism, Counter-terrorism and the *jus in bello*', in *Terrorism and International Law: Challenges and Responses* (San Remo: International Institute of Humanitarian Law, 2002).

28. President George W. Bush, Address to a Joint Session of Congress and the American People, 2001.

29. Adam Roberts, 'Counter-terrorism, Armed Force and the Laws of War', *Survival* 44, no. 1 (2002), p. 9.

30. Colin Powell, 'U.S. Forces: Challenges Ahead', *Foreign Affairs* 73 (1992), pp. 32–45.

31. Grimes, Rawcliffe and Smith (eds), *Operational Law Handbook*; Joseph B. Berger, Derek Grimes and Eric T. Jensen (eds), *Operational Law Handbook* (Charlottesville, VA: The Judge Advocate General's Legal Center and School, 2004), pp. 14 and 15.

32. While DoD, The Law of Land Warfare, *Field Manual*, vol. no. FM-27-10 (1956). , para. 41, refers to the principle of proportionality by stating that '… loss of life and damage to property incidental to attacks must not be excessive

in relation to the concrete and direct military advantage expected to be gained', AP1 article 51(5)b and 57(2)a(iii) consider that an '... attack which may be expected to cause incidental loss of civilian life, injury to civilians, damage to civilian objects, or a combination thereof, which would be excessive in relation to the concrete and direct military advantage anticipated should be cancelled or suspended'.

33. The author is involved in this training at Sandhurst.

34. DoD, Law of War Program, *Directive*, vol. no. 2311.01E (2006), para. 4.1.

35. DoD, Law of War Program, *Directive*, vol. no. 5100.77 (1998), para. 5.3.1.

36. Grimes, Rawcliffe and Smith (eds), *Operational Law Handbook*, p. 12. The DoD, Implementation of the Law of War Program, *Chairman of the Joint Chiefs of Staff Instruction (CJCSI)*, no. 58101.01A (1999) adds 'unless otherwise directed' by competent authorities, to the quote above. Later versions have dropped the sentence completely.

37. For more details see, on EBA, MoD, *UK Military Effects-Based Operations – An Analytical Concept*, Joint Doctrine and Concept Board, 2005; MoD, The UK Military Effects-Based Approach, *Joint Doctrine Note*, vol. no. 1/05 (2005); MoD, Incorporating and Extending the UK Military Effects Based Approach, *Joint Doctrine Note*, vol. no. 07/06 (2006); DoD, *Major Combat Operations – Joint Operating Concept*, 2004); DoD, *Effects-based Operations*, edited by USJFC, *White Paper Version 1.0*, 2001); DoD, *Operational Implications of Effects-Based Operations (EBO)*, Joint Doctrine Series, Pamphlet 7 (2004c); DoD, *Commander's Handbook for an Effects-Based Approach to Joint Operations*, edited by USJFC, 2006; Edward Smith, *Effects Based Operations – Applying Network Centric Warfare in Peace, Crisis, and War*, DoD Command and Control Research Program, 2002.

38. Mission Command espouses the delegation of authority and the freedom to carry out actions consistent with the intent of the commander. As a philosophy, it attempts to maximise human creativity, initiative and diligence. Having clarified what effect subordinates are to achieve and the reason why it needs to be achieved, commanders allocate appropriate resources, but use a minimum of control measures so as to allow subordinates to decide within their delegated freedom of action how best to achieve their missions. See MoD, British Defence Doctrine, *Joint Warfare Publication*, vol. no. 0-01 (2001), pp. 3–7.

39. 'The manoeuvrist approach to operations is one in which shattering the enemy's overall cohesion and will to fight, rather than his material is paramount. [...] It aims to apply strength against identified vulnerabilities.' *Ibid.*, pp. 3–5.

40. Peter Wielhouver, 'Toward Information Superiority: The Contribution of Operational Net Assessment' *Air & Space Power Journal* 19, no. 3 (2005), pp. 85–97.

41. EBA emphasises that the efficiency of hitting individual targets must not be confused with the effectiveness of achieving campaign objectives. See Maj. Z. Jobbagy, 'Literature Survey on Effects-Based Operations', in TNO, *Secondary Literature Survey on Effects-Based Operations* (2003).

42. MoD, 'Comprehensive Approach', *Joint Discussion Note*, no. 4/05 (2006).

43. The MoD has defined NEC as 'the enhancement of capability through the effective linkage of platforms and people through a network'. MoD, *Delivering Security in a Changing World: Defence White Paper* (December 2003), p. 3. DoD, *The Implementation of Network-Centric Warfare* (Washington, DC, 2005).

44. See MoD, *Network Enabled Capability: An Introduction*, 1.0 edn (2004); MoD, Network Enabled Capability, *Joint Service Publication*, no. 777 (2005).

45. Clausewitz's concept of absolute war contradicts Ludendorff's idea of total war in this aspect, since the former would not accept the subordination of politics to the war effort proposed by the latter.

46. This term was coined by Gen. Charles Krulak to describe a scenario where troops in an urban environment may be confronted by a spectrum of challenges reaching from humanitarian missions, through peace-keeping and peace enforcement-type actions, to full-blown combat, in the span of a few hours and within the space of three contiguous city blocks. See Charles Krulak, 'The Strategic Corporal: Leadership in the Three Block War', *Marines Magazine* (1999), available at: http://www.au.af.mil/au/awc/awcgate/usmc/strategic_corporal.htm.

47. Terrell Turner, *Coalition Forces Help Repair Girls School*, Defend America, DoD News About the War on Terrorism, 2006, available at: http://www.defendamerica.mil/articles/apr2006/a042706dg1.html.

48. Lindsey Cameron, 'Private Military Companies: Their Status under International Humanitarian Law and its Impact on their Regulation'. *International Review of the Red Cross* 88, no. 863 (2006), pp. 573–98. Peter Singer, 'Humanitarian Principles, Private Military Agents: Some Implications of the Privatised Military Industry for the Humanitarian Community', in V.W. and A. Harmer (eds), *Resetting the Rules of Engagement – Trends and Issues in Military–Humanitarian Relations* (London: ODI, 2006); Mark Maxwell, 'The Law of War and Civilians on the Battlefield: Are We Undermining Civilian Protection?', *Military Review* 84, no. 5 (2004), pp. 17–25.

49. Richard Sele, 'Engaging Civil Centres of Gravity and Vulnerabilities', *Military Review* 84, no. 5 (2004), pp. 32–7.

50. ICRC, *Commentary Protocol Additional to Geneva Conventions of 12 August 1949, and relating to the Protection of Victims of International Armed Conflicts* (1977), para. 2023.

51. Marco Sassòli, *Legitimate Target of Attacks under International Humanitarian Law,* International Humanitarian Law Research Initiative, 2003 [cited 1 Jan. 2008], available at: http://www.ihlresearch.org/ihl/pdfs/Session1.pdf, p. 4. *Final Report to the Prosecutor by the Committee Established to Review the NATO Bombing Campaign Against the Federal Republic of Yugoslavia* [cited 1 Jan. 2008], available at: http://www.un.org/icty/pressreal/nato061300.htm, paras 71–2.

52. UK Reservation, Corrected Letter of 28 January 1998 sent to the Swiss Government by Christopher Hulse, HM Ambassador of the United Kingdom; *Protocol Additional to the Geneva Conventions of 12 August 1949, and Relating to the Protection of Victims of International Armed Conflicts (Protocol I)*, 8 June 1977.

53. Grimes, Rawcliffe and Smith (eds), *Operational Law Handbook*, p. 14.

54. Dinah Pokempner, 'Laws of War – Bending the Rules', *World Today* 59, no. 5 (2003), pp. 14–15.

55. Human Rights Watch, *Off Target – The Conduct of the War and Civilian Casualties in Iraq* (2003), available at: http://hrw.org/reports/2003/usa1203/usa1203.pdf, pp. 42–9.

56. ICRC, *Commentary Protocol Additional to Geneva Conventions of 12 August 1949, and relating to the Protection of Victims of International Armed Conflicts* (1977), para. 3479.
57. Smith, 'The New Law of War', p. 367.
58. Human Rights Watch, 'Civilians under Assault – Hezbollah Rocket Attacks on Israel in the 2006 War', available at: http://hrw.org/reports/2007/iopt0807/iopt0807webwcover.pdf.
59. Cannizzaro, 'Contextualizing Proportionality', p. 790.
60. Human Rights Watch, *Fatal Strikes – Israel's Indiscriminate Attacks Against Civilians in Lebanon*, available at: http://hrw.org/reports/2006/lebanon0806/lebanon0806webwcover.pdf; Amnesty International, 'Israel/Lebanon – Deliberate Destruction or "Collateral Damage"?'
61. Joel Greenberg, *Illegal Targeting of Civilians*, Crimes of War Project (2008), available at: www.crimesofwar.org/thebook/civilian-illegal-target.html.
62. Marten Zwanenburg, Hans Boddens Hosang and Niek Wijngaards, 'Humans, Agents and International Humanitarian Law: Dilemmas in Target Discrimination', *BNAIC*, ed. K.T. Katja Verbeeck, Ann Now, Bernard Manderick and Bart Kuijp (Koninklijke Vlaamse Academie van Belie voor Wetenschappen en Kunsten, 2005).
63. Quéguiner, 'Precautions', pp. 798–9.
64. Michael Schmitt, 'The Impact of High and Low-tech Warfare on the Principle of Distinction', International Humanitarian Law Research Initiative, available at: http://www.michaelschmitt.org/images/Hi%20Tech%20Low%20Tech%20Schmitt%20formatted.doc.
65. Schoenekase, 'Targeting Decisions', pp. 26–31.
66. Human Rights Watch, *Off Target*, p. 42.
67. US Air Force, *Operation Iraqi Freedom – Key Themes*, Air Force link, available at: http://www.af.mil/airforceoperationscenter/operationiraqifreedom.asp; Smith, 'The New Law of War', p. 363.
68. Schmitt, 'The Impact of High and Low-Tech Warfare'.
69. Smith, 'The New Law of War'.

8
The Paradox of Value Discourses

Helen Dexter

The president has maintained the US commitment to the Geneva Conventions, whilst recognising that the Convention simply does not cover every situation in which people may be captured or detained by military forces, as we shall see in Afghanistan today … [The president] arrived at a just, principled and practical solution to a difficult issue … *The president did so because, as Americans the way we treat people is a reflection of America's values. The military operates under a code of conduct that upholds these values based on the dignity of every individual.*[1]

PARADOX: A STATEMENT OR PROPOSITION THAT SEEMS
SELF-CONTRADICTORY OR ABSURD BUT IN REALITY
EXPRESSES A POSSIBLE TRUTH[2]

This chapter aims to put the current assault on the Geneva Conventions in its wider political context. The US and its allies fight brutal wars, restrict civil liberties, deny human rights and denigrate humanitarian law in the name of democracy, liberty and the good of humanity. Given the definition above, a paradox may be the best way for us to understand the apparent contradiction between contemporary discourses of humanitarianism and cosmopolitanism and the violence that accompanies them. The chapter begins by tracing the development of a norm of humanitarian intervention after the end of the Cold War. It is important to put the war on terror and its humanitarian motivations within a context where, to quote Lawler,

[f]rom the point of view of the key members of the international community at least, armed 'humanitarian intervention' is no longer just a form of war but has become virtually synonymous with permissible war itself.[3]

The chapter then examines NATO's controversial air campaign in Kosovo and the perceived legality/legitimacy gap that has opened up. The Kosovo campaign is important because it places the US's assessment of the Geneva Conventions within a context where the applicability of international law in an apparently changed international environment was already in question.

Finally, this chapter puts the current treatment of the Geneva Conventions by the Bush administration within the context of neo-conservative political thought. The US's vision of global politics saw itself engaged in a battle between good and evil upholding values that derive their legitimacy from God. As such, the US answered to a law above and beyond international law. From the birth of their nation, Americans have believed that the values on which they based their government are universal. As such, any force that may be required to uphold these values is considered benign. Violence may be a necessary, but *unintended* consequence.

Today, debate about the nature of international security threats and the way to counter them is dominated by discussions of values. For the resort to force to be considered legitimate it must be seen to serve the interests of humanity as well as the state that employs it. Indeed, as Weiss admits, in the post-Cold War world, 'little else besides humanitarian impulses and human rights often seems to inspire Western foreign policy'.[4] In the post-Cold War world (yet, one should add, before the situation in Iraq had descended into a protracted and bloody insurgency) a norm of humanitarian intervention had developed in the international community.

In the new normative context of the post-Cold War era where states were no longer threatened by external powers, debate about the concept and role of state sovereignty developed both within academia and policy circles. The culmination of this debate has been the 2001 Report of The International Commission on Intervention and State Sovereignty (ICISS) entitled *The Responsibility to Protect.*[5] *The Responsibility to Protect* was a project organised by the Canadian Government in response to UN Secretary-General Kofi Annan's calls for a new consensus on the question of intervention, following the controversy of NATO's actions in Kosovo. In 1999, NATO launched an air campaign against Serbian forces in Kosovo without the backing of the UN. Serbian leader Slobodan Milošević had been carrying out a policy of ethnic cleansing in Kosovo yet likely vetoes from Russia and China in the UN Security Council led to suggestions that international law guiding the recourse to armed force was ill suited to post-Cold War world.

Kosovo also highlighted the apparently new, degenerate nature of the warfare that the West was encountering. This was war where civilians rather than soldiers were primary targets. Ethnic cleansing, systematic rape and mutilation driven by identity politics and criminality characterised these new types of conflicts as experienced in the Balkans and sub-Saharan Africa in the 1990s. Mary Kaldor argued that these new conflicts blurred the lines between war and human rights abuses.[6] Faced with such moral outrages politicians and academics alike argued that force could not be guided by such sterile legalism that would, as in Rwanda in 1994, allow genocide to happen. Rather, a more flexible, ethically guided framework was appropriate. The war on terror has also been portrayed as new kind of war fought by networks of terrorists who deliberately target civilians. Again, the degenerate nature of warfare led to disparaging of international law, in particular the denial by the Bush administration of the applicability of the Geneva Conventions to al-Qaeda suspects held in Guantánamo Bay detention centre. A White House spokesman explained:

> The war on terrorism is a war not envisaged when the Geneva Conventions was signed in 1949. In this war global terrorists transcend national boundaries and intentionally target the innocent.[7]

The post-Cold War era has, then, seen a return of Just War reasoning demonstrated not only in the justifications offered by the US for the war in Iraq but in the 'doctrine of the International community' as variously set out by the then British Prime Minister Tony Blair in 1999, in the Kosovo Report,[8] the ICISS document and recent reports by the UN. Recent developments have, then, moved to separate humanitarianism from international law. International law concerning intervention is presented as simply not living up to western moral standards. Blair's comments here are illuminating:

> It may be that under international law as presently constituted, a regime can systematically brutalise and oppress its people and there is nothing anyone can do when dialogue, diplomacy and even sanctions fail, unless it comes within the definition of a humanitarian catastrophe (though the 300,000 remains in mass graves already found in Iraq might be thought by some

to be something of a catastrophe). *This may be the law, but should it be?*[9]

By 2001 and the launch of the war on terror by the Bush administration in the US, the use of armed force by western states was deeply enmeshed in progressive politics. 'War', as George Bernard Shaw concluded, 'is no longer the prerogative of international criminals but the first resort of the righteous.'[10] The war in Iraq served to demonstrate this. Not sanctioned by the UN, opinion about the legitimacy of the invasion fractured the political spectrum, with hawks and doves on both the left and the right. How do you justify the illegal use of force, asked the doves? How do you justify leaving Saddam Hussein, a man who has used chemical weapons against his own people, replied the hawks. In March 2004 President Bush posed these questions himself:

> Who would prefer that Saddam's torture chambers still be open? Who would wish that more mass graves were still being filled? Who would begrudge the Iraqi people their long-awaited liberation? One year after the armies of liberation arrived, every soldier who has fought, every aid worker who has served, every Iraqi who has joined in their country's defence can look with pride on a brave and historic achievement. They've served freedom's cause, and that is a privilege.[11]

Our paradox, then, is that the war on terror has seen international law labelled as morally redundant: the US derogation from the Geneva Conventions; rendition flights; abuse and torture at Abu Ghraib; the alleged massacre of civilians by western troops;[12] around 80,000 civilian deaths from violence in Iraq alone;[13] indefinite detention without trial or charge in the UK;[14] and the erosion of civil liberties in the name of freedom, democracy and *humanity*.

The actions of the US and UK, then, seem to contradict entirely the humanitarian rhetoric that is used to justify them. It could be argued that humanitarian motives for warfare are simply a mask for more traditional power politics. As this chapter will demonstrate, the relationship between values and violence is in fact far more complex. To return to the definition that opens this chapter, a paradox is 'a statement or proposition that seems self-contradictory or absurd but in reality *expresses a possible truth*'. Rather than arguing that the actions of the US and UK simply contradict the language of values, this chapter seeks to demonstrate how those values have in fact enabled violence by creating and maintaining moral identities.

A NEW WORLD ORDER

'From the start the Kosovo problem has been about how we should react when bad things happen in unimportant places.'[15] So said Thomas Friedman of the *New York Times*. But the question of whether and how to act when strangers' lives are threatened has been pondered over since the end of the Second World War and the establishment of the UN Charter. The UN Charter was designed to limit all recourses to force by national governments. Only in self-defence could a state resort to military engagement. Military interventions have of course continued after 1945 – many of which were condemned by the UN.

The rule of non-intervention established in the Charter was reinforced in the 1970s by the Declaration on Principles of International Law Concerning Friendly Relations and Co-operation, which stated:

> The practice of any form of intervention not only violates the spirit and letter of the Charter, but also leads to the creation of situations which threaten international peace and security.[16]

In a search for international stability, the Charter was interpreted as putting the right of state sovereignty above all else. A textual interpretation of the Charter makes any interference by a foreign state into the domestic politics of another illegal. During the Cold War, it was maintained that the use of force to save non-nationals from human rights abuses was a violation of the Charter. The UN could only sanction force if 'international peace and security' was threatened.

The end of the Cold War convinced (western) states that their existence was no longer threatened by their neighbours. The realist 'security dilemma' has been reversed; threats to the state are now more likely to be found within borders than from outside them.[17] Untied from superpower confrontation, and emerging from the shadow of the nuclear threat, the end of the Cold War saw the international community finally in a position to bring about a new world order. No longer did the logic of the Cold War prevail. As the British Prime Minister proclaimed in the now often-quoted speech to the Chicago Economic Club: 'Now our actions are guided by a more subtle blend of mutual self interest and moral purpose in defending the values we cherish.'[18]

The end of the Cold War framework, it has also been suggested, made it less likely that interventions would escalate into larger conflicts. The so-called new threats to international security identified after the Cold War – intra-state war, ethnic cleansing, genocide and terrorism – have the victimisation of civilians at their heart. The revolution in communications technology has meant that atrocities in the farthest corners of the world can be broadcast on TV sets in cosy western homes. That pleas for help can be posted on the Internet makes it all the more difficult for the distress of others to be ignored. The resulting pressure from an emotive electorate has made national governments more likely to act to 'save strangers'.

The change in international normative context has also come from the growth of human rights law. Stemming originally from the UN Charter itself, the obligation of states to respect their citizens was consolidated in the 1948 Universal Declaration of Human Rights and the Genocide Convention of the same year, and again in the two International Covenants on human rights written in 1966.[19] Limits have been set on how governments can treat their citizens, and a culture of 'individual rights' has developed in the West. A massive growth in Non-Governmental Organisations (NGOs) dedicated to the promotion of human rights has seen pressure for governments to be more involved in this work develop from these new grass-roots organisations.

This change in public attitude has been officially acknowledged. The 2002 paper, *The Future Strategic Context for Defence* issued by the British Ministry of Defence, stated that:

> Increasing emotional attachment to the outside world fuelled by immediate and graphic coverage and a public desire to see the UK act as a force for good is likely to lead to public support and possibly public demand for operations prompted by humanitarian motives.[20]

This led the analyst to conclude that: 'Pressure to mount military operations for "moral" reasons will increase.'[21]

It was during the war in the former Yugoslavia that the term 'ethnic cleansing' entered the political vocabulary. The much-criticised 1992 UN mission in Bosnia demonstrated the futility of traditional peace-keeping principles when there was in fact, 'no peace to keep'.[22] This, combined with the disastrous militarised humanitarian mission in Somalia, meant that when warned of, and then confronted with genocide in Rwanda, calls from the UN for troops were ignored, and the 'international community' stood by and let it happen.

Particularly since the international community's unwillingness (or, as President Clinton would have it, simple inability) to act in the face of genocide in Rwanda in April 1994, the United Nations is now criticised for intervening too little rather than too much, as Tony Blair's comments above illustrate. By the 1990s it was generally accepted that the UN should take a more interventionist role to prevent and cope with crimes that shock the conscience of humankind. The change in international norms that has been under way since the Cold War ended was most decisively demonstrated in the NATO military intervention on Kosovo in 1999 – an intervention that did not have prior authorisation by the UN Security Council.

It was the NATO bombing of Serbian targets in Kosovo in 1999 that has caused the most controversy surrounding humanitarian intervention. Much of this controversy arose because NATO powers, led by the United States and the United Kingdom, took the decision to act in Kosovo without prior UN authorisation. The military intervention in Kosovo brought the notion of the legality of humanitarian intervention directly into the spotlight and raised questions about the very utility of the UN Charter in the new international environment. Louis Henkin summarised some of the issues that Kosovo raised:

> Was the military intervention by NATO justified lawful under the UN Charter and international law? Does Kosovo suggest the need for reaffirmation or clarification or modification of the law as to humanitarian intervention? What should the law be and can the law be construed or modified to what it ought to be?[23]

The Independent International Commission on Kosovo (IICK) and *Report of the International Commission on Intervention and State Sovereignty* that followed the conflict aimed to answer many of these questions and made a substantial step forward in redefining sovereignty and responsibility of states in order to set a clear foundation for the right of intervention by the international community.

No one could argue that there had not been a humanitarian crisis in Kosovo. Ethnic Albanians were suffering at the hands of the Milošević government, although atrocities were being carried out to some extent by all parties to the conflict. Continuing media coverage only added to the sense that something needed to be done. NATO's actions in Kosovo have split opinion. On the one hand, those who support the intervention argue that with no territorial gain, no desire for regime change and no national interest other than restoring peace to Europe, NATO acted in the truest humanitarian fashion. At the other end of the spectrum are those who believe that in Kosovo NATO simply committed a criminal act.[24]

After its perceived failure in both Bosnia and Rwanda, the Clinton administration, Richard Falk argues, did not believe the UN was capable of dealing with the situation in Kosovo, and this belief was shared by many of the European leaders.[25] The stakes were high in Kosovo, and the embarrassing paralysis demonstrated by the leading nations over the genocide in Rwanda in 1994 could not be repeated. The fiftieth anniversary of NATO was also approaching and the credibility of the alliance was on the line. Those calling for intervention claimed that all efforts to find a diplomatic solution had been exhausted. With Russia and China clearly willing to veto any UN resolution to authorise action, the only response was to deal with the situation from outside the framework of the UN.

Having not condemned the intervention after it began, and by accepting the responsibility of post-conflict peace-keeping and reconstruction, the UN could be interpreted as having given its approval to NATO's intervention in the only way it could, given the deadlock in the Security Council. For those opposed to the intervention, the veto, rather than hindering the functioning of the UN, worked exactly as it should, limiting the use of force in a situation where there was not full agreement in the Security Council for its need. Thus Falk summarises,

> In this reading of the Charter, all uses of non-defensive force are strictly controlled by the UN Security Council, and to bypass its authority on the basis of a self-serving evasion of prospective vetoes is to take the law into one's own hands unacceptably.[26]

Yet, Falk continues, to condemn the intervention solely because it was not legal on paper is not *morally* appropriate within the new normative context, arguing that,

> To regard the textual barriers to humanitarian intervention as decisive in the face of genocidal behaviour is politically and morally unacceptable, especially in the view of the qualifications

imposed on unconditional claims of sovereignty by the expanded conception of international human rights.[27]

The Kosovo Report, compiled by the IICK, of which Falk was a member, also took this view, concluding that NATO's action were 'illegal, but legitimate'.[28]

THE WAR IN IRAQ: 'ILLEGAL BUT LEGITIMATE?'

Tony Blair, on a number of occasions, had linked changing norms in regard to humanitarian intervention and his decision to go to war in Iraq. In an interview with the BBC Arabic Service, Blair reiterated that even with the benefit of hindsight not only would he have gone ahead with the war but that the military action in Iraq was part of an important change in international relations:

> I think there is something else that is going on at a broader level here in international relations where we are slowly learning that this doctrine that has held sway for a long period of time, that it doesn't matter how brutally a country's people are oppressed, the outside world stands by and does nothing, that that doctrine has not really got a place in the 21st century. We should be saying that there are certain basic principles of human justice that should be upheld everywhere, and that it should be the function of the international community, working together and operating on a proper basis, to try and bring that hope to all the people of the world.[29]

In an interview on the BBC programme *Newsnight*, hosted by Jeremy Paxman, the then British International Development Secretary Hilary Benn explicitly linked the case of Kosovo to that of Iraq. When questioned as to how the UK and US justify their role as global policemen Benn replied thus:

> *Benn:*
> Kosovo is another very good example where you could make exactly the same argument. Why did we take military action in Kosovo? We went in, in that case to save lives despite the fact that there wasn't UN support for that action because there had been a veto in the Security Council. So in the end people made a judgment in those circumstances. The UN *is* a very important institution and the role it has played in Iraq subsequently to the

military action has helped to move the political process along which is what the Iraqi people want because frankly after thirty years of trauma and brutalisation and impoverishment, which is what the Iraqi people had under Saddam ...

Paxman:
That is another point altogether; that is not why we went to war.

Benn:
No it isn't. But it is a consequence of having taken the military action to enforce the UN resolutions that the Iraqi people now for the first time have a chance of a better life, and I for one think they deserve it.[30]

THE REVIVAL OF THE 'JUST WAR'

NATO's intervention into Kosovo is now at the centre of debate about the appropriate justification for military conflict – a debate that has intensified since the military intervention in Iraq. Is a war justified because it is legal, or because it is considered legitimate? What would be the appropriate source of such legitimacy? The failure of the UN to sanction an intervention in Kosovo prompted the argument that international law is not the appropriate mechanism to guide humanitarian intervention.

The gap that opened up between the illegality of NATO's operations in Kosovo and its apparent legitimacy is being filled by a revival of Just War theorising. The rising prominence of human rights, media coverage of humanitarian disasters and the changing understanding of sovereignty mean that for many commentators, politicians and academics alike, a new ethical approach was needed when considering recourse to armed force in response to humanitarian catastrophes. The apparent changing nature of conflict that now saw civilians as primary targets meant that a new approach was called for, one that lay between 'sterile legalism' and 'political nihilism'.[31] Given that the UN failed to sanction a second resolution, one that would have endorsed the use of force in Iraq in 2003, the final judgment of the Iraq war may now rest within this legality/legitimacy gap that Kosovo opened up. In the new era of the war on terror, Falk writes,

[t]he relevance or obsolescence of international law has become a matter of intense controversy and relates to whether the just

war framework provides a solution for those who seek to bring principles discussion to the debate.[32]

Indeed, from the start the war on terror and its military operations to date have been justified from within a Just War framework.[33] Making the distinction between *jus in bello* (just methods in war) and *jus ad bellum* (just motivations for warfare), for a war to be considered just it must meet three conditions: first, that it be properly declared by a sovereign authority; second, there must be a just cause; and third, that it must employ just means.[34] These principles have long been and continue to be debated.

In Richard Jackson's opinion the public language used to discursively construct the War on Terror has been 'moulded closely on what has become known as traditional just war theory':

> In part, this close reading of just war theory is designed to appeal to the Bush administration's conservative Christian supporters who are more likely to endorse a theologically defined just war – as opposed to one solely justified by national security. At the same time, it is moulded on popular 'good guy' versus 'bad guy' binaries, as well as the Pentagon's public relations template for 'selling' wars to the public.[35]

However, this 'just war' rationale has extended beyond the war on terror directly to justification for the use of force by the international community more widely. Although it is true that a theologically based justification for the war on terror would have appealed to President Bush's Christian supporters, the choice of a Just War framework in which to situate the wars in Afghanistan and Iraq is by no means unique to the neoconservatives.

In the immediate aftermath of NATO's intervention in Kosovo and before George W. Bush had taken power in the US, British Prime Minister Tony Blair was already espousing a Just War framework to guide recourse to armed force in his Doctrine of International Community. When deciding when to intervene Blair argued that there were five factors to take into consideration:

> First, are we sure of our case? War is an imperfect instrument for righting humanitarian distress, but armed force is sometimes the only means of dealing with dictators. Second, have we exhausted all diplomatic options? We should always give peace every chance, as we have in the case of Kosovo. Third, on the basis of a practical

assessment of the situation, are there military operations we can sensibly and prudently undertake? Fourth, are we prepared for the long term? ... And finally, do we have national interests involved? ... I am not suggesting that these are absolute tests. But they are the kind of issues we need to think about in deciding in the future when and whether we will intervene.

It should be noted that Blair's final criterion here, that national interests should be involved, is not a condition of traditional Just War theory. A war cannot be considered just if national interests are paramount in the decision to take military action. Right intent, however, is a condition of Just War theory, and it is questionable to what extent right intent can be divorced entirely from national interests. Nevertheless, Blair's speech serves to demonstrate that policy-makers and academics alike were seeking to situate debates about the justification for the use of force within an *ethical* framework rather than a strictly legal or instrumental one. Both the Kosovo Report and the International Commission on Intervention and State Sovereignty can, according to Falk, be best understood as a rewriting of Just War theory to fit the dilemmas of humanitarian intervention. Just War was apparently also embraced by the former UN Secretary-General Kofi Annan as demonstrated in his March 2005 report, *In Larger Freedom*. Setting out the future direction of the institution in the wake of the 2003 invasion of Iraq, the report proposed that:

> When considering whether to authorize or endorse the use of military force, the Council should come to a common view on how to weigh the seriousness of the threat; the proper purpose of the proposed military action; whether means short of the use of force might plausibly succeed in stopping the threat; whether the military option is proportional to the threat at hand; and whether there is a reasonable chance of success.[36]

The principles set out by the Secretary-General to guide any recourse to force replicate almost exactly the principles of the Just War doctrine.

VIOLENCE AS MORALLY REQUIRED: THE RETURN OF THE 'GOOD WAR'

In the current Just War revival, just cause is linked explicitly to humanitarian values rather than state security. A war is considered just if it is deemed morally motivated. Just War theory has its origins in the theology of St Augustine and his break with Christian pacifism. Augustine argued that violence was sometimes required in the search for justice, rather than peace.[37] Just War theory presents itself as the moderate middle ground between two extreme positions: realism, which views war as a rational continuation of politics, and pacifism, which denies absolutely the use of force:

> The Just War position has the virtue of accommodating both our deep desire for peace and commitment to what might be termed 'human rights'. War is rightfully considered an evil, but it is nevertheless deemed necessary under certain circumstances to combat the evil or violated rights or what Augustine refers to as 'unjust peace'.[38]

Although Just War theory rejects the use of violence for imperialist gains, as an act of aggression, or as a preventative strike, by linking warfare to the search for justice, Just War theory creates what Burke refers to as 'a norm of war'.[39] Pacifism, Geller argues, becomes an argument struggling to be heard with 'the call of justice beckoning in the background'.[40] According to this argument, violence is not only on occasion morally acceptable, it is morally *required*. Failure to act then becomes immoral.

The belief that violence is not merely justifiable but in fact morally required complements Shaw's belief that the end of the Cold War has seen not merely a revival of Just Wars but the return of 'Good Wars'. A 'Good War' is not merely a rational and justifiable response to a threat but rather a moral response to an injustice – an act of good.[41]

> For most of the last century, the liberal conscience found most war and war preparation irredeemably bad. The Allied fight in the Second World War and some liberation struggles were major partial exceptions. The former was further legitimated retrospectively by the Holocaust; nowadays, the ever-growing commemoration of that old evil lends authority to military action against its present day echoes. War is struggling out of the closet and into the limelight of progressive approval.[42]

Good Wars are fought not simply to defeat an enemy but rather as an expression of values. The attacks of September 11, 2001 presented the Bush administration with their just cause. Labelling these instances of terrorism as an act of war, the war on terror was presented as a legally acceptable act of self-defence. More than this, the war on terror has been portrayed as a crusade for freedom, a war fought in defence of liberty, a quest for justice. The operation in Iraq extended this rhetoric further: democratic values would be transferred and the oppressed would be liberated. The war on terror has been presented as nothing less than a 'virtuous' campaign.[43]

AMERICAN VALUES AS UNIVERSAL VALUES

For the neoconservatives in the Bush administration, the conflict in which they were involved was not merely to defeat insurgency in Iraq and the Taliban in Afghanistan; and the war on terror did not represent a wider battle between East and West, or even a clash of civilisations. In the neoconservative vision of international politics, the war on terror was nothing less than a battle of good versus evil. Although in practice the military action of the war on terror so far has been the antithesis of humanitarianism, it has been inspired and legitimised by an appeal to universal values. This appeal to values is often taken as a public relations exercise. Humanitarian language can too easily be viewed as a mask for traditional, realist power politics. The analysis in this chapter, however, supports Rhodes's assertion that '[i]t is necessary to take seriously the Bush administration's vision of global politics':

> It is important however to avoid the temptation to dismiss the Bush administration's rhetoric as window-dressing or to assume that it obscures more cynical, but also more traditional approach to politics ... the Bush administration's actions make sense if one accepts that the president actually means what he says.[44]

It is more comfortable to assume that bad things (the detention and torture of terrorist suspects and the denial of their human rights, for example) are only undertaken for what we consider to be 'bad' reasons. It is less comfortable to believe that very bad actions stem from a genuine desire to do good.

Great evil is stirring in the world,' Bush warned in 2002.[45] This evil did not merely threaten the US. Rather it threatened all who share in those values that the US holds dear: liberty, democracy and free markets. For neoconservatives, people regardless of nationality or culture share a common view of how the world should be – all except, of course, for a few rogue elements, Saddam Hussein and Osama bin Laden being among them.[46] Therefore, when America acts in its own interests, it in fact acts in the interests of all. 'We know', William Bennet wrote in 2000, 'that in nations where political stability, the rule of law, basic freedoms and economic prosperity take root, American values are advanced.'[47] Yet, '[b]ehind our attempts to advance American ideals abroad has been the belief that basic rights are unalienable, universal, God-given and therefore that all people, wherever they may be, are deserving of them'.[48]

Although embodied in the founding of the American nation, the ideals enshrined in the Declaration of Independence are not considered within neoconservative thought to be particular in any way to America – they are universally valid. Take, for example, Caesar who argues:

> We know from experience that when acting for universal principles as we understand them we can often count on the support of many allies who have come to share the same fundamental views, not because they are American ideas, but because they have a rational claim to universal validity.[49]

According to Robert Kagan, the principles of the Declaration of Independence are not merely the choices of a particular culture but are 'universal, enduring, "self-evident" truths'.[50]

AMERICAN VIOLENCE AS BENIGN VIOLENCE

Because rights in the neoconservative tradition are inalienable, universal and God-given, in order to protect and advance them the US answers to a law above both national and international law. In a remark that helps us contextualise the Bush administration's relationship to the Geneva Conventions George W. Bush states:

> [A]ll these duties and all these rights are ultimately traced to a source of law and justice above our wills and beyond our politics – [to] an author of our dignity who calls us to act worthy of our dignity.[51]

It is the universal foundations of neoconservative political philosophy that leads the Bush administration to wholeheartedly believe that the US wields *benign* power. Although some of the methods necessary to defeat terrorism may have unfortunate consequences, be they the deaths of innocent civilians, the denial of human rights, derogating from the Geneva Conventions or the restriction of civil liberties, these are always *unintended* effects, sacrifices made in the name of a higher purpose. To quote again from Caesar:

America is not interested in territorial conquest, subjugation of others or world domination. ... Because the political values that are at the core of the United States' existence are honourable and estimable, the judgement of history is likely to be positive.[52]

This benign use of violence is contrasted sharply with the violence that characterises the so-called 'new' warfare that the US is having to counter. To refer back to the position of the White House, '[t]he war on terrorism is a war not envisaged when the Geneva Conventions was signed in 1949'. Colin McInnes suggests that the events of September 11, 2001 indeed represent a transformation warfare arguing that, 'they appear to break the pattern of war established by the West in the 1990s'[53] In part what characterises these acts as something novel is that they did not try to avoid collateral damage: 'The terrorist attacks either did not accept any distinction between legitimate targets and collateral damage or did not care about it.'[54] 'This', concludes McInnes, 'appeared to be some new form of warfare which passed not only traditional understandings of instrumental force, but acceptable norms of conduct in war.'[55] Whereas the US invaded Iraq with 'overwhelming force', emotive terms like 'genocide', 'slaughter' and 'ethnic cleansing' establish non-western warfare as qualitatively different to the kinds of killing that the West is involved with. This, as Jackson argues, 'functions as a means of distancing our purportedly civilised, humane and technologically-driven forms of warfare from their uncivilised and "dirty" kinds of warfare'.[56]

IN THE NAME OF HUMANITY: THE PARADOX OF VALUE DISCOURSES

Although at first glance humanitarianism may seem a very inclusive concept, it can also be a divisive linguistic tool cleanly separating the humane (or human) from the inhumane (or non-human), 'demarcating the democrat and the despot, the human rights advocate and the human rights abuser, and ultimately the human and the sub-human...'[57] The Bush administration claimed both to represent and preserve the 'international community', 'civilisation' and 'humanity'. These terms, as Jeremy Moses and Helen M. Kinsella[58] acknowledge, have become synonymous.[59] The significance of this is not widely acknowledged. Within international relations theory, the term 'international community' is accepted as being somewhat ambiguous.

When using the term, an effort should be made to establish who exactly is and is not a member of the international community. Is it the preserve of states alone or perhaps only a core set of democratic states, the 'West'? Are international institutions, NGOs and civil society also members? If international community is now synonymous with humanity, does this mean that the international community includes all of humanity, or that 'humanity' consists only of those entities said to make up the international community? According to the Bush administration, terrorism had never threatened the US alone, nor has the war on terror been solely the fight of the US. In November 2001, Bush told the United Nations that:

> Civilization, itself, the civilization we share, is threatened. History will record our response, and judge or justify every nation in this hall. The civilized world is now responding.[60]

For any community to exist it must identify itself in relation to an 'other'. For membership to be inclusive it must at the same time be exclusive – that is to say, in order for membership in that community to make sense, there must also be non-members. Can this also be true for humanity? Who could exist outside of global humanity? Humanity, used in this sense, is less a biologically descriptive word but rather a political, and normatively powerful term. It is only by identifying those who oppose civilisation, who defy the international community or display inhumanity that the Bush administration could claim itself to be not only representing, but leading, global humanity. In order for there to be humanity there must exist a sub-human.

Jackson argues that each age has its own 'bogey man', and that in recent years the 'communist spy' has been replaced by the terrorist. In Tony Blair's Doctrine of the International Community inspired by NATO's 'humanitarian' war against Serbia, rogue states, failed states, tyrants and barbarians all represented the 'sub-human'.[61] Within the rhetoric of the war on terror, it is the terrorist who clearly exists 'outside' humanity and hence is not entitled to the same human rights as others – including the Geneva Conventions. 'Specific rights of war are granted only to those identified as already within the ambit of civilisation and, so it appears, humanity itself.'[62]

The US approach to the Geneva Conventions in particular demonstrates the complex relationship that existed between the

Bush administration and international law. As Kinsella points out, the US has only argued that the Third Geneva Convention, that which sets out the rights of prisoners of war (POWs)[63] is not applicable to the changed circumstances of the war on terror while continuing to uphold the Fourth Geneva Convention relative to the protection of civilians. It may be mistaken to believe that the US only upholds international law where it serves its strategic purposes. There appear to be few if any strategic reasons for not giving POW status to battlefield detainees from Afghanistan. A POW may be detained until the holding state feels that they are no longer a threat to security; therefore, denying POW status does not alter the length of time for which detainees can be held. POWs can be questioned; therefore, this legal status does not prevent intelligence-gathering. There is also no clear relationship between the status of the detainee and the manner in which trials for breaches of the laws of war were to be carried out by the US.[64]

There is, of course, much evidence from both Afghanistan and Iraq that the US had employed methods of interrogation that contradict the principles of the Geneva Conventions. When pushed on this matter the US has maintained that the denial of POW status to Afghani prisoners thought to be linked to al-Qaeda is not so that harsher methods of interrogation may be used. Under the Bush administration the position of the US was that while such detainees are not legally entitled to the protection of the Geneva Conventions they will be treated in a manner 'consistent with the principles of the Geneva Convention'.[65] This position then reinforces the moral superiority of the US, which extends 'humane' treatment to those it classes as unworthy of it.

In contrast, the US has been at pains to up hold the Fourth Convention relative to the protection of civilians in war.[66] In order to defend civilisation, the US must defend civilians. In the Bush administration's bifurcated moral universe the 'evil' terrorist is offset by the 'innocent' civilian. It is the protection and care shown to civilians that marks the civilised world from the barbarians. On the first anniversary of the terrorist attacks on the US Bush told the American people: 'Our deepest national conviction is that every life is precious, because every life is the gift of a Creator who intended us to live in liberty and equality. More than anything else, this separates us from the enemy we fight. We value every life; our enemies value none – not even the innocent, not even their own.'[67]

The Fourth Geneva Convention serves to constrain the strategic actions of the US in the war on terror far more significantly than the Third.[68] Yet, the US complies with the Fourth Convention because it is essential to its own identity as 'civilised' and 'humane/human' and to the identity of the terrorist as uncivilised, inhumane/sub-human. The disparity between US compliance with the Fourth Geneva Convention but not with the Third is not simply *because* of these opposite moral identities; rather, US compliance and non-compliance with the Geneva Conventions *creates* and *sustains* these moral identities.

The value-driven security policies of both the US and, one could argue, the UK, not only set out the identity of those who exist beyond humanity, it actively seeks to eliminate those who would challenge that agenda. In his speech to the Chicago Economic Club, Tony Blair made this appeal to the American nation to join with Britain to, 'work with you, *fashion with you* the design of a future built on peace and prosperity for all, which is the only dream that makes humanity worth preserving' (emphasis added).[69] There are two implications in this statement. First, that the future designed by Britain and America is the only design that is worthy of humanity. Second, that this is a design that need not necessarily come about unaided. It must be *fashioned*. A shared belief in the doctrine of Just War means that both Bush and Blair shared the belief that violence can be not only morally justifiable, but also *morally required* in certain circumstances. Violence, in the context of humanitarian intervention, can be used as a progressive tool as well as 'corrective discipline'.[70]

How can one purport to represent humanity and at the same time carry out a foreign policy that denies basic human rights to others? The answer is that those others exist outside of global humanity. And so, then, we return to our paradox. It does indeed seem self-contradictory and absurd that illiberal practices are being pursued by western states in the name of liberty and democracy and that human rights are denied in the name of humanity. Yet to view these value discourses as simply a way of excusing violence is to miss the complex relationship between morality, values and violence.

NOTES

1. Statement by the US White House Press Secretary on the Geneva Conventions, 7 May 2003, available at: http://www.whitehouse.gov/news/releases/2003/05/20030507-18.html [consulted 11 November 2007].

2. Paradox: Dictionary.com Unabridged (v 1.1), Random House, Inc., available at: http://dictionary.reference.com/browse/paradox.
3. Peter Lawler, 'The Good War After September 11th', *Government and Opposition* 37, no. 2 (2002), p. 151.
4. Thomas G. Weiss, 'Researching Humanitarian Intervention: Some Lessons', *Journal of Peace Research* 38, no. 2 (2001), p. 421.
5. *Report of the International Commission on Intervention and State Sovereignty, The Responsibility to Protect* (Ottawa: International Development Research Centre, 2001).
6. Mary Kaldor, *New And Old Wars: Organised Violence in a Global Era* (Cambridge: Polity Press, 2001).
7. Statement by US White House Press Secretary, 7 May 2003.
8. Independent International Commission on Kosovo, *The Kosovo Report*, available at: http://www.reliefweb.int/library/documents/thekosovoreport.htm.
9. Tony Blair, speech on the threat of global terrorism, 5 March 2004, available at: http://www.number10.gov.uk/output/Page5461.asp (italics added).
10. Martin Shaw, 'The Return of the Good War' (2001), available at: http://www. theglobalsite.ac.uk/press/104shaw.htm [consulted 2 November 2007].
11. George W. Bush, Remarks by the President on Operation Iraqi Freedom and Operation Enduring Freedom, delivered in the East Room, 2004, available at: http://www.whitehouse.gov/news/releases/2004/03/20040319-3.html [consulted 2 November 2007].
12. The Subhani district in Haditha, Iraq, was the sight of an alleged massacre of 15 Iraqi civilians by US marine troops in November 2005. The official version of events claims that civilians were killed by a roadside bomb blast. Eyewitnesses claimed that civilians were shot dead by US soldiers. See: http://new.bbc.co.uk/2/ hi/middle_east/5033648.stm.
13. http://www.iraqbodycount.org/. At the time of writing, the Iraq Body Count estimate civilian deaths from violence in Iraq to be between 77,323 and 84,240.
14. The Anti-terrorism, Crime and Security Act 2001 allowed the UK Home Secretary to detain indefinitely any non-British citizen suspected of terrorist activity pending deportation. In 2004 the House of Lords ruled that this was contrary to human rights law. For more information, see: http://news.bbc. co.uk/2/hi/uk_news/4100481.stm.
15. Noam Chomsky, *The New Military Humanism, Lessons From Kosovo* (London: Pluto Press, 1999), p. 5.
16. Cited in Adam Roberts, 'Humanitarian War: Military Intervention and Human Rights', *International Affairs* 69, no. 3 (1993), p. 433.
17. The 'war on terror' arguably still leans upon the language of 'external threat' plus the risk of an 'enemy within'.
18. Tony Blair, 'Prime Minister's Speech: Doctrine of the International Community at the Economic Club' (1999), available at: http://www.pm.gov.uk/output/ Page1297.asp.
19. Nicolas Wheeler, *Saving Strangers: Humanitarian Intervention in International Society* (Oxford: Oxford University Press, 2002), p. 1.
20. 'The Future Strategic Context for Defence' (2001), available at: http://www. mod.uk/NR/rdonlyres/7CC94DFB-839A-4029-8BDD-5E87AF5CDF45/0/ future_strategic_context.pdf.
21. *Ibid.*

22. Jonathan Gilmore, 'What Peace to Keep? The International Community's Response to the War in Bosnia-Herzegovina, 1992–95', unpublished MA thesis, University of Manchester, 2003.

23. Louis Henkin, 'Kosovo and the Law of "Humanitarian Intervention"', *American Journal of International Law* 93, no. 4 (1999), p. 24.

24. Richard Falk, 'Kosovo, World Order, and the Future of International Law', *American Journal of International Law* 93, no. 4 (1999), p. 848.

25. *Ibid.*

26. *Ibid*, p. 850.

27. *Ibid*, p. 853.

28. Independent International Commission on Kosovo, *The Kosovo Report.*

29. Prime Minister Tony Blair interview with the BBC Arabic Service, 16 December 2003, available at: http://www.number-10.gov.uk/output/Page5060.asp.

30. Hilary Benn interviewed on *Newsnight*, broadcast Wednesday, 17 March 2004 on BBC2, available at: http://news.bbc.co.uk/1/hi/programmes/newsnight/3513850.stm.

31. Richard Falk, 'Legality to Legitimacy: The Revival of the Just War Framework', *Harvard International Review* 26, no. 1 (2004), available at: http://hir.harvard.edu/articles/1215.

32. *Ibid.*

33. Here, these principles are as defined by Joseph McKenna in 1960: (1) the war must be declared by the duly constituted authority; (2) the seriousness of the injury inflicted on the enemy must be proportional to the damage suffered by the virtuous; (3) the injury to the aggressor must be real and immediate; (4) there must be reasonable chance of winning the war; (5) the use of war must be the last resort; (6) the participants must have the right intentions; (7) the means used must be moral. Joseph McKenna, 'Ethics and War: A Catholic View', *American Political Science Review*, cited in Donald A. Wells, 'How Much Can "The Just War" Justify?' *Journal of Philosophy* 66, no. 23 (1969), p. 821.

34. Jenny Teichman, *Pacifism and the Just War* (Oxford: Basil Blackwell, 1986), p. 46.

35. Jackson, *Writing the War on Terrorism*, p. 124.

36. *In Larger Freedom: Towards Development, Security and Human Rights for All*, Report of the Secretary-General, 21 March 2005, UN Doc A/29/2005, p. 33.

37. Anthony Burke, 'Just War or Ethical Peace: Moral Discourses of Strategic Violence', *International Affairs* 80, no. 2 (2004), p. 336.

38. Jeffrey L. Geller, 'Justifying War, A Philosophical Critique', in *Culture and International Relations*, ed. Jongsuk Chay (New York: Praeger Publishers, 1990), p. 75.

39. *Ibid.*, p. 336.

40. Geller, 'Justifying War', p. 78.

41. Burke, 'Just War or Ethical Peace', p. 334.

42. Shaw, 'The Return of the Good War'.

43. Jackson, *Writing the War on Terrorism* pp. 124–46.

44. Edward Rhodes, 'The Good, the Bad and the Righteous: Understanding the Bush Vision of a new NATO Partnership', *Millennium Journal of International Studies* 33, no. 1 (2004), p. 125.

45. George W. Bush, 'Remarks to the Atlantic Student Summit', Prague, 20 November 2002, available at: http://findarticles.com/p/articles/mi_m2889/is_47_38/ai_96266744.

46. David Reiff, 'Kosovo: The End of an Era?', in *In the Shadow of 'Just Wars'*, ed. *Fabrice Weissman* (New York: Cornell University Press, 2004), p. 294.
47. William J. Bennett, 'Morality, Character and American Foreign Policy', in *Present Dangers*, ed. Robert Kagan and William Kristol (San Francisco: Encounter Books, 2000), p. 294.
48. *Ibid.*
49. James W. Caesar, 'The Great Divide: American Interventionism and its Opponents', in *Present Dangers*, ed. Kagan and Kristol.
50. Robert Kagan, cited in Michael C. Williams, 'What is the National Interest? The Neoconservative Challenge in IR Theory', *European Journal of International Relations* 11, no. 3 (2005), p. 323.
51. George W. Bush, 'Remarks by the President in Address to Faculty and Students of Warsaw University', 15 June 2001, available at: http://www.whitehouse.gov/news/releases/2001/06/20010615-1.html [consulted 11 November 2007].
52. Caesar, 'The Great Divide', pp. 294–5.
53. Colin McInnes, 'A Different Type of War? September 11 and the United States' Afghan War,' *Review of International Studies* 29 (2003), p. 171.
54. *Ibid.*, p. 172.
55. *Ibid.*, p. 173.
56. Richard Jackson (forthcoming), *What Causes Intrastate War? Towards an Understanding of Organised Civil Violence* (Manchester: Manchester University Press), p. 26.
57. Helen M. Kinsella, 'Discourses of Difference: Civilians, Combatants, and Compliance with the Laws of War', *Review of International Studies* 31 (2005), pp. 163–85; Jeremy Moses, 'The Bush–Blair Nexus: Recognising the Violence of Liberal Internationalism', paper presented at the Oceanic Conference on International Studies, University of Melbourne, 5–7 July 2006, p. 5.
58. Kinsella, 'Discourses of Difference', pp. 163–85.
59. *Ibid.*
60. 'President Bush Speaks to the United Nations November 10th 2001', available at: http://www.whitehouse.gov/news/releases/2001/11/20011110-3.html.
61. *Ibid.*, p. 6.
62. Kinsella, 'Discourses of Difference', p. 183.
63. Geneva Convention (III) relative to the Treatment of Prisoners of War. Geneva, 12 August 1949.
64. Kinsella, 'Discourses of Difference', p. 174.
65. Statement by the US White House Press Secretary on the Geneva Conventions, 7 May 2003.
66. Geneva Convention (IV) relative to the Protection of Civilian Persons in Time of War. Geneva, 12 August 1949.
67. 'President's Remarks to the Nation, September 11 2002', available at: http://www.whitehouse.gov/news/releases/2002/09/20020911-3.html [consulted 14 January 2008].
68. Thomas E. Ricks, 'Target Approval Delays Cost Air Force Key Strikes', *Washington Post*, 18 November 2001, available at: http://www.washingtonpost.com/wp-dyn/articles/A46827-2001Nov17.html [41/0108].
69. Tony Blair, 'Prime Minister's Speech: Doctrine of the International Community at the Economic Club', Chicago, 24 April 1999, available at: http://www.number-10.gov.uk/output/Page1297 [consulted 11 November 2007].
70. Moses, 'The Bush–Blair Nexus', p. 16.

9
Freeing Force from Legal Constraint

Jim Whitman

INTRODUCTION

Violations of the Geneva Conventions are nothing new: wars, insurgencies and violent conflicts of every description routinely entail not only human rights abuses but also contraventions of international humanitarian law – the latter embodied in the Geneva Conventions. While human rights law is in large measure an attempt to bring an end to absolute power as an acceptable form of human relatedness, the standards set down in the Geneva Conventions have a more immediate purpose: constraining means and ends in the conduct of war. As the capacity to wage violent conflict advances technically and extends politically to non-state actors, the importance of the Geneva Conventions has increased – not only in terms of their specific remit, but also more generally as an indispensable part of the human rights prospect. In short, the broadly shared, post-Second World War normative consensus about bringing power relations of all kinds within the compass of international law rests on the willingness of states to accept constraints on their use of power at its most violent and destructive – war. Distinguishing combatants from non-combatants; specifying what counts as a legitimate objective in war; creating legal limits on the treatment of prisoners of war – these and other matters codified in the Geneva Conventions form a key element of what this volume terms 'the normative tenor of international relations'.

It is not difficult to see in human history an unending trail of misery and blood, occasioned by war, tyranny and oppression. Yet that same history has a parallel narrative: the struggles of peoples everywhere to make relations of absolute power anathema; to enable peoples themselves to determine the bases of legitimacy for holding and exercising power; and to make the holders of power accountable. These centuries-long efforts entailed philosophical speculation and religious principle, political risk, raw courage and the great political struggles of history: the fight of nameless millions for a decent life, without domination and fear. Most of those battles were lost; and many of them ended terribly – true instances of 'hope against hope'.

The human rights regime and the Geneva Conventions are the principal legacy of those struggles, because both delegitimize relations of absolute power. This is a matter of greater historical significance than is commonly appreciated. Against the disappointments of our failure to enact and enforce human rights law and international humanitarian law (IHL), we should bear in mind that some of the most important and enduring features of national and international life are now wholly outside international norms: slavery, colonialism and indiscriminate, total war. We might also consider what it means in political terms to have the comfortable and the oppressed alike believe that they are entitled to their human rights and bound by standards of humane decency – not merely because they are enshrined in international law and countless national laws, but also as a lived expectation in the hearts of most human beings. This norm, or shared expectation, is the standard by which states, no less than individuals, are held to account.

At the same time, though, we need to be clear-sighted about the degree to which that parallel narrative to the worst of human history – largely, but not exclusively in the form of codified law – is aspirational. This is not to suggest that IHL and human rights lack either substance or effect, but to recognize some of the blunt facts of national and international life: that the practitioners of *realpolitik* work to maximize the order-creating qualities of law while trying to minimize the degree to which their own behaviours are constrained. This tactic features as a part of the framing of laws as well as their enactment and enforcement. The legal and political counterpart to these pressures can be found in the idealist language adopted for the Geneva Conventions:

> The Geneva Conventions and the Rome Statute even tried to out-Orwell Orwell. They coined the term 'international humanitarian law' to refer to the new law of war. Nothing could be more deceptive than referring to the Rome Statute, which establishes severe punishments for crimes of genocide, war crimes, and crimes against humanity, as a humanitarian measure. There is nothing humanitarian about sending men and women to jail for committing egregious crimes. […] Of course, the Geneva Conventions have a humanitarian purpose of protecting the sick,

civilians, and prisoners of war from the sometimes-indiscrimi-
nate dangers of military hostilities. But criminal law also has the
more general purpose of protecting innocent people from harmful
criminal behavior. If institutions are properly called humanitarian
by virtue of their good purposes, then we might as well call
the entire system of criminal law, including the death penalty,
domestic humanitarian law.[1]

The core of IHL is the Geneva Conventions of 1949. Article 3
of the Conventions, which is common to each, prohibits violence
to life and person; the taking of hostages; deportations; torture,
outrages upon personal dignity; and non-judicial killing. The Fourth
Convention pertains not to the minimum standards of treatment for
combatants and prisoners of war, but to the protection of civilians;
and Protocol II pertains to the protection of victims of non-international conflicts. IHL is *jus in bello*, law in war, while human rights
law concerns itself with the integrity and well-being of persons at
all times and in all places. Although the compass of internationally
recognized human rights extends considerably beyond IHL, many
of the provisions of IHL also find expression as negative human
rights ('freedom from...') in the three documents that comprise the
International Bill of Human Rights.

Yet violations of IHL and of even the most basic provisions of
human rights have been frequent. However, it might fairly be pointed
out that tensions between political impulse and legal stricture are
always present; that instances of law-breaking more often than not
leave the general integrity of the laws in question intact; that states
routinely qualify their adherence to international law – and dispute
its application or interpretation in specific cases; and, perhaps most
importantly, that because the vitality of legally sanctioned public
norms is impossible to quantify, there is no secure means of inferring
that particular acts or general categories of action that run contrary
to the letter of the law will work to undermine it in a general
way. States negotiate the particulars of international agreements
in accord with their political interests – witness the wrangling over
Protocol 1 of the Geneva Conventions[2] – and continue to pursue
them thereafter, within the law as far as possible, but outside it
when they deem it sufficiently important. In short, states can and
do evince both legal and prudential reasoning to justify apparently
illegal acts – and they often employ both together. The humanitarian
intervention debate[3] proceeds on that basis; both the US and UK
offered legal as well as strategic justifications for their invasion of

Iraq in 2003; and there currently exists a debate on preemption, which has legal as well as political advocates.[4] Furthermore, it is striking that the Genocide Convention even survived the 1994 slaughter in Rwanda – the accusation of genocide having recently been invoked by the United States against Sudan. And did the illegal invasion of Iraq destroy Article 2(4) of the UN Charter?

What, then, marks out recent violations of the Geneva Conventions as particularly noteworthy and distressing? After all, legal systems and the individual laws that comprise them must be able to demonstrate resilience by a more general pattern of adherence. This is what is meant by the term 'norms' as they apply to law – routine, unenforced conformity to established standards and a shared expectation that violations can be regarded as unacceptable. It is because the enactment of both IHL and human rights laws has been so patchy and inconsistent that the normative quality of the regimes has grown in importance, since this is the means by which something more than the letter of the law survives outrages such as genocide and keeps open the continuance of that parallel narrative to war and violence: the project of bringing force ever more fully within the orbit of law. Of course, norm maintenance needs to be a shared project of international politics – one requiring regular affirmation and support. Unhappily,

> Those who believe in natural law are inclined to assume that once a human right has been legislated, it will, ipso facto, persist forever: the vital center of the law, ever expanding and infused with new prohibitions, will always hold. But no law made by human beings endures simply by virtue of its own authority. All law requires political support. Principles of international law, like any prescription, are abrogated when their consumers and custodians decide, for better or worse, to change them, whether by explicit abrogation purportedly based on rational self-interest, or by persistent tolerated and unremedied violations, the latter often committed obliviously to rational self-interest.[5]

There are several characteristics of recent violations of the Geneva Conventions which, taken together, suggest that we might have crossed a critical threshold in terms of general normative adherence to their provisions: the number and seriousness of the violations; the fact that some of the most egregious violations have been committed by large and powerful states; and that some of the most serious have been committed flagrantly and/or persistently without concern over international opprobrium. Add to that the political justifications that have sometimes accompanied them – not least variations on the declared exigencies of the 'war on terror' – and it becomes clear that the sum of these actions are undermining the Geneva Conventions not only inadvertently – in an uncoordinated but cumulative way – but also purposefully.

Expressed bluntly, one can see in now-familiar outrages the beginnings of a movement toward releasing the legal constraints on force. This is not an assault on the rule of law *per se*, but something more pernicious: attempts along several fronts to make the law accommodate the exercise of absolute power. But the laws of war cannot be rolled back without impacting other laws (including human rights and civil liberties within states) – and other states' adherence to them. How else might other states – particularly those with a wish to extend or disable the legal boundaries of the Geneva Conventions or diminish the strength of the norm – view recent developments in the United States?

> We now have law-free zones (e.g., Guantánamo); law-free practices (e.g., extraordinary rendition); law-free courts – we call them 'military commissions'; and law-free persons, whom we call 'enemy combatants.' All of these practices the [US] Government claims are exempt from judicial oversight. The [US] Executive branch now infringes upon civil liberties, based not on congressional statements, but on vague legislative mandates. And we now see sharp and growing distinctions between aliens and citizens that have led millions of people to march in the streets.[6]

The worst effect of recent violations of the Geneva Conventions is that they threaten to usher back into public acceptability the exercise of absolute power – and that would be a normative shift of historic proportions. The post-1945 international order is historically unique in being all-inclusive and law-based; and its principal accomplishments – the establishment of human rights, the Geneva Conventions, the end of colonialism, the spread of accountable, representative government – are all structures that invalidate the accrual and use of absolute power at all levels of human interaction, from the inter-personal to the inter-state.

Now, torture has been brought out from the darkest corners of recalcitrant regimes and become another 'issue' to be considered. It is justified not only on prudential grounds, but also on moral and legal ones, or fenced off with definitional niceties – so 'waterboarding' (coerced, simulated drowning) is declared to be within the bounds of acceptable interrogation methods.[7] But the real measure of the damage brought about by reintroducing torture into state conduct can be seen in the way that it now features in the media[8] ('Time to think about torture') – and legal argument in favour of its codification has even appeared in the non-specialist press.[9]

This is terrible in human terms, of course, and also in respect of our Enlightenment heritage and the values we profess to defend. Worse still where normative expectation is concerned, if the logic that ends justify means, or that national security, or the 'war on terror' necessitate 'fighting fire with fire' holds for something so fundamentally gruesome as torture, then the out-of-sight, out-of-mind business of 'extraordinary rendition'[10] of ghost prisons;[11] and the incarceration of 'unlawful combatants' in Guantánamo[12] can also be accommodated. And so they have – not without protest, at least from some quarters;[13] and not without at lest some principled legal challenges. But no combination of legal, political and moral argument halted, let alone reversed, these and similar outrages. That they can be accommodated at all suggests that our national and shared political cultures have already been altered, considerably for the worse, with the prospect that we are moving backward, to force-based rather than law-based relations.

In what follows, there is an emphasis on the actions undertaken by the United States under the presidency of George W. Bush. The reason for this is because of the profile that comes with its political standing, since its own actions are more likely to have a normative effect throughout the international system than the actions of small states, or 'rogue' ones. Nor does the fact of US violations of the Geneva Conventions give it special standing: one need only consider the conduct of the Russian army in Chechnya, the atrocities committed in Bosnia in the 1990s or Israel's 2006 invasion of Lebanon, to cite but three prominent cases. Instead, it is the particular quality of the changed and changing attitude of the US toward the Geneva Conventions under the Bush administration that requires close attention.

What we have witnessed in recent US conduct is not a pattern of discrete violations, of the sort that is often accompanied by 'regrettably necessary', or 'in extraordinary circumstances' – that is, violations of the law which, though defiantly illegal, are committed and subsequently defended in the hope of not unleashing a more general non-conformity by other states. Rather, recent US challenges to the Geneva Conventions are not only numerous and wide-ranging: they were also systematic, institutionalized, embedded in legislation and the assertion of executive power and openly contemptuous – famously captured in the words of Alberto Gonzalez, then-White House counsel and subsequently US Attorney General, who advised the White House that 'the war on terrorism is a new kind of war, a new paradigm [that] renders obsolete Geneva's strict limitation on questioning of enemy prisoners'.[14] Apparent, intermittent concessions to the still-extant international norm have not long disguised the Bush administration's clear, determined drive, a prime example of which is

> ... the signing statement that President Bush attached to a 2005 law prohibiting 'cruel, inhuman and degrading' treatment in interrogation that placed modest new limits on the President. The law was sponsored by Senator John McCain of Arizona and initially opposed by the White House. After weeks of negotiation, President Bush invited Senator McCain to the White House for what the *Washington Post* described as a 'public reconciliation' and a declaration of a 'common objective' to make clear to the world, as President Bush said, 'that this government does not torture and that we adhere to the international convention of torture.' And yet as soon as the bill became law, President Bush issued a statement saying that it might violate his commander-in-chief powers and he might not always act in compliance with it.[15]

Much of the flouting of the Geneva Conventions by the United States in recent years has drawn in other countries, directly and indirectly, particularly with respect to the global network of air links involved in the CIA's extensive 'extraordinary rendition' programme. But the corruption of the international norm extends well beyond some governments (including European ones) turning a blind eye at their airports. In a report produced by the European Parliament,[16] MEPs reported that several EU governments not only knew that the CIA had conducted extrajudicial transfers of prisoners to countries where they were at high risk of torture – they also obstructed investigation into the extent of their own duplicity. Moreover,

> The MEPs singled out Geoff Hoon, the [UK] minister for Europe, saying they deplored his attitude to their special committee's inquiry into the CIA flights. They expressed outrage at what they said was the view of the chief legal adviser to the Foreign Office,

Sir Michael Wood, that 'receiving or possessing' information extracted under torture, if there was no direct participation in the torture, was not per se banned under international law. They said Sir Michael declined to give evidence to the committee.[17]

But the legal and political effects of what has come to be known as 'outsourcing torture' cannot be mitigated by assertions of moral distance, or by claims of unintentional benefit; and neither can either the law or the norm long withstand the crass evasion of wrongdoing.

BREAKING, BENDING, SIDESTEPPING AND SURMOUNTING THE LAW

Because violations of the Geneva Conventions carry such considerable legal meaning, moral weight and human consequence, there is a tendency to concentrate on the acts themselves and their immediate repercussions. But for the purpose of judging whether the norm is being undermined in fundamental ways, the legal and political manoeuvring that enables or excuses an instrumental approach to the law is much more revealing of underlying intentions. In recent years, this has taken a variety of forms: blunt refusal to be bound by the law; making illegal activity established practice, but keeping it secret, or away from public scrutiny; extending definitional boundaries; citing key national interests; asserting ethical justifications if not a moral imperative; and arguing that the conditions for which the Geneva Conventions were devised have changed in important ways, which both necessitates and justifies illegal action.

What is notable about these and other tactics is an implicit concern to maintain the general integrity and vitality of the Geneva Conventions – the intention being that the individual states involved can secure for themselves an instrumental, even *à la carte* approach, while the stability and predictability afforded by the law can be kept in place. When examined in detail, the quality of the legal and political reasoning in support of these positions, the failure to grasp implications beyond immediate, enabling purposes, the shocking photographic evidence of the outcomes and the abuse of language in both specialist and public arenas all signal an outright contempt for the Geneva Conventions that makes the hope of preserving a more general normative adherence to them appear both risky and naïve.

Legal Sophistry

Once the US determined to engage al-Qaeda and the Taliban, there began a remarkable exchange of memos between legal counsel at the highest levels of the administration of George W. Bush concerning the status of detainees under the Geneva Conventions. Although the views expressed were by no means unanimous,[18] the prevailing argumentative line (and subsequent policy) displayed an astonishing attitude toward both domestic and international law. By arguing for a highly selective application of the law, US soldiers and other operatives could, so it was argued, effectively be inoculated from legal wrongdoing. As argued by then-US Attorney General John Ashcroft to President Bush:

> A Presidential determination against treaty applicability would provide the highest assurance that no court would subsequently entertain charges that American military officers, intelligence officials, or law enforcement officials violated Geneva Convention rules relating to field conduct, detention conduct or interrogation of detainees. The War Crimes Act of 1996 makes violation of parts of the Geneva Convention a crime in the United States.[19]

The corollary of this is that individuals regarded by the US as antagonists and even suspects were legally disenfranchised in respect of the law's protections, but were nevertheless still to be bound by its obligations. According to White House Legal Counsel Alberto Gonzalez (who was later appointed US Attorney General), '[E]ven if the [Geneva Conventions provision for the treatment of prisoners of war] is not applicable, we can still bring war crimes charges against anyone who mistreats US personnel.'[20] From this logic much else follows, including the legal basis for the Bush administration's creation of military commissions. According to a memorandum produced by the Legal Counsel's office, trying terrorists under the laws of war 'does not mean that terrorists will receive the protections of the Geneva Conventions or the rights that laws of war accord to lawful combatants'.[21]

A great deal of attention has been devoted to the scope and application of the Geneva Conventions as determined by the lawyers and other senior figures in the Bush administration – much of which turns on the definition of 'combatant'.[22] The intricacies of these exercises in legal sophistry do not stand up to the plain language of the Conventions:

> Common Article 3 assures that any person detained has certain rights 'in all circumstances' and 'at any time and in any place whatsoever', whether the detainee is a prisoner of war, unprivileged

belligerent, terrorist, or noncombatant. Such absolute rights include the right to be 'treated humanely',' freedom from 'violence to life and person'. Freedom from 'cruel treatment and torture', freedom from 'outrages upon personal dignity, in particular, humiliating and degrading treatment', and minimum human rights to due process in case of trial.[23]

In addition, the US distortion of the law in order to facilitate its political ends has the perverse effect of giving international legal status to non-state international actors, which is inconsistent with international law – and even contrary to practice well established within the United States itself, by which 'Acts of terror are not equated with acts of war. While acts of war are regulated directly under international law, terrorism and terrorists remain the subject of national [criminal] law.'[24] The unconsidered and perhaps unintended wider consequences of the catch-all category 'combatant' are considerable.

In 2004, President Bush declared that two persons (Ali Saleh Kahlah al-Marri and José Padilla) arrested in the United States were 'enemy combatants'. However, neither al-Marri nor Padilla was detained in a zone of armed conflict. They are, therefore, not combatants, but the Bush administration has its own definition of 'combatant'. It asserts anyone associated with terrorism is a combatant. This assertion means, according to Marco Sassòli, that we now have the 'absurd result [of] permitting targeted assassinations in the midst of peaceful cities'. For Sassòli, this possibility proves that 'all those suspected to be "terrorists" cannot be classified as combatants'.[25]

More worryingly,

In addition to its weak arguments regarding the definition of combatant, the [US] Administration has also failed to explain the impact of the global war declaration on the US military. If the war is everywhere, members of the US armed services are lawful targets everywhere. Yet most Americans make the common sense assumption that US service members away from an active theater of combat are not lawful targets for killing or detention. The common sense position tracks the law.[26]

What is of the greatest importance in this is not the question of legal competence or the quality of the legal reasoning, but the underlying identification of a keen interest in minimizing legal constraint on the US application of force, from which the legal contortions and practical abuses followed. Under the rubric provided for President Bush by Alberto Gonzalez, the US was to establish a norm to treat detainees 'humanely' – not as defined by the Geneva Conventions, but 'to the extent appropriate and consistent with military necessity'.[27] And once the movement in the direction of legally unconstrained force was begun, the way was open for its extension and refinement. How else could lawyers working at the highest levels of a democratic state come to pore over the legal definition of torture for enabling purposes? Indeed, the Assistant Attorney General at the US Department of Justice, Jay S. Bybee, made a detailed case to Alberto Gonzalez not only that the infliction of pain is not necessarily torture, but that in order for physical pain to count as torture, 'it must be of an intensity akin to that which accompanies serious physical injury such as death or organ failure'.[28]

Once the norm has been breached so severely, by the politicians and lawyers entrusted with its maintenance working to disable it, the corruption of the norm in more public arenas quickly follows. In a non-specialist magazine, a former chief assistant US attorney argued the case for 'torture warrants':

> Then there is the moral argument: torture is an abomination so profound that permitting it, even if limited to rare and dire emergencies, constitutes an indelible blight on a society and its laws. So stated, the proposition has undeniable appeal. But 'torture' is a loaded word. No one, it is fair to say, favors a policy of complete laissez-faire. What is envisioned instead is the administration of pressure that is capable of causing extreme pain – Dershowitz gives the example of sterile needles forced under the fingernails – but is nonlethal.[29]

The photographs that emerged from Abu Ghraib were indeed shameful, but the heart of the matter is not place-specific, or confined to unprofessional command or the psycho-sexual profiles of the personnel in question. Investigations into whether the abuses at Abu Ghraib received direct sanction are worthwhile,[30] but that matter is dwarfed by Guantánamo and by 'extraordinary renditions' – there and to sites unknown. US Vice President Dick Cheney's determination to work 'on the dark side' proved to be far-reaching as well as sinister:

We also have to work, though, sort of the dark side, if you will. We've got to spend time in the shadows in the intelligence world. A lot of what needs to be done here will have to be done quietly, without any discussion, using sources and methods that are available to our intelligence agencies, if we're going to be successful. That's the world these folks operate in, and so it's going to be vital for us to use any means at our disposal, basically, to achieve our objective.[31]

The enablement of 'any means at our disposal' has entailed a progressive disabling of the law – again, by any means at the administration's disposal. One international lawyer has been moved to write, 'Not since the Nazi era have so many lawyers been so clearly involved in international crimes concerning the treatment and interrogation of persons detained during war.'[32]

Legal Selectivity

The (US) Military Commissions Act is perhaps less notable for what it enabled than for what it disabled. Previously, under the War Crimes Act of 1996, US personnel could be legally accountable for violations of Common Article 3 of the Geneva Conventions. Under the Military Commissions Act, this was reduced to torture or cruel or inhuman treatment only if they inflict 'severe physical and mental pain or suffering [if not incidental to lawful sanctions]'.[33] With US personnel thus insulated from international and domestic legal stricture, the way was open for 'waterboarding' – or water torture as it has been known previously, in the US no less than the rest of the world.

The drafters of the [Military Commissions Act] […] were apparently unaware of or ignored past US legal history. Indeed, despite increasing discussion of variations of the technique and their applications on a global scale, nobody seems to remember that, not so very long ago, the United States, acting alone before domestic courts, commissions, and courts-martial, and as a participant in the world community, not only condemned the use of water torture, but severely punished as criminals those who applied it.[34]

As for military commissions themselves, the legal foundation for their establishment in current form rests on a highly selective and remarkably small part of the body of directly pertinent legal principles and international agreements.

> A brief defending President Bush's military commissions [...] declared that 'the history of military practice is legally insignificant' before also identifying claimed historical trials by military commissions. Yet, while participants in any credible common law trial must be familiar with relevant precedents, this knowledge is largely absent from the process followed by today's military commissions, as demonstrated by significant factual errors in both public statements and court filings by responsible officials.[35]

A larger and more disturbing form of legal selectivity has also featured as part of US efforts to fence off the professed demands of the 'war on terror' from the Geneva Conventions: treating the Geneva Conventions and IHL as a realm of law effectively free-standing from human rights law. In their diligent search for means to invalidate the application of Common Article 3 to al-Qaeda and Taliban detainees, Bush administration officials ignored the rights and duties of human rights even though these prohibit many of the measures they were seeking to legitimize.[36] With every legal device employed to shelter US operatives from the strictures of the Geneva Conventions, the larger human rights norms were also impacted. Torture is not only illegal under the Geneva Conventions: it is also a fundamental and integral part of human rights law. What can come of normative adherence to the Geneva Conventions when any one state, on its own determination, can sanction torture without entirely repudiating the Conventions and everything they stand for? And does anyone believe that we can maintain a normative expectation of universal human rights *and* an allowance of torture?

The Corruption of Language

Euphemisms abound: 'extended' and 'enhanced' interrogation techniques for torture and cruel or inhuman punishment; and 'self injurious behavioural incidents' for prisoners' attempted suicides are but two. But the moral insulation provided by antiseptic terminology does not save us from the dehumanizing effects of incorporating brutalities into our accepted practices and political discourse. So it is that three suicides at Guantánamo could be described by the camp commander as '... not an act of desperation, rather an act of asymmetrical warfare waged against us'[37] – to which the US Deputy

Assistant Secretary of State for Public Diplomacy felt moved to add, 'Taking their own lives was not necessary, but it certainly is a good PR move.'[38]

It is unclear whether the declaration of a 'war on terror' was ever intended in strictly metaphorical terms, but it has been presented and reinforced so as to invalidate any nuanced political response or moral engagement that is at odds with the means adopted.[39] As President Bush himself asserted, 'Either you are with us, or you are with the terrorists.'[40] Much else follows from such crude rhetoric – notably, polite glosses on barbarous activities, such as infusing instrumental reasoning with moral purpose, in the 'defense of values' and saving lives, both of which were invoked by US Secretary of State Condoleezza Rice in a speech dedicated to European audiences in which she also asserted that 'The United States does not transport, and has not transported, detainees from one country to another for the purpose of interrogation using torture.'[41]

Worst of all, the law itself and IHL in particular – our best-established means of preventing the kinds of relations that terrorism threatens to reintroduce as acceptable forms of national and international conduct – have been used as a means of extending the prerogatives of states in the 'war on terror':

> Intended as the branch of international law providing protection to all those affected by or involved in armed conflicts, IHL has thus become the justification for denying such people and others any protection afforded by human rights law and domestic legislation.[42]

THE FUTURE OF THE GENEVA CONVENTIONS IN A WEAKENED NORMATIVE ETHOS

Recent US actions are clearly deleterious to more general normative adherence to the Geneva Conventions. As a consequence, other more familiar kinds of violations of IHL are likely to accrue more normative impact than they would otherwise have had. And in much the same way that under ordinary conditions, laws and norms are mutually reinforcing, law-breaking and open contempt for legal norms could produce a downward spiral. Israel's invasion of Lebanon in 2006 entailed serious violations of the Geneva Conventions, yet at a public rally in New York,

Israel's ambassador to the United Nations Dan Gillerman spoke first and struck a particularly aggressive and confident tone. 'From this stage, I would like to send out a clear message to that glass building behind you,' Gillerman said, referring to the United Nations. 'Let us finish the job! You know better than anyone else that what we are doing is doing your own work: fighting terror. ... And to those countries who claim we are using disproportionate force, I have only this to say: "you're damn right we are!"' His comments drew wild applause.[43]

Other, less emotive pronouncements are little less worrying: when asked at a Munich press conference whether the United States is bound by any international system, legal framework or code of conduct, the US Defense Secretary Donald Rumsfeld replied, 'I honestly believe that every country ought to do what it wants to do. ... It is either proud of itself afterwards, or it is less proud of itself.'[44] Where the Geneva Conventions are concerned, what the adoption of such an attitude might amount to in practical terms is a prospect both frightening and horrifying: in February 2008, 'Israel's deputy defence minister [...] warned his country was close to launching a huge military operation in Gaza and said Palestinians would bring on themselves a "bigger *shoah*," using the Hebrew word usually reserved for the Holocaust.'[45]

The more freely and frequently the Geneva Conventions and IHL are either brushed aside as an encumbrance, or declared to be inapplicable to contemporary conditions, the more likely it is that human beings of every disposition and in any situation will find themselves in violent or threatening circumstances, unprotected by law and subject either to the caprices of mercy (possibly subject to 'military necessity') or to the application of indiscriminate force. Combating terror – or indeed any other kind of adversary in this manner – will surely prove counter-productive, as the war in Iraq has already demonstrated amply.[46]

There is certainly a good deal of carefully voiced concern over the precision of IHL in respect of terrorists and terrorism – and over what might count as self-defence by concerned states – a matter that has been brought into sharp focus by the issue of targeted assassinations.[47] This and similar matters require the most careful deliberation, but it is difficult to see how they can be made a matter of high-level politico-legal discussion when states have demonstrated their willingness to argue legal inapplicability or elasticity to suit their immediate ends. The recent diminution of the norm makes considered clarifications or adjustments to the Geneva Conventions and to normative expectation an unlikely prospect for the immediate future – a fix that might well confirm some states in courses of action that are either patently illegal or of dubious legality.

At the same time, the range of violations of the Geneva Conventions and the legal manoeuvres that have in some cases been used to justify them are corrosive of the moral and legal tenor of both domestic and international life, perhaps best captured in Mark Danner's, 'we are all torturers now', as throughout the world, we become habituated to matters that were until recently so shocking because they were widely deemed to be unconscionable:

> The system of torture has, after all, survived its disclosure. We have entered a new era; the traditional story line in which scandal leads to investigation and investigation leads to punishment has been supplanted by something else. Wrongdoing is still exposed; we gaze at the photographs and read the documents, and then we listen to the president's spokesman 'reiterate', as he did last week, 'the president's determination that the United States never engage in torture.' And there the story ends.[48]

The strains placed on habeas corpus – and in the case of the United States, its suspension under the terms of the Military Commissions Act 2006[49] – are widely felt in many countries;[50] and what has been termed 'blind cooperation leading to what is now corrupted complicity'[51] has featured in many countries in conjunction with the 'war on terror' – with everything this entails in terms of professional standards, popular perceptions and community cohesion. The long-term consequences of the assertion of executive power over something so fundamental to law and justice as habeas corpus – especially by the United States – are difficult to calculate, even against the historical background.[52] Foreboding hardly seems out of place:

> It would seem that given the right set of circumstances, a large part of the historic efficacy of the 'great writ' may become subject to summary destruction. Under such circumstances – which are not entirely beyond the imagination – it is not unreasonable to wonder if even a remedial Act of Congress could, in the words of Henry Hallam discussing the intended effect of the habeas corpus statute of Charles II, serve to 'cut off abuses by which

the government's lust of power, and the servile subtlety of [its] lawyers, had impaired so fundamental a privilege'.[53]

On the other hand, the case for a reversal of current trends is not groundless:

[M]uch of the [US] administration's approach to the key legal questions regarding executive power have been rejected – by courts, by the public, by Congress, and in some instances, by subsequent lawyers in the Justice Department. [...] More broadly, one could argue that the administration's extreme views of executive power have not carried the day in the population at large, or in the world of elite legal and educated opinion. To that extent, they may serve as 'anti-precedent,' examples of mistakes we need to avoid in future crises, rather than as precedent.[54]

The larger point is this: although the Geneva Conventions and other provisions of IHL, together with human rights and the constitutional particulars of democratic states regarding the treatment of prisoners and the allowances for combating terrorism occupy distinct realms of law, they are seamless by dint of fundamental norms of humane decency, worked out and refined over centuries. Because the Geneva Conventions exist to limit the worst excesses of war and violent conflict – and to minimize risk and harm to those caught up in it, directly and indirectly – they are not only 'on the front line' in the struggle to bring force within the compass of law; they are also in many ways the most sensitive barometer of our shared commitment to that enterprise. Whether or not one agrees that the Geneva Conventions are under assault, they are most certainly under severe strain – and with them, the principles that comprise the foundation of and prospects for civilized social and political orders, nationally and internationally. Terrorism is an important test of what we say we believe; and we cannot defend our values by acting in ways that directly contradict them.

NOTES

1. George P. Fletcher, 'The Law of War and its Pathologies', *Columbia Human Rights Law Review* 38, no. 517 (2007), pp. 101–2.
2. For the background of which, see Jeremy Rabkin, 'The Politics of the Geneva Conventions: Disturbing Background to the ICC Debate', *Virginia Journal of International Law* 44, no. 1 (2003–04), pp. 169–205; for a contemporary account, see Guy B. Roberts, 'The New Rules for Waging War: The Case Against

Ratification of Additional Protocol', *Virginia Journal of International Law* 26, no. 1 (1985–1986), pp. 109–70.

3. Nicholas J. Wheeler, *Saving Strangers*: *Humanitarian Intervention in International Society* (Oxford: Oxford University Press, 2002).
4. Alan M. Dershowitz, *Preemption*: *A Knife That Cuts Both Ways* (New York: W.W. Norton & Co., 2006).
5. W. Michael Reisman, 'Holding the Center of the Law of Armed Conflict', *American Journal of International Law* 100 (2006), p. 860.
6. Harold Hongju Koh, 'The Future of Lou Henkin's Human Rights Movement', *Columbia Human Rights Law Review* 38, no. 487 (2007), p. 106.
7. BBC interview with President George W. Bush, 14 February 2008, available at: http://news.bbc.co.uk/1/hi/world/americas/7245670.stm; Dan Eggen, 'White House Pushes Waterboarding Rationale', *Washington Post*, 13 February 2008.
8. David Walsh, 'US Liberal Pundits Debate the Value of Torture', *World Socialist Web Site* (10 November 2001), http://www.wsws.org/articles/2001/nov2001/tort-n10_prn.shtml [a short, useful summary of the speed and extent to which a debate about the possible use of torture sprang up in the wake of the 9/11 attacks]; Susan Sontag, 'Regarding the Torture of Others', *New York Times* (23 May 2004), available at: http://donswaim.com/nytimes.sontag.html [a thoughtful reflection on the meaning of the Abu Ghraib photos, particularly with respect to wider social norms]; Mark Danner, 'We Are All Torturers Now', *New York Times* (6 January 2005), available at: http://query.nytimes.com/gst/abstract.html?res=F30810FA3B5D0C758CDDA80894DD404482 [succinct, thoughtful op-ed piece on the political meaning of torture, especially for the United States, before the hearings to confirm Alberto Gonzalez as US Attorney General]; see also an editorial in the *Washington Post*, 'Legalizing Torture' (9 June 2004), available at: http://www.washingtonpost.com/wp-dyn/articles/A26602-2004Jun8.html.
9. Andrew C. McCarthy, 'Torture: Thinking the Unthinkable', *Commentary* (July–August 2004), pp. 17–24.
10. Jane Mayer, 'Outsourcing Torture: The Secret History of America's "Extraordinary Rendition" Program', *New Yorker* (14 February 2005), available at: http://www.newyorker.com/archive/2005/02/14/050214fa_fact6.
11. US President George W. Bush has confirmed the existence of CIA-run 'ghost prisons'. See The White House, Office of the Press Secretary, 'President Discusses Creation of Military Commissions to Try Suspected Terrorists', 6 September 2006, available at: http://www.whitehouse.gov/news/releases/2006/09/20060906-3.html; see also Dana Priest, 'CIA Holds Terror Suspects in Secret Prisons', *Washington Post* (2 November 2005), p. A01.
12. David Rose, *Guantánamo*: *America's War on Human Rights* (London: Faber & Faber, 2004); Michael Ratner and Ellen Ray, *Guantánamo*: *What the World Should Know* (Moreton in Marsh, Gloucestershire: Arris Books, 2004).
13. *Washington Post*, 'Legalizing Torture' (9 June 2004), p. A20, available at: http://www.washingtonpost.com/ac2/wo-dyn/A26602-2004Jun8?language=printer; and *New York Times* (editorial), 'Rushing Off a Cliff' (28 September 2006), available at: http://www.nytimes.com/2006/09/28/opinion/28thu1.html.
14. Alberto Gonzalez, Memorandum for the President, 'Decision Re Application of the Geneva Conventions on Prisoners of War to the Conflict with Al Quaeda and the Taliban', 25 January 2002, in Mark Danner, *Torture and Truth*: *America, Abu Ghraib, and the War on Terror* (London: Granta Publications, 2004), p. 84.

15. Jack Goldsmith, *The Terror Presidency: Law and Justice Inside the Bush Administration* (New York: W.W. Norton & Company, 2007), p. 210.

16. European Parliament, *Report on the Alleged Use of European Countries by the CIA for the Transportation and Illegal Detention of Prisoners*, A6-0020/2007 (20 January 2007), available at: http://www.europarl.europa.eu/comparl/tempcom/tdip/final_report_en.pdf.

17. Richard Norton-Taylor, 'MEPs condemn Britain's role in "torture flights"', *Guardian (*29 November 2006).

18. The US State Department's Legal Director, William H. Taft IV, wrote a riposte to the position adopted by then-legal Counsel to the White House, Alberto Gonzalez, 'Comments on Your Paper on the Geneva Conventions', 2 February 2002, reprinted in Danner, *Torture and Truth*, pp. 94–5.

19. Letter from Attorney General John Ashcroft to President George W. Bush, 1 February 2002, available at: http://news.findlaw.com/wp/docs/torture/jash20102ltr2.html.

20. Gonzalez, Memorandum for the President, in Danner, *Torture and Truth*, p. 86.

21. Tim Golden, 'After Terror, A Secret Rewriting of Military Law', *New York Times (*24 October 2004).

22. See, for example, Anne E. Joynt, 'The Semantics of the Guantanamo Bay Inmates: Enemy Combatants or Prisoners of the War On Terror?', *Buffalo Human Rights Law Review* 10 (2004), pp. 427–41.

23. Jordan J. Paust, 'Executive Plans and Authorizations to Violate International Law Concerning Treatment and Interrogation of Detainees', *Columbia Journal of Transnational Law* 43, no. 3 (2005), pp. 817–18.

24. Mary Ellen O'Connell, 'Enhancing the Status of Non-State Actors Through a Global War on Terror?', *Columbia Journal of Transnational Law* 43, no. 2 (2005), p. 452.

25. *Ibid.*, pp. 455–6; see also Marco Sassòli, 'Use and Abuse of the Laws of War in the "War on Terrorism"', *Law and Inequality* 22 (2004), pp. 195–221.

26. O'Connell, 'Enhancing the Status of Non-State Actors', p. 456.

27. Gonzalez, Memorandum for the President, in Danner, *Torture and* Truth, p. 87.

28. Office of the Assistant Attorney General, Memorandum for Alberto Gonzalez, Counsel to the President, 'Re: Standards of Conduct for Interrogation under 18 U.S.C. sections 2340–2340A', reprinted in Danner, *Torture and Truth*, p. 155. See also Harold Hongju Koh, 'A World Without Torture', *Columbia Journal of Transnational Law* 43, no. 3 (2005), pp. 641–61, in which the author points out that the Bush administration condemned a catalogue of practices in Saddam Hussein's Iraq as reprehensible tortures that would not qualify as such under the Bybee criteria. See also: Stephanie L. Williams, '"Your honor, I am here today requesting the Court's permission to Torture Mr Doe": The Legality of Torture as a Means to an End v. The Illegality of Torture as a Violation of *Jus Cogens* Norms Under Customary International Law', *University of Miami International and Comparative Law Review* 12 (2004), pp. 301–60.

29. McCarthy, 'Torture: Thinking the Unthinkable', p. 23.

30. Seymour Hersh, *Chain of Command: The Road from 9/11 to Abu Ghraib* (London: Penguin Books, 2005). See also: Final Report of the Independent Panel to Review DOD Detention Operations (August 2004), available at: http://www.globalsecurity.org/military/library/report/2004/d20040824finalreport.pdf.

31. Transcript of US Vice President Dick Cheney, 'Meet the Press', 16 September 2001, available at: http://www.whitehouse.gov/vicepresident/news-speeches/speeches/vp20010916.html.
32. Paust, 'Executive Plans and Authorizations', p. 811.
33. Military Commissions Act 2006, available at: http://frwebgate.access.gpo.gov/cgi-bin/getdoc.cgi?dbname=109_cong_bills&docid=f:s3930enr.txt.pdf.
34. Evan Wallach, 'Drop by Drop: Forgetting the History of Water Torture in U.S. Courts', *Columbia Journal of International Law* 45, no. 2 (2007), pp. 468–506.
35. David Glazier, 'Precedents Lost: The Neglected History of the Military Commission', *Virginia Journal of International Law* 46, no. 5 (2005–2006), p. 7.
36. See Paust's analysis of the Yoo-Delahunty memorandum, 'Executive Plans and Authorizations', pp. 830–3. The Memorandum itself, from the US Deputy Assistant Attorney General and Special Counsel, to the General Counsel, Department of Defense (9 January 2002) is available at: http://www.texscience.org/reform/torture/yoo-delahunty-9jan02.pdf.
37. *Daily Telegraph*, 'Guantanamo suicides "an act of warfare", says camp commander' (12 June 2006).
38. Suzanne Goldberg and Hugh Muir, '"Killing themselves was unnecessary. But is certainly is a good PR move"', *Guardian* (12 June 2006).
39. Richard Jackson, 'Language, Policy and the Construction of a Torture Culture in the War on Terrorism', *Review of International Studies* 33 (2007), pp. 353–71.
40. George W. Bush, Address to a Joint Session of Congress and the American People, 20 September 2001, available at: http://www.whitehouse.gov/news/releases/2001/09/20010920-8.html.
41. *The Times*, '"Renditions save lives": Condoleezza Rice's full statement' (5 December 2005), available at: http://www.timesonline.co.uk/tol/news/world/us_and_americas/article745995.ece. For a full account of 'extraordinary renditions' and torture, see: Centre for Human Rights and Global Justice New York University Law School, 'Torture by Proxy: International and Domestic laws Applicable to "Extraordinary renditions"', available at: http://www.chrgj.org/docs/TortureByProxy.pdf.
42. Sassòli, Use and Abuse of the Laws of War', p. 198.
43. Gal Beckerman, 'New York Jews Rally in Support of Israel', *Jeruselum Post* (18 July 2006), available at: http://www.jpost.com/servlet/Satellite?pagename=JPost%2FJPArticle%2FShowFull&cid=1150886029570.
44. Quoted in Jonathan Freedland, 'The war is not yet over', *Guardian* (11 February 2004).
45. Rory McCarthy, 'Israeli minister warns of Holocaust for Gaza if violence continues', *Guardian* (1 March 2008).
46. Suzanne Goldberg, 'Iraq war is breeding a new generation of professional terrorists, warns CIA report', *Guardian* (15 January 2005), available at: http://www.guardian.co.uk/Iraq/Story/0,2763,1391072,00.html.
47. David Kretzmer, 'Targeted Killing of Suspected Terrorists: Extra-Judicial Killings or Legitimate Self-Defense?', *European Journal of International Law* 16, no. 2 (2005), pp. 171–212; W. Jason Fisher, 'Targeted Killings, Norms, and International Law', *Columbia Journal of Transnational Law* 45, no. 3 (2007), pp. 711–58.

48. Danner, 'We Are All Torturers Now'. See also: Clark Butler (ed.), *Guantanamo Bay and the Judicial-Moral Treatment of the Other* (West Lafayette, IN: Purdue University Press, 2007).

49. From the Military Commissions Act 2006: '[N]o court, justice, or judge shall have jurisdiction to hear or consider any claim or cause of action whatsoever, including any action pending on or filed after the date of the enactment of the Military Commissions Act of 2006, relating to the prosecution, trial, or judgment of a military commission [...] including challenges to the lawfulness of procedures of military commissions... '

50. For a survey of this, see John Ip, 'Comparative Perspectives on the Detention of Terrorist Suspects', *Transnational Law and Contemporary Problems* 16, no. 3 (Spring 2007), pp. 773–99.

51. Robert Billyard, 'The Cases of Maher Arar and Omar Khadr: Canada's Disgrace', *Counterpunch* (20 August 2007).

52. Natsu Taylor Saito, *From Chinese Exclusion to Guantánamo Bay: Plenary Power and the Prerogative State* (Boulder, CO: University of Colorado Press, 2007).

53. Morad Fakhimi, 'Terrorism and Habeas Corpus: A Jurisdictional Escape', *Journal of Supreme Court History* 30, no. 3 (November 2005), p. 237.

54. 'David Cole on Waterboarding, Executive Power, and the Legacy of the Bush Justice Department', *New York Review of Books* (21 December 2007).

10
Undermining International Humanitarian Law and the Politics of Liberal Democracies

Sarah Perrigo

INTRODUCTION

This chapter explores one of the contentions of several contributions to this book: namely that the undermining of the Geneva Conventions and international humanitarian law (IHL) resonates outwards with significant implications not just for international politics but also for the internal politics of liberal democratic states. A central argument of this chapter is that in the name of 'waging a war on terror' in defence of the values of freedom and democracy, the United States and countries like Britain are not just disregarding IHL but are profoundly undermining the conditions for freedom and democracy at home.

There has been a good deal of public attention to violations of the Geneva Conventions and the Convention on Torture in the period post-9/11; and there has also been some on the effects of counter-terrorist policies on domestic politics in the USA and UK.[1] One of the intentions here is to demonstrate the connections between norms and laws at both levels. Too often, violations of international humanitarian laws are seen as by citizens of liberal democracies as remote, 'out there' and having little import for the ordinary routines of liberal democratic politics.

The first part of this chapter outlines and explores the key values, principles and preconditions for democratic politics that are fundamental to the practice of liberal democracies. This is not an exercise in political philosophy but simply to suggest that there are in fact certain fundamental values and principles, institutions and practices that cannot be subverted or undermined without threatening this form of politics.

The second part explores the relationship between key principles of liberal democracy and the development of IHL, human rights and the Geneva Conventions. The norms and values that underlie the development of the latter, it will be argued, have historically been profoundly influenced by the former. Further, it is argued that under contemporary conditions it is extremely difficult to separate domestic from international politics. What powerful states do in the international sphere has profound implications for domestic politics; and what governments do in domestic politics further impacts on the international arena. This is nowhere more apparent than the counterterrorism policies adopted by, for example, the US and the UK in the so-called 'war on terror'.

The third part of the chapter, using primarily evidence from the UK, but not exclusively, demonstrates the cumulative effects of counterterrorism polices in eroding a range of key principles of liberal democratic politics, including the rule of law, institutional constraints on arbitrary power, the divide between the public and private spheres, fundamental liberties, principles of equality/non-discrimination and on citizenship debate and dissent.

The final section assesses the costs of the 'normalisation' of these policies for both domestic and international politics.

LIBERAL DEMOCRATIC POLITICS

What are the fundamental features of liberal democratic politics and what are the preconditions for this form of politics? There are, of course, many differences within liberal democracies in terms of institutions, practices and culture. Nevertheless there are a number of crucial principles and characteristics shared by all those understood to be liberal democracies, which I want to argue cannot be abrogated without undermining the distinctiveness and normative strengths of this form of politics. Liberal democracies may not always have achieved these commitments, and liberal democracies are by no means perfect and can be criticised for many failings. However, the primary rules, values, institutions, procedures and liberties that are axiomatic to such a form of politics are, I will argue, being threatened in the present period in new and disturbing ways.[2]

As Farer notes in examining the response of President Bush to 9/11:

It is not just the physical and psychological security of western peoples that is threatened but the norms and institutions embodying and protecting liberties: norms and institutions so painfully constructed over the bloody millennia of western history.[3]

It is important to note that the principles, values and norms that underpin liberal democratic politics are not some kind of timeless abstract universals – the outcome of purely philosophic speculation. The institutions, practices and rules of liberal democracies have developed out of a process of long and protracted struggles of real men and women in specific historical contexts. They are the outcome of those struggles from the seventeenth century to the present to constrain the exercise of power both political and economic, and to do so in ways that recognised the inherent dignity of human beings and their capacity for autonomy and self-determination and which required a commitment to equality, non-discrimination and individual liberty. The lessons were learned slowly and painfully through struggles against tyranny and oppression in revolutions, wars and civil wars. The process was uneven and often riven with setbacks, with reversions to dictatorships, fascism and other forms of authoritarian rule. Only slowly and painfully have political elites accepted that these principles are not simply coercive restraints on political power but are principles that best provide for stability, legitimacy and the peaceful resolution of conflict within nation states. Liberal democracy cannot be a taken-for-granted system of government. Its values, institutions and practices have to be constantly acknowledged and affirmed as an ongoing process.

There have been (and continue to be) tensions between the liberal and the democratic in liberal democratic forms of politics. Liberals have historically been preoccupied with the restraint of political power and the protection of individual liberty in civil society. Thus liberals pay great attention to institutional design and to political institutions that ensure checks and balances. Constitutions, conventions, bills of rights and the separation of powers have long been as a *sine qua non* of liberal politics. Locke's formulation constitutes the classic argument of liberal politics: that the state is set up with limited functions, to protect our rights to life, liberty and property. On the other hand, democracy is concerned with collective decision-making, and with the common good or the good of the community as a whole. The left and many political progressives in the past viewed the liberal element as a constraint on democracy and on popular power. (Later, we will see the way in which appeals to democracy are being used in attempts to delegitimise both judicial powers and fundamental human rights.) However, in much contemporary writing there is a clear recognition that certain liberal principles are essential to the workings of democracy.[4] Beetham, for example, argues that liberalism secures freedom of expression, movement and association – rights that are absolutely necessary to secure popular control over collective decision-making.[5] Further, liberal constitutionalism and the rule of law control political decision-making and ensure that no one is above the law. Parekh draws upon liberal principles in outlining what he considers to be principles of democratic governance:

> People as the ultimate source of political authority, popularly chosen and accountable government, universal suffrage, legal and political equality, freedom of speech, protest and organisation, respect for basic human rights and the rule of law. No form of government that denies these can be called democratic.[6]

Further, in a liberal democracy the democratic will of the majority must be tempered or limited by rules that protect individuals and minorities from being sacrificed for utilitarian calculations regarding the common good. As Dworkin writes in *Taking Rights Seriously*,

> The institution of rights is therefore crucial, because it represents the majority's promise to the minority that their dignity and equality will be respected. When the divisions amongst the groups are most violent, then this gesture, if the law is to work, must be most sincere.[7]

FUNDAMENTAL PRINCIPLES AND VALUES

One of the most fundamental principles of liberal democratic politics, which serves to distinguish it from other forms of government, is its commitment to constraining political power and the use of force and violence, and ensuring the accountability of government decisions to citizens. It is worth remembering Locke's famous critique of Hobbes's advocacy of the sovereign, leviathan state: 'This is to think that men are so foolish that they take care to avoid what mischief may be done to them by pole cats or foxes but are content, nay think it safety to be devoured by lions.'[8]

In practice this means that liberal democratic politics is limited, and crucially the rules are the fundamental defence against the arbitrary exercise of executive power. The rules are also a fundamental guarantee of impartiality in both the making of the law and its administration. The rule of law and the norms and procedures that underlie it are therefore not just basic to this form of politics but constitute the major source of political legitimacy. Though it is often stated that liberal democratic politics is fundamentally procedural, there are good reasons contra the legal positivists for recognising the importance of the substantive normative principles that lie behind the procedures and provide legitimacy and rightness to the procedures. Following Dworkin and Habermas,[9] we cannot grasp the significance of the procedure of liberal democracy without grasping the intimate relationship between norms and procedures. The values of equality, impartiality and liberty, for example, are crucial norms that lie behind the rule of law, due process and fair trial.

Second, liberal democratic politics fundamentally limit the role of the state and government. Though exactly how and where to draw the line between public and private is often contested both in theory and in practice, the acceptance of a distinction between state, civil society and between public and private are crucial concepts in defining liberal democratic politics.

Third, in liberal democracies the people are citizens, not merely subjects. Thus liberal democracies crucially depend upon the existence of a number of fundamental civil liberties or rights possessed by all individuals as of right, in particular freedom of speech, information and assembly. These rights or liberties are not simply negative liberties, necessary to limit political power and defend in some way abstract freedoms but are an essential facet of democratic politics that enable citizens to engage in politics itself.

POLITICS IN LIBERAL DEMOCRACIES: NORMAL TIMES AND TIMES OF EMERGENCIES

To what degree are political leaders of liberal democracies entitled to erode the established norms and principles in times of an emergency? In conventional wars between states there is an inevitable tension between 'normal' politics and what is deemed necessary in order to wage war successfully. In both World Wars, certain individual rights were curtailed, executive power expanded and enemy nationals were interred for the duration of the war. However, these wars were declared, the enemy was usually identifiable and the period of war is itself limited. Further, with the codification of the rules of war in the Geneva Conventions and in the UN Convention on Civil and Political Rights, there are limits to what is permissible in times of war both domestically and internationally. If the Geneva Conventions set minimum standards of treatment for both combatants and civilians in wartime, both the UNCCPR and the ECHR clearly limit the rights from which states can derogate in their domestic politics in times of war. These fundamental rights include the right to life and a fair trial. It is further illegal to discriminate on the basis of ethnicity or religion; and the use of torture is forbidden in any circumstance. Rules on derogation are clear and define both procedures to be followed and time limits on any such derogation states may make.

Since 9/11 the political leaders of at least two leading liberal democracies, the US and Britain, have denigrated and treated with contempt the UN Charter (which they themselves played a prominent role in constructing) and, in the case of the US, attempted to rewrite the rules of war. But they have only simultaneously disregarded their own constitutional rules and conventions and violated the values and norms that are supposed to be protected by those rules. The reasons given draw upon the same language of justification. Both are justified by reference to 'new times'; that the war on terror requires new rules.

However, despite this similarity the ways in which the rules are being challenged, the domestic sphere has required a rather different approach. The dominance of realism, with its scepticism about the role of norms in international relations plus the lack of enforcement mechanisms, allowed the Bush administration to denigrate the laws of war rather more easily than can be done to rewrite the norms and rules of liberal democracy. Liberal democracy is after all the place where justice, equality and freedom are supposed to be protected and arbitrary power constrained. While clearly there has been a concerted effort to change the rules of 'normal' politics (as will be demonstrated later), ironically, it is done in the name of defending the very norms and values of liberal democratic politics itself. As Gearty had perceptively noted when looking at the attack on human rights discourses in Britain in the present period, while at one level it seems to be an explicit conflict between human rights and counter-terrorism, in fact it is 'also something more ominous – a supposed lack of conflict between the two flowing from a redefinition of human rights, the effect of which is to excuse repression as necessary to prevent the destruction of human rights'.[10]

Those who defend the suspension of the normal rules of politics and the violation of human rights (both politicians and academics) use a number of arguments to justify their position.[11] When examining the arguments of politicians in Britain at one end of the spectrum some have explicitly attacked the Human Rights Act (HRA) and the human rights culture as dangerous. David Blunkett, for example, said in 2001 that 'the HRA was the biggest mistake of Blair's first term in office',[12] and Jack Straw in an article in the *Daily Mail* in 2008 criticised judgments made under HRA as fuelling perceptions that it was a villains' charter.[13]

Others have been more circumspect but have argued that Britain faces imminent and dangerous threats that require exceptional measures that legitimate and justify the suspension of the rules. Government has as its first priority a responsibility to ensure safety and security, and that cannot be achieved using the normal system of justice. In so doing they have reframed the meaning of justice, equality, liberty and human rights. Human rights become redefined as for the majority, not the few. Liberty becomes redefined as freedom from fear. Justice is for some, not all. Both human rights and justice become relativised and reduced to one or two values among others, and therefore can be traded in some kind of utilitarian calculus.

Even some of those who are critical of specific pieces of anti-terrorist legislation on the grounds that such a policy is disproportionate to the threat implicitly seem to accept that human rights and the rule of law can in some ways be traded or balanced. The academic literature supportive of counterterrorist measures uses similar arguments, also drawing upon versions of utilitarianism, to argue that in certain circumstances ends justify the means. Bellamy identifies two arguments found in the contemporary literature, what he calls the 'dirty hands' thesis and the 'lesser evil' argument.[14] Both draw upon forms of utilitarianism and accept that rules are important but can be overridden in exceptional circumstances.

What is deeply troubling about these arguments is their failure to critically examine the assumptions behind them. Exactly what is the threat? Why is it exceptional? Who constitutes a threat? Why is the well-established system of criminal justice considered inadequate to deal with this threat? They all accept the initial premise that there is a threat that calls for extraordinary means. Michael Ignatieff's book, *The Lesser Evil: Political Ethics in an Age of Terror*, is a good example.[15] He accepts there are evil people out there (the terrorists) determined to destroy 'our' way of life, which legitimates jettisoning normal rules of civilised behaviour. Not only is there in such an approach a complete failure to interrogate terrorism, its meaning, or the causes of the use of political violence, as writers such as Farer and Gearty have cogently pointed out, but it immediately creates a Manichean world, which divides people and the world into good and bad, civilised West and barbaric 'Others'. No longer are there human beings deserving of respect and reasonable treatment but two kinds of humans, those who are worthy of respect and those who have lost all their rights.

Not only is this to ignore both the huge number of mistakes, the innocent people who have been killed, arrested, tortured and detained without trial in the name of the 'war on terror' and the use of political violence by states themselves, but it is to forget that both international humanitarian law and the fundamental rules of justice in liberal democratic states are not luxuries that can be dispensed with but are meant to apply whatever the circumstances. As Dworkin so eloquently argued in *Taking Rights Seriously*, what is the use of rights when they disappear when they are most needed?[16] What is the point of bragging about freedom, and constitutional rights when they can be violated with impunity? In so doing those liberal democratic states themselves destroy the very distinction between civilised, humane behaviour and barbarism they have themselves constructed.

INTERNATIONAL HUMANITARIAN LAW AND LIBERAL DEMOCRATIC POLITICS

The fundamental desire to constrain absolute power, to protect civilians in war and citizens in all times both in war and peace and to provide guarantees of minimum standards of treatment for all binds the Geneva Conventions and international human rights law with the fundamental principles that underpin liberal democratic politics discussed above.

There is in liberalism a thin universalist or cosmopolitan thread that is apparent in the form and content of human rights law, the Geneva Conventions and humanitarian law more generally. This is manifest in the strong belief that there are minimum standards by which all people should be treated, whether they are one of 'us' or strangers, citizens or outsiders, simply because they are human beings. In exactly the same way as there are fundamental principles that can never be breached whatever the circumstances within a liberal democracy if it is to remain one, so too there are certain rules, norms and procedures that can never be derogated from if the relations between states are to have legitimacy.

These rules need to be considered not simply as constraints on state power and state interests. As we noted earlier, the development of fundamental principles of liberal democratic government is the fruit of experience regarding the kinds of institutions and practices most conducive to peace and security within domestic politics. So too has IHL, the Geneva Conventions and human rights law developed out of experience of war, violence and genocide that characterised the first half of the twentieth century, particularly in Europe. The UN, the UN Charter and the framework of humanitarian law and human rights were directly related to the Nazi genocide of the Second World War (albeit it can also be seen as a framework tempered by realism in that it took cognisance of past failures, particularly of the framework of the League of Nations after the First World War). This move was a great achievement. It was a recognition on the part of the great powers that however just the cause or however dire the threat, there are minimum standards of decency that must be observed and fundamental rules that cannot be breached. Without those minimum standards and without those rules we are in danger of reverting to the kind of barbarism where anything goes.

It is crucially important to acknowledge the fact that the primary drivers in the development of both IHL and international human rights have been the leaders of important liberal democracies, in particular the USA and the UK. They played a key role in drafting and mobilising support for both legal and normative rules on the behaviour of states in both war and peacetime, for the construction of the United Nations and the post-1945 international order. As Cardenas demonstrates (this volume), they did so not just out of humanitarian/ethical concerns but from an understanding of the pragmatic value of such developments and a recognition that they serve the long-term interests of states themselves in developing conditions most conducive to stability, order and legitimacy in the international system. Similar arguments are made by Vincent and some prominent neo-realists who recognise the importance of the role of law and norms in international relations.[17] The increasing saliency and normative force of, for example, human rights (or for that matter democracy) in international relations since 1989 cannot be wholly explained by reference to the strategic interests of the US as the hegemonic power. As with domestic politics, the interplay of norms, values and interests that determine policy is complex and cannot be explained by a simple dichotomy of strategic interests or normative commitments, as debates on humanitarian intervention in Somalia, Rwanda and Kosovo illustrate.[18]

Though the Cold War and the bipolar rivalry between the US and the Soviet Union constrained the effectiveness of the both IHL law and human rights conventions, it is apparent that the period since the end of the Cold War has seen a resurgence of commitments to building norms and institutions that serve to both constrain sovereign power and also to provide a framework for a safer world. As noted by Gordon (this volume), we have witnessed, at least until the events following the New York bombing, a growing consensus around the needs to protect civilians from threats of genocide and crimes against humanity. Further, the setting up of the ICC, despite the vigorous objection of the US government, and steps to remove impunity from violators of gross abuses of human rights was seen by many as a sign that IHL and human rights were moving up the agenda of international politics. During the 1990s and up to 9/11, it seemed to many that significant progress was being made.

Of course, there were counternarratives, with state and international practices that breached legal and normative principles of international law and contradicted or subverted this progress. There are many instances when the great powers turned a blind eye to blatant abuses of human rights for strategic political reasons or where international intervention was not seen as a priority, as for example in Rwanda. Nevertheless, those violations of IHL were never justified by political leaders with the claim that those rules were not valid, or could be disregarded with impunity. What makes the change in both language and practice since 2001 so significant is that that the rules were broken unilaterally by the leader of the most powerful state, the US (with the implicit collusion of the British Prime Minister) with the argument that in the face of the attack on America the rules were obsolete, that everything was permissible in the fight against the 'terrorist threat'. The so-called 'new times' sometimes explicitly and sometimes implicitly justified the use of unconstrained power both in international affairs and in domestic politics.

The import of this move cannot be underestimated. As Connor Gearty has observed, 'where the United States and the United Kingdom go, other countries follow … in the way these states conduct themselves vis à vis human rights they matter out of all proportion to their sovereign space'.[19] It gives the green light to authoritarian leaders around the world to violate with impunity not just IHL but to disregard the rights of their own citizens and any non-citizen populations that they control. The behaviour of Israel in the recent past in Lebanon and at present in Gaza is only one example of what can happen when the legitimacy of the United Nations and the rules are blatantly flouted.

It further undermines the efforts of the UN generally and western states in particular to strengthen compliance with human rights norms and the basic rules of democratic governance. The cultural and political effects of globalisation mean that violations of human rights and the rule of law, and the unequal treatment of peoples on the basis of race, ethnicity and religion by countries such as the US is observed by peoples across the globe. What they see is much more likely to breed cynicism and hostility rather than respect for those ideas.

Globalisation itself means that international and the domestic, inner and outer, are no longer separate (if they ever were) but are inextricably intertwined. The 'enemy' in the discourse of the so-called 'war on terror' is no longer a foreign state and its nationals but potentially can be anywhere and everywhere. Enemies are no longer 'out there' but are seen to reside deep in the homeland. Citizens and non-citizens alike are vulnerable to the arbitrary exercise of power, to detention without charge, to the denial of a fair trial, to surveillance and a denial of basic rights. Further, in disregarding international law and the rule of law the governments of the US and the UK have involved and implicated a large number of their own citizens in the process. Not just politicians, but a range of professions and 'experts', including lawyers, jurists, doctors, policemen and military personnel have all in different ways colluded in, for example, sanctioning torture and detention without trial. This process is insidious: it not only corrupts the individuals implicated in these practices but also eats away at the ethical heart of the body politic. It is to the evidence of this corruption that we now turn.

COUNTERTERRORISM AND THE POLITICS OF LIBERAL DEMOCRATIC STATES

As the undermining of aspects the UN Charter and of IHL was always one trend in international politics prior to the bombing of the Twin Towers, so too threats to the health of liberal democracies did not begin with 9/11. The diminution of the powers of legislatures to increasingly powerful executives, increasing surveillance of the population and encroachment on civil liberties, the increasing cynicism of citizens to government and politics shown in rising voter apathy and cynicism and declining voter turnout were all clearly apparent well before 2001. In some ways, the policies post-9/11 in the UK, for example, could be seen as taking place on a terrain already partially prepared for it, if one examines a raft of legislation over immigration, asylum seekers, young people and protestors that preceded the events of 2001. However, the cumulative effects of polices designed to counter the so-called 'terrorist threat' arguably have had a detrimental effect on the working of politics in liberal democracies well beyond what had occurred previously and have intensified many of those pre-existing trends. There are clear signs too that these policies are being normalised into the routines and practices of everyday politics.

In what follows the focus will be primarily on what I consider to be several of the most important areas where policy has impacted to significantly undermine the important/fundamental principles and values of liberal democratic politics. The first section focuses on the institutions and practices of government and explores the impact on the rule of law and the increase in unconstrained power of the executive and the consequential diminution of both legislative and judicial scrutiny. The second examines the effects on private life, and the third the effects on civil society, democratic culture and the possibilities for debate, dissent and wider political activity. Though these areas have been separated out for discussion here it is important to note how each impacts on other areas. For example, increases in executive discretionary powers erode both rights of privacy and the autonomy of civil society organisations. It is also important to note that what has occurred had not gone unchallenged. There is a growing if rather belated recognition of the cumulative effects that present counterterrorist policies are having on both national and international politics.[20]

IMPACT ON THE INSTITUTIONS AND PRACTICES OF GOVERNMENT

Common effects of counterterrorist policies can be discerned across countries with rather different institutions and practices such as the US and the UK. In both countries, anti-terrorism legislation broke with certain fundamental principles of the rule of law and due process. Second, legislation passed was drafted in such terms as to grant enormous discretionary powers to the executive. It was further drafted in such a way as to enable executives to apply the new laws to peoples and activities that had nothing to do with terrorism, however defined. Third, key legislation was passed with great haste, denying legislatures the opportunity to fully debate the provisions of the legislation and often resulting in very weak or inadequate provision of measures for scrutiny or oversight by either the legislature or the judiciary. The result has been to remove wide areas of policy from proper scrutiny and debate, and to severely weaken the normal checks and balances or institutional constraints that have hitherto been seen as essential to the working of normal politics in the making of law and its implementation.

1. Legal Justice: The Rule of Law, Habeas Corpus, Due Process and Fair Trial

In both international law and in the domestic law of states such as the US and the UK, there are rules regulating when and in what circumstances individuals can be arrested, how they are to be treated and what rights such individuals have. Nowhere is the connection between undermining international law, human rights and domestic politics clearer than in issues related to the rule of law, habeas corpus and detention without trial. Blackstone makes this absolutely clear in the UK context:

> The glory of the English law consists in clearly defining the times, the causes, and the extent, when wherefore, and to what degree, the imprisonment of the subject may be lawful. This induces an absolute necessity of expressing upon every commitment the reason for this which it is made; that the court upon an habeas corpus may examine into the validity; and according to circumstances of the case may discharge, admit to bail, or remand the prisoner.[21]

The rule of law and the right to a fair trial are not just enshrined in domestic law but also in human rights covenants such as the UNCCPR, the ECHR and the Geneva Conventions. Since 2001 both the US and the UK have made significant moves to bypass the normal system of justice, to limit the role of the courts and judicial review, ignore habeas corpus and deny individuals their right to a fair trial. In their US hearings the ICJ Eminent Jurists Panel report warned that 'the continual erosion of judicial safeguards within the United States could precipitate an international decline in the strength of human rights and humanitarian law'.[22] Justice Chaskalson further declared, 'You cannot look at this as if a few people who are affected ... it is a whole legal structure ... you must look at the cumulative effect of what has happened.'[23]

In both the USA and the UK detention without trial was introduced in the wake of 9/11. Three days after 9/11, President Bush proclaimed a state of emergency, giving the executive sweeping powers including the powers to indefinitely hold in detention without trial non-citizens and denying either Congress or the judiciary any power against those decisions. This decision allowed the detention of prisoners at Guantánamo Bay who have been held indefinitely as some have described it in a 'legal black hole'[24] where their rights to a trial in an ordinary court have been denied. They were further denied access to a lawyer. The vast majority have not been charged with any offence. Many others, both citizens and non-citizens, were detained and questioned without charge.[25]

In the UK the 2001 Antiterrorism, Crime and Security Act (ATCSA) also introduced detention without trial for foreign nationals 'reasonably suspected of being a terrorist' and defined a terrorist broadly as anyone with links to terrorist organisations. When that decision was overturned by the House of Lords in 2004 on the grounds that it contravened Articles 5 and 14 of the European Convention on Human Rights (ECHR), in 2005 the British government introduced 'control orders', in effect a system of 'house arrest', under the Prevention of Terrorism Act, which could be used against nationals and non-nationals alike. Control orders enable the authorities to impose a wide range of restrictions on individuals who have not been arrested or charged. The decision to impose such orders is made by the executive alone without any involvement of the judiciary. In addition, the Terrorism Act of 2000 granted powers for holding suspects in terrorism cases from seven days without charge, which was extended to 28 days in 2006. At the time of writing there are proposals to increase this time to 42 days.

Along with the clear breach of habeas corpus, a second fundamental principle, the right to a fair trial, has been significantly weakened. In the USA, prisoners held at Guantánamo Bay have been denied a fair trial *tout court*. The Bush administration set up special military tribunals. These were held by the Supreme Court in *Hamden v Rumsfeld* in 2006 to be in violation of the Uniform Code of Military Justice and the Geneva Conventions (in particular Common Article 3) as they allowed hearsay evidence, unsworn testimony and evidence obtained by torture. The US government refused to accept these findings in that it then passed through Congress and the Senate the Military Commissions Act of 2006, which redefined Common Article 3 of the Geneva Conventions and in effect codifies the incremental erosion of defendants' judicial rights that had occurred since September 11, 2001. The Military Commissions Act, with its redefinition of Common Article 3 (which many would argue lies at the heart of the Geneva Conventions), has huge import for both international and national politics. As Jumanta Musa of Amnesty International has noted,

> What is more worrisome is that there are several other countries that have done similar things in setting up military commissions. In the past we have influenced these countries, and now the US is losing its ability to influence other countries. Hosni Mubarack, President of Egypt declared this movement of the US to military commissions validates the historic use of military commissions elsewhere.[26]

The UK has a history the use of special courts in relation to Northern Ireland, and has to date not proposed to introduce such courts under its counterterrorism initiatives. In fact, it has recognised their ineffectiveness in counterterrorism policy. However, the UK government has introduced changes that directly affect the possibilities of a fair trial. Under the Criminal Justice Act of 2003, the right to trial by jury was withdrawn from certain cases. The bill allowed for a single judge to sit in complex fraud cases or cases where there was significant danger of juries being tampered with. The same bill removed the right to silence without inference being drawn. Though access to lawyers is still the norm in the UK, there have been a number of cases where the police and security services have breached client/lawyer confidentiality (there have also been cases where MP/constituent confidentiality has also been breached).

As worrying as these developments are, it is the systematic use of torture in clear contravention of both international and domestic law that has created most attention. The public sanctioning of torture has been the most controversial and (along with extraordinary rendition), many would claim, the most morally reprehensible of all the actions taken by the Bush administration post-2001. Though the Bush administration had at times denied using torture and has gone to great lengths to redefine the meaning of torture, there is now a wealth of evidence to demonstrate its routine and systematic use in Guantánamo as well as in other countries including Afghanistan, Pakistan and Iraq and in a number of so-called 'black sites' in countries as far afield as Egypt, Romania and Poland.[27] Many of those tortured remain unidentified, have been charged with no offence, and have had no access to lawyers and on release, no redress.

I do not intend here to repeat the wealth of literature from academics, lawyers and even from the security services and the military that torture is not only illegal and counterproductive in preventing terrorism but is unlikely to produce reliable evidence – and that the so-called 'ticking time bomb' scenario is a hypothetical that is extremely unrealistic. In my view there are at least two important and overriding arguments against both torture and rendition. First, it corrupts a wide range of persons, not just those who actually practise it but also the wide number of people complicit in the practice. This includes states like Britain and other European states that have failed to speak out against torture or have turned a blind eye to extraordinary rendition.[28] Second, and closely connected, it makes any liberal democratic state that practises torture or colludes with it no different from those so-called 'rogue states' that are routinely condemned by those same liberal democratic states. The treatment of those detained and the use of torture strikes at the very heart of the values of liberal democracies. A government and society that professes itself committed to liberal values and minimum standards of humanitarian treatment of others both inside and outside the democratic state can never countenance torture, whatever the circumstances.

In many ways the practices described above have been enabled by the increase in discretionary and arbitrary powers granted to the executive since 9/11 and the failures of other branches of governments to control, scrutinise and monitor executive power.

2. Unconstrained Executives: The Increase in Discretionary and Arbitrary Power

Counterterrorist policies have seen a very significant shift in power towards the political executive and its agents, specifically the police and security services, and a corresponding diminution of the legislature and the judiciary, thus severely weakening the effectiveness of checks and balances in the system.

Although the strategy in the US and the UK differed to some extent, the former immediately declaring itself at war while the latter adopted a stronger law enforcement approach, policies and legislation in both cases have allowed a huge expansion of executive powers. On 18 September 2001 Congress authorised the President

to use all necessary means and appropriate force against those nations, organizations or persons he determines planned, authorized, committed, or aided the terrorist attacks that occurred on September 11th 2001, or harboured such organizations or persons in order to prevent any future acts of international terrorism against the United States.[29]

In pursuance of this, the Patriot Act, the National Security Strategy and the setting up of the Department of Homeland Security delegated enormous discretionary powers to the President and his administration. In addition, this significantly expanded the areas where executive agencies could intrude in all areas of life (an issue that will be raised later in the discussion of the erosion of privacy).

In the UK, the Terrorism Act of 2000 had already made terrorist groups illegal and had enhanced police powers including wide stop-and-search powers with the authority to detain suspects for up to seven days without charge. It also introduced a number of new criminal offences, including inciting terrorist acts and seeking to provide training for terrorist purposes. The Anti Terrorism, Crime and Security Act of 2001 went further, not only introducing detention without trial but significantly increasing powers for the police and the security services with little room for oversight of decisions made. The 2006 Terrorism Act further expanded areas of discretionary powers of the executive arm of government, making a number of further acts criminal, such as acts preparatory to terrorism and the dissemination of terrorist publications, and made it an offence to glorify terrorism. It further expanded police powers with the introduction of warrants for police to search any property owned by a terrorist suspect, extending police stop-and-search powers and extending the power to detain suspects without charge up to 28 days.

In addition there have been a number of other pieces of legislation, which while not explicitly related to terrorism, in effect widen the discretionary powers of the executive and undermine the civil liberties of citizens. The Serious Crime and Police Powers Act of 2005, for example, criminalises certain forms of protest and dissent; it bans unauthorised protests within one kilometre of Parliament, introduces a new criminal offence of trespass on 'designated sites' on grounds of national security as well as widening the scope of those who may seek Anti Social Behaviour Orders (ASBOs).

One of the impacts of the expansion of discretionary powers, as with the failure to respect the rule of law in general, is the discriminatory effects the use of those discretionary powers have had on a range of minorities, targeting particularly ethnic and religious minorities, but also asylum seekers, the young and anyone thought to be 'deviant' by the police, the security services or by government itself. The effect is not just to undermine polices on social cohesion but to contradict the principle of equality and non-discrimination central to liberal democratic politics. There is strong evidence to demonstrate that stop-and-search powers are disproportionately targeted at black and Asian people, and that in the name of counterterrorism asylum seekers are routinely identified as potential terrorists, denied a fair hearing and are held in arbitrary detention.

3. Detrimental Effects on Checks and Balances

In both countries there has been an explicit intent to constrain the powers of the legislature and the judiciary in terms of effective scrutiny, oversight and monitoring of the increases in executive powers. The result has been to severely weaken the checks and balances essential to the constraint of political power.

In liberal democratic theory the legislature is the place where government policy is openly debated, scrutinised and amended. However, in both countries the role of the legislature as a site for deliberation, debate and scrutiny of government policy has been severely curtailed. Counterterrorist legislation has been passed using special measures restricting time for proper deliberation and usually without provision for review of the legislation, clear time limits or adequate oversight of the effects of the legislation. Elected members have come under extraordinary pressure to support government proposals.

In the US, not only were members of Congress and the Senate subject to the accusation by President Bush that 'either you are with us or you are with the terrorists',[30] but were subjected to public pressure for strong action, in large part the result of government- and media-orchestrated campaigns to whip up fear and panic among US citizens in the post-9/11 period. The Bush administration further benefited from a Republican majority in both the House of Representatives and the Senate, which rendered the checks and balances system inherent in the constitutional separation of powers ineffective.

In Britain too the opposition and backbenchers came under pressure to support government counterterrorist legislation. Though there has been significant opposition to some of the counterterrorist legislation, the government dominance of Parliament, party discipline and the whipping system assured the passage of government legislation, at least in the House of Commons. Ironically, the main opposition to the government's counterterrorism policy has come from the unelected House of Lords and from elements of the judiciary.

If the powers of the legislature have been crucially diminished, governments in both countries have also sought ways in which to prevent the judiciary from intervening in counterterrorist legislation. As noted earlier, special courts such as the military tribunals were established by the US and were designed to keep suspect terrorists out of the normal criminal justice system. Even when suspected terrorists are dealt with by the ordinary criminal justice system, new rules regarding evidence and habeas corpus have been introduced that limit the role of the judiciary. However, the judiciary have also been sidelined as an effective check on executive power. In the UK, without a written constitution and with the doctrine of parliamentary sovereignty, the role of the judiciary in challenging government is circumscribed. The HRA, although it is law, has no special standing that would allow the judiciary to strike down legislative provisions that contravene the Act. Judicial review is limited to issues related to whether actions are *ultra vires* rather than substantive legislative matters.

Further, as Donohue notes, the judiciary in the UK has been reluctant to interfere in matters of security.[31] When the judiciary has legitimately challenged counterterrorist legislation as, for example, on detention without trial (when it argued that the provisions were contrary to the ECHR), the executive attempted to discredit the role of the judiciary. It responded by talking about the need to strike a new balance between the executive and the judiciary in the name of democracy. A succession of UK Home Secretaries (Blunkett, Straw, Clarke) have argued that the executive is democratically elected and therefore expresses the will of the people to whom they are accountable, whereas the judiciary is unelected and accountable to no one. The Home Secretary in 2001 bluntly stated: 'politicians not judges are the guardians of citizens' rights'.[32]

PUBLIC/PRIVATE: A SURVEILLANCE SOCIETY?

The blurring of the distinction between the state and civil society, between the state and the private lives of individuals, has always been an issue in liberal democracies, and the encroachment of the state into private realms is not new. However, the speed and intensity of intrusions into private life under counterterrorist legislation has led some to talk of the real danger of liberal democracies becoming surveillance societies where citizens and non-citizens alike are subject to constant scrutiny, their communications monitored and data relating to their private lives stored indefinitely. In relation to the US and Britain, Donohue goes so far as to assert that

> the combination of national security, counter terrorism laws and technology has brought both countries to the point where psychological, not just physical surveillance is possible. ... The impact goes well beyond the security, freedom dichotomy.[33]

In what follows, the UK systems of surveillance are outlined. However, the trends are similar in the US, and the Patriot Act significantly increased the surveillance powers open to the US administration. Among the new powers central to these developments in the UK are the collection and storage of a wide range of data on individuals including DNA, the interception of communications, the use of surveillance cameras and the introduction of identity cards. All this is in addition to the extremely wide expansion of police powers of stop and search that have been described earlier.

In Britain until the 1980s neither the gathering of information nor the security services were regulated by statute. It was only after a series of high-profile legal cases in which the UK was found in breach of EU rules that the government was forced to introduce a statutory framework.[34] In 1985 the Interception of Communications Act was passed, which established a legal framework for the interception of communications and set up a complaints procedure. The intelligence services were placed on a legal footing by the Security Services Acts of 1989 and 1996 and the Intelligence Services Act of 1994.

Since that time powers to collect and store data and monitor communications have been dramatically increased. The Regulation of Investigative Powers Act (RIPA) of 2000 significantly expanded the powers of the executive for intercepting communications, including the use of electronic bugs and access to encrypted data. At the time of writing, further new legislation is being proposed. The Data Communications Bill proposes to give the government powers to keep records of all electronic communications, including emails, landline and mobile phone conversations and text messages, and providers will have a duty to supply the government all their records.

In addition, the government is in the process of introducing a compulsory identity card system, which it argues is crucial to the prevention of both terrorism and crime. The Identities Card Act was finally passed in 2006 despite opposition in both houses, the House of Lords twice defeating the bill. ID cards became compulsory in

2008 for all non-EU foreign nationals working or studying in the UK, and from the same year everyone renewing a passport will also be issued with an ID card. The details of all ID cards are to be held on a National Identity Card database.

In addition to this, from 1995 a DNA database has been set up, which allowed the police to take DNA samples from all those arrested and detained by the police in connection with a recordable offence. Initially, the police were required to destroy DNA evidence from those subsequently acquitted. However, under the Criminal Justice and Police Act of 2001 data may be retained even where a suspect is not charged or is acquitted. This change is subject to a European Court hearing on whether retaining data of those not charged or acquitted is in breach of the ECHR rights to privacy. At present, over 3 million people or 5.2 per cent of the population are on the database, including some children.[35]

A final example of the intrusion of the state into the lives of its citizens is the increasing and widespread use of surveillance cameras. Britain has more surveillance cameras than any other country in the world. In 2003, according to the *National Geographic*, there were more than 4 million such cameras in place.[36]

In all these areas there are real concerns about the possibilities for abuse of the information held, for how it will be used and for what purpose. As Donohue asks, 'what is the state's aim in gathering data? How is the information used? How long is it retained? Who sees it?'[37] In effect, many important issues relating to surveillance and data collection have been removed from the normal processes of politics. First, there is a strong culture of secrecy in relation to the kinds of information gathered by the security services, which means that both legislators and citizens alike have no way of assessing or questioning the efficacy of the various forms of surveillance in preventing either terrorist acts or serious crime.

Further, the public have no way of knowing what information is held on them or whether or not it is accurate. If an individual does not know what data is held how can they check its accuracy? Judicial oversights are weak, and the Data Protection Act of 1998 and the Freedom of Information Act of 2000 are inadequate and exclude information held by intelligence and security services. The Home Affairs Select Committee of 9 June 2008 frankly admitted: 'the expansion of state surveillance has been as relentless as it has been under discussed'.[38]

Much of data being collected has nothing to do with security and public safety, but there are very legitimate fears that such information can and is being used against a variety of minorities including the young and legitimate protestors, and those who hold particular beliefs that the government considers to be undesirable, regardless of whether they have broken any law or constitute a real threat to public safety.

In the arguments used to justify increased levels of surveillance there is little or no recognition of the importance of the value of privacy to living a life of dignity and freedom. The argument that those who have nothing to hide have nothing to fear is beside the point. The knowledge that we may be watched at any time, our phone recorded or our lifestyle monitored affects us all and leads to self-monitoring and forms of self-surveillance that is inimical to freedom and democracy.

IMPACT ON CIVIL SOCIETY AND DEMOCRATIC CULTURE: FREEDOMS TO DEBATE AND DISSENT

The issue of surveillance is closely connected with the assault not only of the right to privacy but to the erosion of free speech, assembly and the ability of citizens to freely debate and dissent, all of which are essential to any form of democratic politics. Without these rights the ability of citizens to hold governments to account for their actions and policies is clearly diminished. In addition, without these rights an independent civil society and a democratic culture cannot flourish.

Freedom of speech, considered rightly as a fundamental right in a free society, is not an unqualified right. There are criminal rules, for example, relating to slander and libel and in the past for sedition and treason. While recognising the right of free speech, the ECHR allows for its curtailment where national security is threatened. Both in the UK and the US there have been times when free speech was severely curtailed in the recent past. The McCarthy period in US history and the ban on broadcasting by Sinn Fein in the 1980s are but two obvious examples. Race-hate speech was also criminalised in the UK following the 1965 Race Relations Act.

Counterterrorist legislation, however, has significantly widened and extended the criminalisation of speech acts. The Terrorism Bill of 2006, for example, has made the 'glorification of terrorism' a criminal act. The Act was explicitly aimed at Muslims, immigrants and asylum seekers and allowed the state to deport foreigners who 'fostered hatred'. Leaving aside the crucial questions of how we define terrorism, a terrorist or a terrorist act, quite what constitutes the offence of the glorification of terrorism is extremely unclear. Does glorification of terrorism include support for the Palestinians, some of whom use violence in their struggle for self-determination? Does it include support for animal rights supporters? Does it include those who justified or justify the African National Congress's use of violence in the struggle against apartheid? Universities and schools have expressed deep concern over the Act's impact on academic freedom and their ability to discuss a wide range of issues relating to history or contemporary politics with their students.

A further restriction of speech acts is to be found in the regulation of certain kinds of scientific knowledge. Again, restrictions are not new. Under the D Notice system in the UK and under the 1951 Invention Secrecy Act in the US publication of certain material considered by the government to constitute a security threat was prevented. The Anti Terrorism, Crime and Security Act of 2001 gave wide-ranging new powers to control publication of what is considered sensitive biological chemical and nuclear research, which has also given rise to concerns by the academic community related to academic freedom.

It is not just the 2006 Act that is important to free speech: new police powers along with terrorism laws and antisocial behaviour legislation are all combined to suppress various forms of dissent in a desire to inculcate a culture of conformity and obedience. For example, an elderly man and life-long Labour Party member, Walter Wolfgang, was arrested under anti-terrorist legislation for heckling Jack Straw, the then Home Secretary at a Labour Party conference.[39] Protestors wearing so-called inflammatory slogans on T-shirts have been fined.

The culture of dissent and debate is further restricted by laws restricting freedom of movement and legitimate protest. The Serious Crimes and Police Act of 2005 forbids unauthorised protests within a kilometre of Parliament. Maya Evans and Miler Rai were arrested for merely reading out a list of names of those killed in Iraq. The 1997 Protection from Harassment Act was updated in the same 2005 Act and has been used to prevent legitimate protests against militarism, environmental change and the proposed extension of Heathrow Airport.

CONCLUSION

The so-called 'war on terror' has, I have argued, led to the erosion of fundamental norms of both international humanitarian law and of liberal democratic government. The undermining of IHL and the weakening of institutions and practices of liberal democracies are clearly interconnected. In the contemporary interdependent world it is impossible to separate clearly what states do abroad from what they do at home. Freeing force from legal constraint, to use Jim Whitman's phrase, is not just a cogent way of describing what is happening in terms of international relations and IHL in the present period, but can be applied to what is happening to politics in liberal democratic states. In both cases the movement is towards the exercise of arbitrary, unconstrained power.

In the process, the norms of what have come to be regarded as minimum standards of 'civilised' behaviour due to all people regardless of their differences are inevitably weakened and discredited. Both human rights as minimum entitlements for all, and citizens' rights as the rights of all who belong to a political community, are simultaneously threatened. The protection of the rights of citizens and non-citizens, combatants and civilians, become dependent on the whim of the holders of power. Both citizens and non-citizens become vulnerable to the arbitrary exercise of political power. The meaning of the rule of law and of liberty, equality, impartiality, democracy and human rights are being reframed to become emptied of any binding normative force.

There is a real danger that the trends described here are becoming embedded in what some have described as the 'new normal',[40] where violations of international law and the rule of law more generally, and intrusions into the lives of citizens by unconstrained executives become routine and everyday events. However, there are signs that such trends are being increasingly contested. The costs of the strategy pursued by countries such as the UK and the USA and their counterproductive effects are belatedly being recognised. The damage done to the standing of the USA in the world under the Bush administration has been publically acknowledged by President Obama, and the importance of the Geneva Conventions and the rule of law and the prohibition of torture reaffirmed in his inaugural address. In Britain there are an increasing number of voices being raised by politicians, judges, academics, the media and segments of the population pointing to the erosion of civil liberties and calling for a rebalancing of the institutions of government, improved scrutiny and accountability of the executive and the security services.[41]

We need to support and strengthen such voices and to create spaces for alternative strategies for confronting present dangers that do not require the abandonment of the rule of law and the erosion of liberal democratic norms. The future is not set in stone; there are ways of reversing the 'new normalcy' but only if those ways work with, rather than against, those very norms that the 'war on terror' strategy was meant to protect.

NOTES

1. Tom Farer, *Confronting Global Terrorism and American Neo-Conservatism: The Framework of a Liberal Grand Strategy* (Oxford: Oxford University Press, 2008); Laura K. Donohue, *The Cost of Counterterrorism: Power, Politics and Liberty* (Cambridge: Cambridge University Press, 2008); Dirk Haubrich, 'Modern Politics in an Age of Global Politics: New Challenges for Domestic Public Policy', *Political Studies* 54, no. 2 (June 2006), pp. 399–423.
2. Farer, *Confronting Global Terrorism*; Conor Gearty, *Can Human Rights Survive? The Hamlyn Lectures 2005* (Cambridge: Cambridge University Press, 2006).
3. Farer, *Confronting Global Terrorism*, p. 4.
4. David Beetham, 'Liberal Democracy and the Limits of Democratization', in *Prospects for Democracy: North, South, East, West*, ed. David Held (Cambridge: Polity Press, 1993); David Held, 'Liberalism, Marxism and the Limits of Democratization', in *Modernity and its Futures*, ed. Stuart Hall, David Held and Antony McGrew (Cambridge: Polity Press, 1992); Bhikhu Parekh, *A New Politics of Identity: Political Principles for an Interdependent World* (Basingstoke: Palgrave Macmillan, 2008).
5. Beetham, 'Liberal Democracy and the Limits of Democratization'.
6. Parekh, *A New Politics of Identity*, p. 262.
7. Ronald Dworkin, *Taking Rights Seriously* (London: Duckworth, 2006), p. 205.
8. John Locke, *Two Treatises on Government* (Cambridge: Cambridge University Press, 1963), p. 373.
9. Dworkin, *Taking Rights Seriously*; Jurgen Habermas, *Between Facts and Norms: Contributions to a Discourse Theory of Law and Democracy* (Cambridge: Polity Press, 1998).
10. Gearty, *Can Human Rights Survive?*, p. 108.
11. Anastassia Tsoukala, 'Democracy in the Light of Security: British and French Political Discourses', *Political Studies* 54, no. 3 (October 2006), pp. 607–27.
12. David Blunkett, *Independent* (12 August 2001).
13. Jack Straw, *Daily Mail* (11 December 2008).
14. Alex Bellamy, 'Dirty Hands and Lesser Evils in the War on Terror', *British Journal of Politics and International Relations* 9, no. 3 (August 2007), pp. 509–26.
15. Michael Ignatieff, *The Lesser Evil: Political Ethics in an Age of Terror* (Edinburgh: Edinburgh University Press, 2004).
16. Dworkin, *Taking Rights Seriously*.
17. R.J. Vincent, *Human Rights and International Relations* (Cambridge: Cambridge University Press, 1986).
18. J.L. Holgrefe and Robert O. Keohane (eds), *Humanitarian Intervention: Ethical, Legal and Political Dilemmas* (Cambridge: Cambridge University Press, 2003).
19. Gearty, *Can Human Rights Survive?*, p. 107.

20. See, for example, President Obama's inaugural speech and the growing pressure from UK politicians both for an inquiry regarding accusations of UK complicity in torture and rendition and pressure from both politicians and the media for greater scrutiny of counterterrorism legislation in the UK.

21. Blackstone, quoted in Donohue, *The Cost of Counterterrorism*, p. 35.

22. Mark Vorkink and Erin M. Scheick, 'The War on Terror and the Erosion of the Rule of Law: The US Hearings of the ICJ Eminent Jurist Panel 2006', Washington College of Law, American University, available at: http://www. wcl.american.edu/hrbrief/14/1vorkink.pdf?rd=1.

23. Justice Chaskalson, in Vorkink and Scheick, 'The War on Terror', p. 3.

24. Philippe Sands, *Lawless World*: *Making and Breaking Global Rules* (London: Penguin Books, 2006).

25. Donohue, *The Cost of Counterterrorism*, pp. 72–9.

26. Jumana Musa of Amnesty International, quoted in Vorkink and Scheick, 'The War on Terror'.

27. *The Guardian* has covered much of this evidence that has accumulated over a number of years. See, for example, Richard Norton Taylor, *Guardian* (9 March 2009).

28. There is increasing evidence of British complicity in the use of torture and rendition, and the Home Secretary, after mounting pressure from the judiciary, some senior politicians and the press, has agreed to set up an inquiry into the allegations made by Binyamin Mohamed, a British resident held in Guantánamo Bay.

29. Donohue, *The Cost of Counterterrorism*, p. 7.

30. *Ibid.*, p. 13.

31. *Ibid.*, p. 20.

32. Hugo Young, 'David Blunkett holds liberty and the judges in contempt', *Guardian* (15 November 2001).

33. Donohue, *The Cost of Counterterrorism*, p. 186.

34. *Ibid.*, p. 190.

35. Editorial, *Guardian* (9 June 2008).

36. Donohue, *The Cost of Counterterrorism*, p. 215.

37. *Ibid.*, p. 186.

38. Editorial, *Guardian* (9 June 2008).

39. Walter Wolfgang, an 82-year-old long-time member of the Labour Party, was arrested at the Labour Party Conference in September 2005 under anti terrorism legislation for heckling the Foreign Secretary Jack Straw.

40. See, for example, Lawyers' Committee for Human Rights USA, 'Assessing the New Normal: Liberty, and Security for the Post September 11 United States' (2003), available at: http://www.humanrightsfirst.org/pubs/descriptions/ Assessing/AssessingtheNewNormal.pdf.

41. See for examples the numerous articles in the *Guardian*, the *Independent* and the *Observer* since 2001 for a summary of these debates articulating dissent from counterterrorist strategies.

About the Contributors

Sonia Cardenas is Associate Professor of Political Science and Director of the Human Rights program at Trinity College, Hartford, Connecticut.

Helen Dexter is a Teaching Fellow in International Relations in the School of Politics, International Relations & Philosophy, Keele University.

Stuart Gordon is a Senior Lecturer at the Royal Military Academy, Sandhurst with responsibility for the Law of War and Peace Support programmes. His current research is focused on the politics of the contemporary battlefield and he is currently completing a book, *Alms and Armour* for Manchester University Press. He has also worked for the UK's Stabilisation Unit (formerly Post Conflict Reconstruction Unit), advising on the Quick Impact Project Programme and conflict issues.

Françoise Hampson is Professor of Law at the University of Essex. She is a member of the UN Sub-Commission on the Prevention of Discrimination and Protection of Minorities and a Governor of the British Institute of Human Rights.

Nick Lewer is Director of the Diploma and Capacity Building Programme, based at the Social Scientists Association in Colombo, Sri Lanka. Prior to this he was a Senior Lecturer and Director of the Centre for Conflict Resolution at the Department of Peace Studies, University of Bradford, UK. His practitioner and research interests include peace education, non-violent conflict resolution and mediation, and new weapons.

Wade Mansell is Professor of International Law and Director of the Centre for Critical International Law at the University of Kent. He convenes postgraduate international law degrees in both Canterbury and at the Brussels campus of the University of Kent.

Björn Müller-Wille first pursued a career in the Swedish Armed Forces. He gained a PhD from the Westfälische Wilhelms-Universität after studies in Münster and the Sorbonne. He was a Marie Curie Fellow in the EU Commission-funded research training network, ESDP-Democracy and a Visiting Fellow at the EU Institute for Security Studies in Paris. Since 2004 Björn has held a post as Senior Lecturer at the Royal Military Academy, Sandhurst.

Keiichiro Okimoto is the Legal Adviser, Delegation in Iraq, International Committee of the Red Cross (ICRC). He holds a PhD from the University of Cambridge and an LLM from the London School of Economics and Political Science.

Karen Openshaw practised as a solicitor before returning to university to complete a postgraduate diploma in international law. She is now completing a PhD in international law in the area of international debt and state succession at the University of Kent.

Sarah Perrigo is a senior lecturer in the Department of Peace Studies, University of Bradford, where she directs the PhD programme.

Jim Whitman is a senior lecturer in the Department of Peace Studies, University of Bradford and is the general editor of the Palgrave *Global Issues* series. His latest book is *The Fundamentals of Global Governance* (Palgrave Macmillan).

Index

Abu Ghraib, 34, 182, 211
Afghanistan, 28, 75, 80, 94, 155, 161, 164, 167, 170, 179, 189, 192, 196, 236
Allhoff, F., 141
Al-Qaeda, 26–9, 31, 32, 51, 155, 181, 196, 208, 213
Amnesty International, 85, 236
Annan, Kofi, 76, 180, 190
Antiterrorism, Crime and Security Act, 235

Benn, Hilary, 187
Bennet, William, 193
Betts, Richard, 84–5
Blair, Tony, 181, 185, 187, 189–90, 197, 278
Blunkett, David, 228, 240
Bosnia, 94, 184, 186, 206
Bouchet-Saulnier, Francoise, 89
Bybee, Jay, 32, 33, 211
Bush, George W., 26–9, 31–4, 139, 150, 161, 180–2, 189, 191–7, 206, 207, 209–14, 223, 227, 234, 234–3, 239, 245

Caesar, James, 193, 194
Chechnya, 206
Chemical Weapons Convention, 7, 139, 145, 149
Cheney, Dick, 211
Clark, Wesley, 84
Cold War, 1, 4, 8, 11, 163, 172, 173, 179, 180, 181, 183–5, 191, 231
Comprehensive Approach, 156, 163, 165, 167, 170
Convention Against Torture, 7, 32, 87
Council on Foreign Relations, 19
Counter Insurgency, 78, 82
Coupland, Robin, 142, 143

De Neveres, Renée, 13
Dershowitz, Alan, 141, 211

Detter, Ingrid, 22
Distinction, 4, 23, 27, 42, 65, 77, 80, 82, 84, 88, 91, 102, 108, 133, 143, 155–7, 161, 162, 166–9, 170, 171, 173, 189, 194
Doctrine, 4, 49, 78, 82–4, 147, 155, 156, 159–63, 166, 170, 172, 173, 181, 190
Doswald-Beck, L., 148
Dunant, Henry, 12
Dworkin, Ronald, 225, 226, 229

Economic Community of West African States (ECOWAS), 76
Effects Based Operations (EBO), 78, 82, 156, 163, 165, 166, 170, 172
European Court of Human Rights, 25
European Union (EU), 76, 142, 207, 241, 242

Falk, Richard, 24, 186–8, 190
Farer, Tom, 223, 228
Fentanyl, 140, 149–51
Fidler, David, 144, 149, 151
Fréchette, Louise, 75, 90
Friedman, Thomas, 183

Gaza, 43, 48, 58, 59, 215, 231
Gearty, Conor, 227, 229, 231
General Assembly, 7
Genocide Convention, 184, 204
Gillerman, Dan, 215
Gonzalez, Alberto, 32, 207, 209, 211
Gruber, Aya, 30
Guantánamo, 15, 27–30, 33, 171, 181, 205, 206, 211, 213, 235, 236

Habeas Corpus, 28, 29, 216, 234, 235, 240
Habermas, Jurgen, 226
Hague Conventions, 3, 146
Hallam, Henry, 216
Hamas, 48

Hezbollah, 85–7
Holt, Victoria, 91–3, 95
Hoon, Geoff, 207
Human Rights Act, 25, 228
Human Shields, 58–60, 155
Hutchinson, John, 11

Ignatieff, Michael, 228
Improvised Explosive Device (IED), 47
Imseis, Ardi, 24, 25
Independent International Commission on Kosovo, 185
International Commission on Intervention and State Sovereignty, 75, 180, 185, 190
International Committee of the Red Cross (ICRC), 9, 10, 12, 44, 47, 64, 77, 89, 100, 101, 111–14, 123–30, 142, 147, 159
International Criminal Court (ICC), 8, 24, 25 65, 76, 77, 169, 231
Israel, 24, 25, 43, 48, 64, 85–7, 139, 169, 170, 206, 214, 215, 231
Israeli Defence Forces (IDF), 59
International Armed Conflict, 2, 8, 43, 64, 100–2, 107–10, 114–18, 120, 122, 125, 136
Iraq, 28, 34, 94, 139, 141, 150, 155, 161, 164, 167–71, 180–2, 187–90, 192, 194, 196, 204, 215, 236, 244

Japan, 22
Jus Ad Bellum, 6, 42, 43, 87, 161, 173, 189
Jus In Bello, 6, 84, 87, 152, 161, 173, 189, 203

Kagan, Robert, 193
Kaldor, Mary, 181
Kinsella, Helen, 194, 196
Kosovo, 59, 84, 87, 94, 155, 169, 180, 181, 183, 185–90

Lauterpacht, Hersch, 74
Lawand, K., 147
Liberal Democracy, 223, 229
Lieber Code, 20, 145, 174
Ludendorff, Erich, 157, 166

McCain, John, 207

McInnes, Colin, 194
Martens Clause, 21, 45, 146
Médecins Sans Frontières, 89
Mileham, Patrick, 82, 83
Military Necessity, 30, 212, 216, 235
Milošević, Slobodan, 84, 94, 155, 169, 180, 185
Military Commissions Act, 30, 212, 216, 235
Millennium Declaration, 75
Moses, Jeremy, 194

Neff, Stephen, 23
Network Enabled Capabilities (NEC), 165
New York Times, 183
Non-International Armed Conflict, 43, 64, 77, 100, 101, 108, 109, 113, 117, 118, 121, 123, 124–7, 129
Non-Proliferation Treaty, 7
Non-Refoulement, 114
Norms, 1, 4–7, 12, 13, 31, 80, 81, 83, 89, 95, 185, 187, 194, 202–4, 213, 214, 217, 222, 223–7, 229–32, 244–6
North Atlantic Treaty Organization (NATO), 59, 76, 84, 85, 138, 144, 148, 168, 180, 185–9, 195

Obama, Barack, 47, 245
Operation Desert Storm, 171, 172
Operation Iraqi Freedom, 171
Operational Law Handbook, 162, 168
Operations Other Than War, 136, 163
Ottawa Convention, 77, 145, 151

Parek, B., 225, 246
Paris Declaration, 21
Patriot Act, 238, 241
Paxman, Jeremy, 187, 188
Pentagon, 153, 154, 189
Proportionality, 42–65, 91, 145, 155–8, 161, 162, 166, 168, 169, 171, 175

Red Crescent, 11, 124, 126, 129
Red Cross, 20, 44, 124, 126, 129, 142
Reisman, Michael, 42
Responsibility to Protect (R2P), 75, 95, 180

Rice, Condoleezza, 214
Rieff, David, 93–5
Rumsfeld, Donald, 29, 139, 150, 215, 235
Russia, 21, 34, 140, 149, 150, 189, 186, 208
Rwanda, 94, 112, 181, 185, 186, 206

Saddam Hussein, 28, 58, 155, 182, 192
St Petersburg Declaration, 3, 21, 22, 78, 97, 145, 148
Sassòli, Marco, 78, 82, 90, 91, 120, 210
Schofiled, S., 142, 148
Security Council, 12, 24, 25, 75, 92, 180, 185–7
Shaw, George Bernard, 182, 199
Simpson, Brian, 20
Slim, Hugo, 94
Stanton, Jessica, 80, 81
Straw, Jack, 228, 240, 244

Taliban, 28, 31, 38, 80, 208

Torture, 211–14, 216, 222, 227, 229, 232, 235–7, 245
Total War, 4, 10, 155, 157, 202

Uniform Code of Military Justice, 29, 30, 235
United Nations, 1, 6, 7, 18, 185, 195, 215, 230, 232
United States, 13, 15, 19, 20, 26, 31, 33, 47, 52, 55, 161, 185, 194, 204–7, 209, 210, 212, 214–16, 218, 222, 231, 234, 238
Universal Declaration of Human Rights (UDHR), 1, 6, 7, 8, 9, 184

War on Terror, 1, 26, 32, 141, 179, 181, 182, 188–92, 194–7, 205–7, 213, 214, 216, 222, 223, 227, 229, 232, 244, 246
Weston, B.H., 24
Wood, Sir Michael, 208

Zegveld, Liesbeth, 90, 91